Essentials of Cultural Anthropology

SECOND EDITION

A.R.N. SRIVASTAVA
Visiting Faculty
Sam Higginbottom Institute of Agriculture, Science and Technology
(SHIAST)
Deemed University
Naini, Allahabad

PHI Learning Private Limited
Delhi-110092
2013

₹ 250.00

ESSENTIALS OF CULTURAL ANTHROPOLOGY, Second Edition
A.R.N. Srivastava

ISBN-978-81-203-4653-6

Second Printing (Second Edition) ... ... January, 2013

Published by Asoke K. Ghosh, PHI Learning Private Limited, Rimjhim House, 111, Patparganj Industrial Estate, Delhi-110092 and Printed by Mudrak, 30-A, Patparganj, Delhi-110091.

Presented to

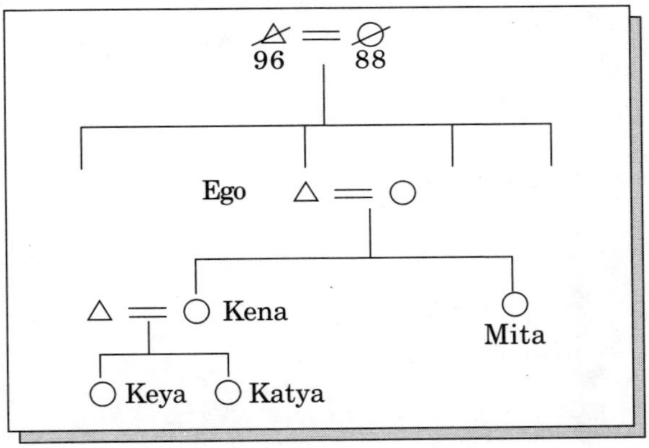

Contents

Preface

Over the years I have received some comments and suggestions both from the students and colleagues. And therefore, I have added two new sections: one on the fundamental concepts of Sociology viz society, community and association, and other section in the form of an Appendix on Tribal movement in India, giving an overview of tribal communities of the country. However, the organization of the chapters is retained in the revised edition with some subtle changes.

It must, be emphasized that the book has been written by keeping both students and the teachers in mind.

Special thanks are due to my student—Dr. Nisheeth Rai, an Assistant Professor at International Hindi Central University, Wardha (M.P.). I also thank the editorial and production team of PHI Learning especially Ms. Babita Misra, who assisted me in many ways.

The book is presented to my grand-daughters—Keya and Katya who, I believe, upon crossing teen threshold will understand what Anthropology is all about.

A.R.N. Srivastava

Preface to the First Edition

No field of study has had more influence on twentieth-century thought than anthropology—a holistic science of human being, which aims to study human origins, human variation, human nature and human culture as evolved through time. Although scholars and thinkers of ancient times have talked about these and other related topics, yet as a professional discipline, Anthropology is barely 125 years old. It blends the biological and cultural facts and perspectives. As such, Anthropology shares with natural sciences, social sciences and humanities.

The primary purpose of this book is to present social-cultural anthropological concepts and theories that have guided our thinking in the past twentieth century; more specifically, spanning the years between 1965 and 2000. The author also identifies some of the concepts that would continue to direct anthropological thought in future.

The book is written in an easy-to-understand manner and is intended for advanced readers with a little knowledge of Anthropology. The topics discussed in the book are as per University Grants Commission (New Delhi, 2002) Curriculum for Master level core course in cultural anthropology. Cultural spheres of domestic life of simple and traditional cultures, their institutions such as marriage, kinship, economy, polity, religion are thoroughly illustrated. In addition, it also includes a discussion on relationship between language and culture, art, folklore, and culture change. Hopefully, it should interest those who want to learn more about achievements in emerging sub-fields of anthropology, viz. visual anthropology, ecological anthropology, urban anthropology and medical anthropology.

In order to make the text materials more understandable, a list of annotated references is presented at the end of each chapter. Names of some popular anthropologists, their works and concepts have been presented in Appendix.

It is impossible in a textbook, dealing with varied concepts and facts, to give credit for the origins of all of author's ideas; nor he would try of doing it. Most of the anthropologists are unable to remember when and where they first became familiar with many of the notions and findings.

The author gratefully acknowledges the modest grant-in-aids by the UGC [9-3(96) BP], New Delhi, towards initial cost of preparation.

A.R.N. Srivastava

Chapter 1

Anthropology
The Study of Man

Anthropology is defined as 'the study of man and his works'. The broader definition of anthropology virtually includes all varied aspects of man and theoretical interests of people who call themselves anthropologists. The anthropologists of different categories come in several varieties. There are digging anthropologists, there are measuring anthropologists, testing anthropologists and field anthropologists. Yet, they all are primarily one, i.e. the people engaged in the study of human beings. The term 'anthropology' has been present in the English language for some centuries, albeit no exact time can be established. Derived from the Greek word, it means 'the study of man' (*anthropo* = man; suffix *logy* used in forming the names of science). By the middle of 19th century, this word was used for the philosophical forerunners of modern social scientists including humanists. By the beginning of twentieth century, Anthropology found its place among the many scientific disciplines, both in British and American universities.

ANTHROPOLOGY: ITS DIVISIONS

Anthropologists all over the world claim that they are studying man. It is interesting to note how do they view man. First of all, man is a mammal and primate of the highest order. Secondly, man is a being who lives by culture.

From the above two perspectives on man, two main divisions or branches of anthropology have emerged—Physical anthropology and Cultural anthropology. Anthropologists, irrespective of their interests, cannot overlook any of the characteristics covered in two aspects, viz. biological and cultural.

The Core Branches of Anthropology

As a scientific discipline, anthropology covers a very broad range of investigation of man. It is commonly divided into four sub-fields, viz. Physical, Cultural, Linguistic and Archaeological anthropology. Each of them examines human beings from a different angles yet, as we shall examine later on, they all work with similar assumptions. It also be noted that these recognized four core areas of anthropology are intimately connected with two main divisions noted earlier. Further, these four core areas are not recently established. Rather, they are included in anthropology eversince the subject was established in the academic world. It was Paul Broca who during 1865–67 attempted to define the field of anthropology, noting the interest areas like man's biological characteristics as well as his intellectual and social traits under anthropology. More specifically, he mentioned linguistics, ethnology, archaeology, races, craniometry and music (Broca, 1868). In the American academic circles, the above noted four branches of anthropology have been recognised since the turn of the 20th century.

A brief look at each of the core areas can help us understand the vast subject matter of anthropology, the theoretical interests and to see why anthropologists value them.

Physical Anthropology

Before World War II, much of physical anthropology was concerned with the description and measurement of external physical (biological) characteristics of men of different places at different time, i.e. men of earlier time (*Homo sapiens*) and anatomically modern time (*Homo sapiens sapiens*). Two main traditional topics of physical anthropologists were Human origins and human evolution on the basis of fossil remains and racial characteristics of contemporary people. These topics were studied under Paleoanthropology and Anthropology of Races. During the past fifty years, Human Genetics and Comparative Primatology have been firmly established under the general title of physical anthropology. In recent decades, physical anthropology has undergone a phenomenal shift. Focusing on constitutional or physiological aspect of contemporary human beings has been a major area of interest for those who are researching in the field on human growth and nutrition. The new emphasis is on the genetic make up of human groups. On the basis of these developments the physical anthropology has come to be known as New physical anthropology. There have been some suggestions that this field be termed as *Biological anthropology*.

In essence, physical or biological anthropologists concentrate on the study of genetically transmitted characteristics of men of past and present times.

Archaeological Anthropology

Archaeology is a specialised science dealing with remains of past human cultural activity. Within Anthropology, prehistoric archaeology (or prehistory and archaeology) extends the field of both cultural and physical anthropology back through time. It tells us how earlier and extinct human societies interacted with their habitats. Archaeologists do it on the basis of remnants of stone tools, broken animal bones, fire-blackened rock, pottery and living sites including hearths. During the past several years, the specialists have turned their attention to study the literate civilizations of the past. Usually this comes under *Classical archaeology*.

In a nutshell, archaeological anthropologists try to reconstruct the cultural phenomena and subsistence patterns of the past recovered from the ancient sites.

Linguistic Anthropology (Anthropological Linguistics)

Linguistics, i.e. the study of languages is a very specialised academic discipline. Its two important branches—Historical and Descriptive linguistics are intimately connected with cultural anthropology. Language is commonly regarded as a functioning part of culture. Like culture, it is learned rather than genetically transmitted.

The major aims of Linguistic anthropology are:

- to establish the evolutionary relationship between human languages and
- to understand the present social and cultural functions of linguistic behaviour.

In recent decades, a number of specific approaches have been developed by the American anthropologists to study the cultural behaviour. Notable among them are: *ethnolinguistics*, *sociolinguistics* (language and culture studies), *componential analysis* and *semantics* (see entries under Appendix-I and Chapters 3 and 10).

Cultural Anthropology

Modern cultural anthropology carves out similarities and differences among the contemporary cultures and societies. In doing so, cultural anthropologists collect facts through fieldwork across cultures and analyse them to arrive at theories. The former is called *Ethnography* while the latter is known as *Ethnology*. Thus, cultural anthropologists play the roles of both ethnographer and ethnologist (see Appendix I).

Cultural anthropologists agree that some socio-cultural features are universal, i.e. common to all. Some features are generalised while others are particularised, i.e. they are common to some members only. However, all members do not share particularised characteristics. A brief note on the traditional framework of cultural anthropology is required here.

In the traditional framework of anthropological teaching and research, ethnology and social anthropology were included under cultural anthropology, but many British anthropologists following the French and English traditions regarded themselves different from general ethnologists or cultural anthropologists. *Ethnology* is regarded as a major field of cultural anthropology. It is defined as the descriptive and comparative study of the world's cultures, usually non-literate or *pre-literate* (not illiterate) societies in order to formulate some generalisations about human societies (cultures). The term pre-literate society refers to those societies which are outside the realm of introduction to formal education. These scholars are social anthropologists. Ethnological study includes study of habitats (technology and environment), economic organisation, kinship system, government and legal system, religion, art, folklore and personality and communication system. Any of these topics may be treated as an area of specialisation within cultural anthropology. During the past 30–40 years, several subfields with specialisation have emerged within cultural anthropology. Some of them are *Economic anthropology, Political anthropology, Kinship and Social Organisation, Comparative religion or Anthropology of religion, Culture and Personality or Psychological anthropology, Urban anthropology, Ecological anthropology, Visual anthropology* and *Medical anthropology.*

Anthropologists of the Great Britain are more interested in those aspects of ethnology that involve social relations within and among the societies. These anthropologists regard themselves social anthropologists following the French and British traditions in Sociology. Although in this book at many places social anthropology is equated with cultural anthropology, but it must be noted that the former conveys specific point of view in understanding human behaviour. They study social system in terms of institutions and values by which people live. It is the job of social anthropologists to identify the components of social systems and analyse them. In essence, like ethnologists, social anthropologists try to arrive at some general (or theoretical) regularities or principle. *A.R. Radcliffe-Brown* and *Bronislaw Malinowski* were two celebrated social anthropologists of the United Kingdom. Both have influenced American cultural anthropologists and anthropologists of Africa and India. More details on cultural anthropology such as its scope, method and subject matters are provided in Chapter 3.

THE UNIQUENESS OF ANTHROPOLOGY

The uniqueness of anthropology lies in its four approaches, which may, in turn, be thought of as trademarks of anthropologists. They are: biocultural, holistic, comparative, and fieldwork. All of these approaches of anthropology contribute to the breadth of anthropology as a discipline. We must then briefly note what these approaches are.

Biocultural Approach

Anthropological studies are partly biological and partly humanities and social science. It is because of the heavy emphasis on both biology and culture that anthropology emerged as a distinct scientific discipline. The biocultural approach requires any meaningful study of human beings whether past or present, to examine both biological and cultural information. Anthropologists are careful in noting what man has inherited biologically, i.e. genetically and what he has learned as the consequence of culture became possible as a product of 'unique sequence of events' and that all human beings while living in various groups/areas share the common biological basis of culture. It looks like a tautological, i.e. circular statement, but the following statements clarify the situation.

In the course of long biological evolution, man became human because of a powerful factor he developed, i.e. culture. This could not have been possible without some changes in genetic make-up of our early ancestors, which gave rise to opposable thumb, erect posture/bipedalism, and increased brain size. These and other elements working in 'complex sequences' gave rise to culture and language. That is why the anthropologists make statement: "development of the 'capacity' for culture was a result of biological evolution alone, not that man has a culture".

Anthropologists of all specialities classify the above-mentioned two processes of evolution under 'biocultural approach'. In strict evolutionary terms, this also implies that natural selection as well as cultural selection contributed to the development of *Homo sapiens*.

The above biocultural approach was in vogue in anthropology from the very beginning, but it became more popular when Mischa Titieve, the American anthropologist explicitly used it in his book the *Science of Man,* 1963 : 18.

The Holistic Approach

According to the philosophers of social sciences of the doctrine, viewing the whole context of human behaviour is termed *holism*. This is the fundamental theme of anthropology. Anthropologists of all specialists insist on putting together what is being learned (or observed) about human biology and culture.

Anthropologists employ a wide range of information from many academic disciplines like biology, sociology, psychology, ecology, political science, economics, etc. The holistic approach combines the ideas of several disciplines on the understanding that all parts of a culture are interrelated. Since culture is the central theme of cultural anthropology within itself, the holistic approach is more pronounced. Robert Redfield (1960) noted that in studying a small community, whether in terms of social structure, world view or as an ecological system, the effort is to understand the community "in its entirety, as a whole". This holistic approach is further reflected in the use of the term integration to describe the consistency inherent in cultures, which is taken by anthropologists to be the most important of a cultural wholeness.

The Comparative Approach

The distinctiveness of anthropology lies in its use of comparative method. In a sense, all the anthropological work—biological and social-cultural is directed on a comparative theme, and all anthropologists agree that their science is fundamentally comparative. This view springs from the very concept of culture and from its interest to mankind in a holistic approach. To be sure, comparison involves not only the study of concepts and practices, which differ from one society to another, but also the analysis of various aspects at various levels within the same society.

A number of methods of comparison were developed by the anthropologists of early and late 20th century such as *controlled comparison, cross-cultural comparison, and statistical comparison* (see Appendix-1).

The Fieldwork Approach

A fourth distinctive feature of anthropology is its emphasis on the fieldwork for obtaining data. Its importance has been realised in all the core branches of the discipline. Often, this approach has been branded with Cultural and Linguistic anthropologists but we must keep in mind that Physical and Archaeological anthropologists, though not always, are engaged in fieldwork among the 'living people'. Traditionally, they were confined to uncovering fossil tools and remains of withered hominids. Presently, archaeologists are very active in the study of contemporary hunting and gathering populations while physical anthropologists are studying the non-human primate behaviour. But, their methodological 'orientations' are different. They are called Ethno-archaeologists. For cultural anthropologists, 'fieldwork' has a specific program, which will be taken up separately in Chapter 4.

To sum up, anthropology studies mankind as a whole following biocultural, holistic, comparative and fieldwork approaches.

THE RELATIONSHIP OF ANTHROPOLOGY TO SOCIAL SCIENCE, LAW, BIOLOGY AND MEDICINE

In the preceding section, the general nature and subject matter of anthropology have been discussed. It is evident that this discipline concentrates on understanding of mankind as a whole and no known discipline in academic world emphasise biological and cultural dimensions on equal footing. We know that, in general, political science studies man's government, economics man's production and distribution of goods, sociology human society, history concentrates on man's past, geography systematically explains man's relation to the physical world. Among all the subjects mentioned above and the other subjects, anthropology is a solitary discipline studying human activity in a unified way. This does not mean that anthropology is unrelated to other disciplines. The relationship of anthropology with various subjects has been illustrated in Fig. 1.1.

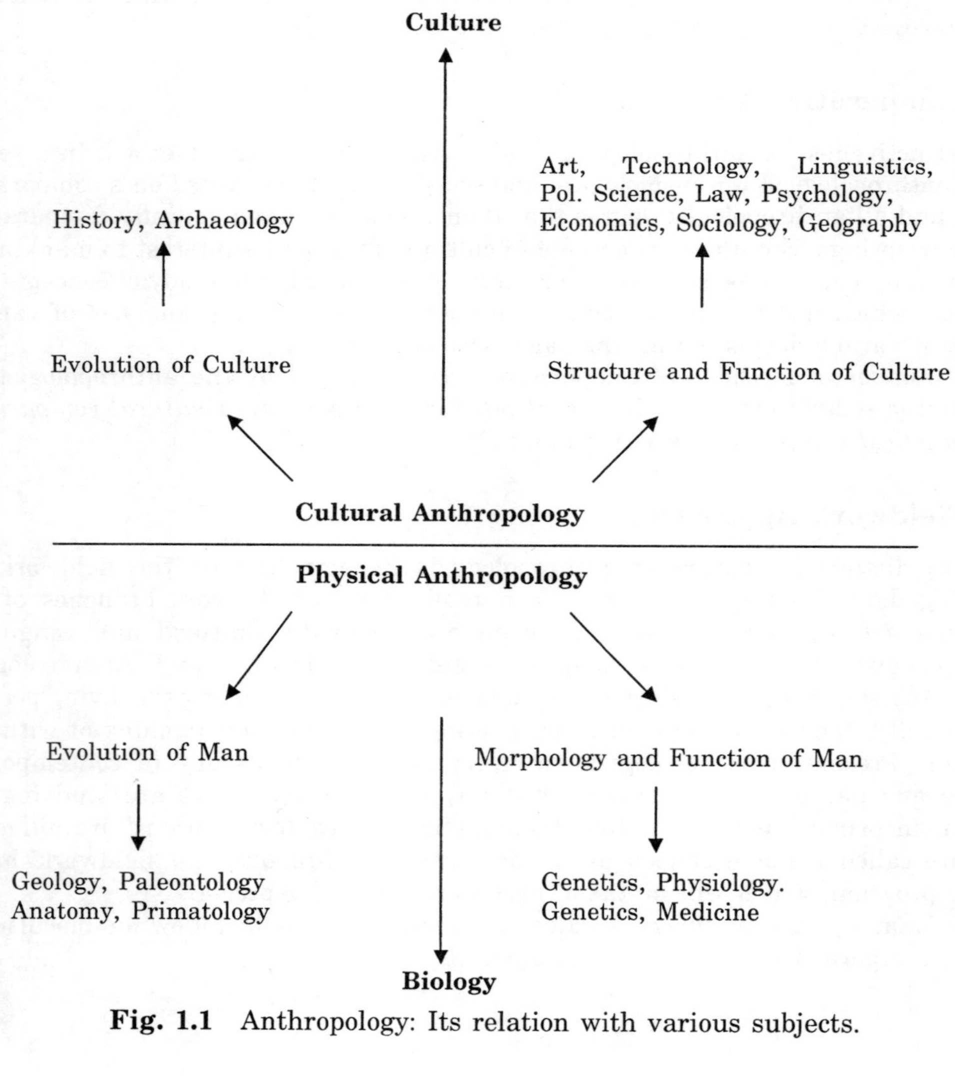

Fig. 1.1 Anthropology: Its relation with various subjects.

The crucial issue still to be answered is how anthropology is related to the above-mentioned subjects. For this, we have to establish the linkage in some specific ways. We will now consider some subjects to illustrate our point.

Sociology

Among all the social sciences, sociology is the closest kin of cultural anthropology. In many countries including India, anthropology and sociology are found in the same department. Their similarity is their interest in social organisation and social system. Many basic concepts (see Chapter 2) such as social status, norms, role, social structure, function, stratification, culture are common to both the subjects. Yet, anthropology and sociology are different subjects. Sociologists do not concentrate on biological dimension of human beings and do not give much emphasis on archaeology and linguistics. In their methodology, sociologists do not necessarily stick to participant observations. They usually work with larger sample and population and employ methods of survey and experimental research.

The celebrated British anthropologist Radcliffe-Brown looked at social anthropology as a branch of sociology, which he and his students called *comparative sociology*. To them, social anthropology focused on pre-literate (primitive) societies while sociology concentrates on industrial societies.

History

Anthropologists realise very well that culture and societies are not momentary things. They were present in the past, they are found presently, and they will continue in the future. In this sense, anthropology is related to history. In fact, under archaeological anthropology, history of mankind of different time is thoroughly studied.

The anthropological ways of organising knowledge are different from the historical methods. Like anthropologists, historians do not study mankind in totality. The historiangs interpret the facts available as the written sources. Their field of operation is library while anthropologists' laboratory is the field.

Several decades ago, George Dalton (1975), the American cultural anthropologist, had remarked that Africa had two kinds of history—the conventional history available through the European exploration of colonial accounts and unconventional history that is prepared by the field anthropologists.

One of the contemporary trends in cultural anthropology is studying native cultures from the native's point of view. This approach is known as *Ethnohistory* (see Chapter 3).

Psychology

Both anthropology and psychology study human beings and borrow certain concepts from each other. During the period 1930–1960, some American cultural anthropologists devoted much of their interest towards social psychology, which gave rise to the emergence of culture and personality school in American anthropology (see Chapter 3). The processes of learning and socialisation developed in psychology left enduring impact on cultural anthropology. In recent years, some American cultural psychologists have made valuable cross-cultural studies. This area is well covered by cultural anthropology.

The main difference between psychology and anthropology lies in research strategies. The psychologists study individual behaviour through controlled laboratory techniques while for anthropologists their laboratory is 'field' (see Chapter 4).

Law and Political Science

Law is one of the best-studied topics by sociocultural anthropologists. In doing so, anthropologists have borrowed several terms and concepts from these subjects. It is usually held that the study of primitive law has contributed to the growth of modern jurisprudence. In Chapter 8, we will deal with those subjects which are, usually, considered as subject matter of Law.

Like social science subjects, anthropology also overlaps biological and medical sciences. In this way, biological and medical sciences are more related to physical anthropology. In Chapter 12, contributions of modern medical science are discussed under medical anthropology.

RELEVANCE OF ANTHROPOLOGY

The celebrated American anthropologist Margaret Mead in her introductory textbook *Anthropology: Human Sciences* had remarked, "If anthropology is about human beings, past and present, it must serve and belong to all humankind" (1964:2).

What Mead wanted to convey was that anthropological knowledge must not be confined to classroom, museum, laboratory, annual meetings and conferences, but it must reach the general public including the 'people' studied by the anthropologists.

Relevance of anthropology can also be realised in the context of its theory and method and their impact on other natural, biological and social sciences.

Terms like 'cultural relativity', 'primitive religion', 'primitive law', 'comparative method', 'wholistic (*holistic*) view', 'participant observation', etc. are no longer confined to anthropological text books. Rather, their usages in other disciplines are also visible.

Worldwide technical-assistance programmes for economic and social development, World Bank and UNESCO projects, military mission, population bureau, and health care are areas in which professional anthropologists have found their places.

In each area of specialisation within General anthropology, trained anthropologists have collaborated with related disciplines specialists. In true sense of the term, anthropology has become a multidisciplinary subject.

The contents of this book reflect the wide range of subjects studied in cultural anthropology.

With this general background on cultural anthropology we will now move on to examine certain concepts and terms related to culture and society in next Chapter.

SUGGESTED READING

Introductory sections of practically all popular textbooks contain some account of the points discussed in Chapter 1. The following are some suggestive titles; a few are more specific:

- Fried, Morton. (Ed.), *Explorations in Anthropology: Reading in Culture, Man and Nature*, Chapter 1, Thomas Y. Crowell, New York, 1973.
- Hoebel, E. Adamson, *Anthropology: The Study of Man*, McGraw Hill Book Company, New York, 1975.
  Practically all chapters are comprehensive and up to date.
- Kluckhohn, Clyde, *Mirror for Man: The Relation of Anthropology of Modern Life*, New York, 1949.
  A good summary of anthropology.
- Mead, Margaret, *Anthropology: A Human Science*, Mentor, New York, 1964.
  Selected papers written between 1939–1960 on aspects of anthropology as a means of studying man, culture and societies.
- Peacock, James L. and A. Thomas Kirsch, *The Human Direction* (An evolutionary approach to Social-Cultural Anthropology), Appleton Century–Crofts, New York, 1970.
- Redfield, Robert, *The Little Community*, University of Chicago Press, Chicago, 1960.
- Tax, Sol, *Horizons of Anthropology*, Aldine, Chicago, 1964.
  Twenty anthropologists have highlighted significant development in the various core branches of anthropology. Some relevant essays related to the contents of the present chapter are 'The setting of the science of man' by Sol Tax, 'The Transition to Humanity' by Geertz, 'The harmonization process' by Clark Howell and 'A perspective for linguistic anthopology' and 'The uses of anthropology' by Dell Hymes.

Chapter 2

Culture and Society and Related Concepts

THE CONCEPT OF CULTURE

Culture is the core concept in anthropology. Specialists of all the branches of anthropology use it in various ways. The only problem with this concept is that there is little agreement about how to define the term. The scientific use of the term corresponds to the original meaning of culture, which is derived from the Latin words *Coletre* (to cultivate and instruct) and *Cultus* (cultivation and training). In its broadest sense, culture is cultivated behaviour, i.e. man's learned and socially transmitted behaviour. This is the general anthropological meaning of the term.

However, anthropologists have operationalised the concept of culture in more than one way. Kroeber and Kluckhohn (1952) have uncovered over 160 definitions of the term. A few representative views are discussed below:

(i) That complex whole which includes knowledge, belief, art, morals, law, custom and any other capabilities and habits acquired by man as member of society (Tylor 1871 : 1).

(ii) All the historically created designs for living, explicit and implicit, rational, irrational and non-rational, which exist at any given time as potential guides for the behaviour of men (Kluckhohn and Kelley 1945 : 78).

(iii) The mass of learned and transmitted motor reactions, habits, techniques, and ideas and valued the behaviour they induce (Kroeber 1948 : 20).

(iv) The man made part of the environment (Herskovits 1955 : 1).

(v) Culture consists of "standards for deciding what is, what can be, how one can feel about it, what to do about it and how to go about doing it." (Goodenough, 1961 : 22–23).

We may present some statements relevant in the use of the term 'culture' used by anthropologists. It must also be noted that from anthropology, the concept has spread to other social sciences and is used in one of the following ways:

(i) Culture is concerned with actions, ideas and artefacts that individuals in the tradition concerned learn and share. The process by which a child learns his/her culture is called *enculturation*.

(ii) Culture can be studied as historical phenomenon. Its elements originate through innovation and spread through diffusion.

(iii) Culture can be studied as a regional phenomenon. Its elements, at any time, are locally distributed in a given geographic area. This is known as *culture area* which will be described shortly.

(iv) Culture tends to be *patterned*. Here, pattern refers to integration. That is, elements of culture (custom, belief, value, institutions, etc.) are interrelated. If one element gets changed, then other elements change as well.

(iv) Culture is a 'continuum', i.e. cultural traditions have accumulated without any break in continuity.

(v) Culture is symbolic. It is a series of man-made objects and personal motivations and actions to which meanings are attached. Anthropologist Lesile White (1959) had viewed culture as symbols consisting of tools, implements, utensils, clothing, ornaments, customs, institutions, beliefs, rituals, art, language, etc.

(vi) In the item (iv) above, we have noted the integration aspect of culture. Related to this is *function* of elements of culture. People use their culture *creatively*. That is, they learn and interpret their culture. They also manipulate the same in different ways. Cultural anthropologists try to distinguish between *ideal* and *real* culture. The former refers to what people say they should do, while the latter is their actual behaviour, observed by the researchers (Linton, 1936).

(vii) A few contemporary cultural sociologists have introduced another dimension of culture, viz. *national culture, international culture* and *subculture* (Clifton, 1968). National culture refers to the experiences, beliefs, learned behaviour and values shared by the citizens of the same nation. Margaret Mead and Ruth Benedict, among others were once interested in study of national character (see Chapter 3). International culture is a term used for cultural traditions beyond national boundaries. Here, cultural borrowings or diffusion of traits become important. Today's multinational organisations such as McDonald, Coca cola, Pepsi, IBM and UND are playing a major role in development of international business. They are trying to impose their own culture on the products.

Although, in a country, the people share common culture and traditions of their nation-state, the individuals may differ in respect of family, region, class, religion and other subgroups. A subculture has different traditions in the same complex societies. Blacks (Negroes) in West-North America is an example of Black subgroup within the American and National character study.

(viii) A culture is static as well as dynamic. Upon a given time, researchers may observe culture of the people as if static, but a culture, indeed, always tends to be on the move. Anthropologists study various processes of culture under the mechanism of culture change. This mechanism consists of diffusion, acculturation, independent invention, culture convergence and most recently, globalisation. These terms are defined at appropriate places in this book (Chapter 3).

Analysis of Culture

Anthropologists of all kinds try to explore the nature of culture. In the ensuing chapters of this book, we will examine the various orientations through which the cultural anthropologists have developed conceptual schemes in understanding culture. These schemes are about how to look at the human behaviour orienting societal or cultural base and the ways to be employed in understanding people and their cultures. The inherent working mechanism of cultural anthropologists, however, is based on the principle of four approaches (biocultural, fieldwork, holistic and comparative) which are discussed in the preceding chapter.

The Construct of Culture

A *construct* is a framework used to explain phenomena that are perceived only partially. No person can perceive everything signified by the term culture. At a construct, culture has two major uses:

(i) as a general category for the classification of phenomena and

(ii) as a tool in predicting social behaviour.

Kroeber and Kluckhohn's edited volume on *Culture: A Critical Review* (1952) contains a discussion on use of culture as a construction.

TAXONOMY OF CULTURE

Taxonomy means scientific scheme of classification. We have seen briefly, how anthropologists have handled the concept of culture. They have also devised several categories or divisions of it. These categories have yielded various insights into the nature of culture.

One scheme is to categorise culture into its *material and non-material* aspects. The former includes things like tools, food, house, etc. Non-material culture, on the other hand, is composed of beliefs, values and ideologies. It is significant to note that this breakdown of culture has contributed to the problem of rate of change in culture. In other words, anthropologists and other social scientists put forth the question which culture changes more rapidly—material or non-material? The difference in rates of the two is termed as *culture lag,* which was introduced by American sociologist William Ogburn.

Material culture and *material objects:* A distinction must be made between culture and objects. Any object made by the man is material culture, e.g. tools, houses, etc. People use a number of objects—organic and inorganic as source of livelihood. They are the goods such as land and cattle. Both material culture and material objects influence social relationships. A single small artefact may be a nexus between persons, e.g. a spear among several African tribes, passed from father to sons by gift or inheritance, is a symbol of their relationship.

Another scheme categorises culture into ideal and real categories. Ideal culture is what ought to exist (norm). It should be noted that a researcher often finds difference between what people say, 'should be' (Norm) and what they do. Discrepancies between norm and behaviour occur in all societies. In their fieldwork, anthropologists are very careful in accounting for ideal and real culture.

American anthropologists of early 20th century developed a third way to breakdown culture into simpler parts. The smallest part which is the most basic element of culture, is called *culture trait*. But, it should be noted that many of the cultural elements which are recognised as traits can further be divided into significant parts, which, in turn, can be recognized as culture traits. For example, the smoking of a ceremonial pipe as a symbol of friendship and brotherhood is a basic unit of culture, but it can be analysed into a number of parts meaningful to the people. There is the formation of the circle of men to whom the pipe is to be passed; there is the fact that the pipe is to be passed in a clock-wise direction, and in this way, there may be other elements which are viewed as traits.

The implication of the above depends how the observer views a culture. Therefore, anthropologists believe that cultural traits must be explained in reference to time and context. It is apparent that a number of traits are closely related. When these traits are in a set, the situation is what anthropologists call *trait complexes*. Thus, a culture consists of not only cultural traits but of complexes of traits. When *trait complexes* are eventually grouped in a larger unit, it is referred to a *pattern*.

In above-mentioned ways, anthropologists have provided several schemes for descriptions of a culture.

SOCIETY AND CULTURE

The terms culture and society are frequently used interchangeably. There is no harm in doing so as long as we know what the difference is. In simpler words, the society (see below) is always made up of people, and the way they behave is culture. In other words, a society is not a culture; *it has a culture.*

Society, although composed of people, is more than an aggregation of human beings. The aggregation of people is necessary to have a society. When this aggregation is bonded together by common people (behaviour), the aggregation is said to be society. Society, in simple terms, therefore, refers to grouping and arrangements of people.

Culture is a product of society, especially since culture presupposes the existence of a human group interacting in a patterned, repetitive manner. Culture refers to the ideas, meaning and knowledge, both conscious and unconscious, that people share.

Societies exist within definite boundaries and occupy a definable space. Members interact in a *network of social relations,* ordered and patterned according to prevailing customs. Members of a defined group know each other well. Structure and behaviour of members occur in a network. Homogeneous networks generally have similar attitude. There is pressure on the members to follow normative pattern of behaviour. Defined boundary makes it possible to control the behaviour of the members and also to assist them at the time of distress. Generally, the members of a society share a common language and a set of symbols. There is no definite number of people required for a society to exist. In contrast to the term culture, we may use the term society in reference to animals other than man.

Relation between Culture and Society

Students of sociology and anthropology often confront with the problem of understanding culture and society and their relationship. Much about culture has been discussed above.

Culture, simply, is the common position of a body of people who share the same tradition. This is expressed in 'social relational' terms, and such a body is a *society*. Obviously, these terms are interrelated. Usually, this is expressed by using the term 'sociocultural'. One cannot be separated from the other. While society and culture are two dimensions of social life; nevertheless, a British social anthropologist Radcliffe-Brown truly remarked that emphasis on culture and society leads to two different kinds of studies—social anthropological study and cultural anthropological study (see Chapter 3). In the former, the emphasis is on the interactions of people living in a society and not on the personal characteristics of individuals, even when they are thought of as the product of their culture. Putting it differently, social anthropologists look for 'social relation' in a group or society; cultural anthropologists look for 'patterns' in a society.

Clifford Greetz (1957) has aptly stated that culture is the fabric of meaning through which human beings interpret their experiences and guide their actions. Social structure is the form these actions take place. Culture and society are but the abstractions of the same phenomenon. This is termed as *sociocultural pattern.*

CIVILISATION

The term 'civilisation', originally derived from the verb to 'civilige' from *civis* and *civilities,* describes the acquisition of qualities over a period of time. Scholars on society have used the term civilisation to connote different things. Arnold J. Toynbee (*A Study of History*, 1933–54) points to civilisations in the known history of the world. Anthropologist E.B. Tylor (1871 : 1) used culture and civilisation synonymously. Many anthropologists used the term culture referring to the patterned ways of all people, no matter how simple or complex their way of life may be. They use civilisation to characterise certain phase with written language, an urban life and a complex economic, political and religious organisation. In the conceptual system of cultural evolutionism, the term civilisation has a precise meaning. It stands for a definite stage in the development of society and culture. In this sense, Lewis Morgan used the term civilisation to mark the attainment of stage 'invention of writing'. Gordon Childe identified the attainment of civilisation with the growth of 'urbanism', e.g. the Sumerian cities.

However, the American neo-evolutionists have clearly shown that the processes of growth of civilisation must be reappraised in the light of data from 'native' Americans, i.e. the Red Indians of America. In Meso-America, urban revolution does not go along with the rise of civilisation. The scholars have clearly shown that the rise of civilisation can be seen as the outcome of a process of *ecological adaptation.* We must also remember that the term civilisation does not imply 'better than' but 'more complex in certain ways than other types of culture'. Some writers have used the term 'Great society' to refer to civilisation as a whole. Civilisation, in our view, is the product of a long-range cultural process. In this sense, experts in prehistory have called earliest Stone Age culture as 'Dawn of civilisation'.

Both cultural and archaeological anthropologists view civilisation as culture of complex societies, which are organised around *stable* socio-economic organisation and around 'state' formation and social stratification. In this sense, the first civilisations arose in the Old world between 6000–5000 B.P. (before present) or 4000–3000 B.C.

Modern anthropologists employ the term civilisation on the basis of empirically derived criteria such as the presence of a high level of food production, the development of managerial skills to handle developing institutions (economic, military, social), control of the means of production by ruling classes (legal, theological), professional merchant classes working within a highly developed exchange network radiating outward from the major urban centres and full-time specialists freed from manual toil who, often, are responsible for the development of arithmetic, geometry, astronomy, writing, numerical notation, standards to time, space and weight. Civilisation is also marked by the development of institutions that take over the functions previously handled by extended kinship ties, for example, redistribution of foodstuffs in times of need. The need for organisation tends to codify and regularise the value system of the culture involved.

SOME SOCIOLOGICAL-ANTHROPOLOGICAL CONCEPTS

While describing a particular culture, ethnographers have frequently used the terms society, community, institution, association, group, structure and organization. Each of these terms carries precise meaning though a few of them, particularly society and community, structure and organization, are used interchangeably. There is no harm in doing so as long as we know what the difference is. It would be useful here to note conceptual meaning of these terms.

Society

In ethnographic writings, many anthropologists have used the term society to refer to a group, small or large, whose members are united by—social, economic, political and religious affiliation such as a Tribal society, a Hindu society or an African society. But, many sociologists have defined society not as group of people, but the "complex pattern of relationship found among the people of a group". Sociologist MacIver (1987: 5) stated it is "a web of relationship, and is always changing". By this he meant myriad of relationships. For example, a simple nuclear family is said to have as many as eight types of relationships among its members, viz. wife-husband relation, mother-son, mother-daughter, father-son, father-daughter, siblings, male siblings and female sibling. Beyond family, the relationship is unlimited or uncountable. MacIver (1987:5), has stated,

"Society is a system of usages and procedures, of authority and mutual aid, of many groupings and divisions, of controls of human behaviour and of liberties. This ever-changing, complex we call society".

In other words, the essential elements of the society are—usages and procedure, mutual aid, authority pattern, grouping, control of behaviour of members. Society involves both likeness and differences. The sense of likeness is focussed in simple societies on kinship, in a complex society it is in the sense of nationality or one world.

Difference between 'the society and a society'

Those who define society as a group of people interpret it in the sense of 'a society' as distinguished from society defined above in abstract sense. In this book we have frequently used the term *a society* in the sense of a community (see below); nevertheless, the abstract sense of the society has not been ignored.

Community

One of the simplest definitions of the community has been set out by Arnold W. Green in his *The Society* (McGraw-Hill, New York 1956: 274) as "cluster of people, living within a contiguous small area, which share a common way of life". Nearly, all sociologists and cultural anthropologists have emphasised the *aerial* as well as *ecological* aspect of a group following an integrated system of social life. A community may be small or large, and invariably is a named group which reflects sentiment and identity. A community is concrete while society is abstract. A society refers to a community. The difference between community and society is well illustrated by the use of Tonnies' terms *gemeinschaft* and *gesellschaft* (described elsewhere).

Association

In general terms, association is meeting together of people to achieve some purposes. According to MacIver, "it is an organisation deliberately formed for the collective purpose of some interest or set of interest, which its members share. Family, church, work group, music-dance club are examples of various types of association. It may be temporary or permanent on the basis of functional and legal power. According to the sociologists, the difference between society and association is that the former refers to the social relationship while the latter is a functional group. An association is not a community but it exists within it. Several associational groups, viz. age group or specific task group exits among the tribal communities such as the youth dormitory (i.e. Gond's *ghotul*), ceremonial-dance group (i.e. Hopi's sun dance). It is in this sense, the term has been used in this book.

Institution

In popular writing, the term institution is used to mean an organisation with some specific purpose such as educational institution (college, university) or a professional or charitable group such as the Indian Institute of Anthropology or the Ram Krishna Mission. This term is also used to denote a set of persons in organised interaction as family, or government. Thus, when college is referred as a body of teachers and students it talks about its associational aspect, but when the system is considered as a whole it talks about its institutional features. Both in cultural anthropology and sociology it carries a specific meaning referring to well established procedures centered on certain focal interest.

In a simple (tribal level) society, the culture provides an unwritten manual according to which tasks are performed by the members, and this British anthropologist Malinowski called the Charter of institution. By this he meant statements explaining why the institutions exit and for what purpose. In many tribal societies institutional charter is present in the form of customs. In various chapters of this book several institutions such as family, marriage, kinship, economic, political, religion and recreational, are described in detail. These institutions within a society overlap, i.e. they are mutually inclusive. It is the task of anthropologists to analyze and present them in a meaningful way. Because of this, it is held that all institutions are integrated.

SOCIAL STRUCTURE AND SOCIAL ORGANISATION

The term 'social structure' and 'social organisation' are frequently used interchangeably. Some anthropologists use social structure what other anthropologists call social organisation or vice-versa. Confusion persists if the users do not define it.

Social structure and social organisation both are *constructs*. As discussed above, a construct is always devised by the researchers. Constructs represent abstract model of social phenomena. Anthropologists maintain that the structure of a society involves two things—first, there is division into smaller social units what we call groups; and second, there are recognised social positions (*statuses*) and appropriate behaviour patterns (*roles*) related to those positions. In brief, social structure is accepted as a component group of role arrangements. The totality of structure and status is known as social organisation.

Social anthropologists examine both social structure and social organisation in terms of *action* and *meaning* to the actors. Action denotes the nature of act and subsequent consequences. We must always take into account not only what and how the action was done (the level of action) but the people's interpretation for the action (the level of meaning).

Distinction between Social Structure and Social Organisation

While distinguishing between social structure and social organisation, Raymond Firth took a lead and insisted that:

"...In the aspect of social structure is to be found the continuity of principle of society; in the aspect of organisation is to be found the variation and change principle—by allowing evaluation of situations and entry of individual choice ... (we find) in the social organisation, the systematic ordering of social relations by acts of choice and decision... Structural forms set a precedent and provide a limitation to the range of alternatives" (Firth, 1951 : 40,31).

It appears that Firth recognises two aspects of every social system, viz. idealised conception of social structure as static and dynamic notion attached to social organisation (Firth 1975 : 1–28). However, not all anthropologists think of 'individual choices' as prime mover in the operation and change of social systems.

How to Investigate the social structure of a society?

The ethnographer identifies the social groups (discussed subsequently) which make up a society (community). He, then, identifies the members of these groups and their domestic and kinship ties, in terms of roles and statuses of the members and so on. The ethnographers also consider the relationship between or among the social groups, viz. domestic group, lineage, clan, kindred and so on.

In brief, anthropological study of social structure involves description and analysis of social groups which make up a society and the ways in which they function.

ROLE AND STATUS

Ralph Linton introduced the concept of social role into anthropology. Each social role has one or more attributes (behaviour) concerned with *recruitment* to the role. Recruitment is a process by which individuals become entitled to perform roles. Ralph Linton (1936 : 113–3) distinguished two general types of recruitments—the recruitment that takes place by *achieved*, i.e. one must do something in order to perform the role and the recruitment that takes place by *ascription*, i.e. a role is ascribed to an individual by 'born into' a group (family, caste, nation). Some time it is difficult to make a neat distinction very easily between achieved and ascribed roles. Many roles are a combination of both. Each type has its merits and demerits. Social structure emphasizes on one or the other type of recruitment. Linton also used the term 'status' to refer to the category (or social position) or a social role. It was S.F. Nadel who eliminated the term 'status' from the description of social structure (Nadel, 1957).

In the analysis of social structure and social organisation, anthropologists emphasise on kinship roles, sex and age roles, occupational roles, political (leadership) role and personal/societal role in varying degrees. The point to be emphasised is the role of the organisational side of status. It is the manner in which the behaviours culturally associated with status are acted out in overt and covert behaviour.

SOCIAL GROUP

Anthropologists and sociologists have defined group in different ways for different analytical purposes. Ferdinand Tonnies' (1855–1936) classical distinction between *Gemeinshaft* and *Gesellschaft* is usually translated as 'communal' (community) and 'associative' (association) groups. Some of the authors have emphasised on differences between familiastic or kin groups and non-familiastic groups. Some distinguish groups with volitional as opposed to ascribed groups. Groups may be residential, spatial, territorial or special purpose groups. Though all the groups are useful, social anthropologists are more interested in *residential* as well as *corporate* nature of groups. Thus, for the analysis of social structure and social organisation, anthropologists frequently make references to domestic groups (family, households), descent groups (lineage, class), bands, etc. Virtually all the groups are residential except clans, which, often, are dispersed. When not specified, groups are residential in character *(corporateness)*. It is the task of the ethnographer to define the nature of corporate character of group. Relatively, a permanent group which controls property is referred to as *corporate group*.

In brief, a residential group exists because it is there, and it has some common (manifest) functions, viz. economic, political, biological and others.

Some anthropologists (Lowie, 1948; Service, 1962) have used the term *sodality* to refer to a 'special purpose group' which is non-residential but display some characteristics of corporateness. It is close in spirit to *gesellschaft*. It may also be noted that the changes in residential groups are essentially demographic matters; sodalities are not directly affected by demographic variables. Service is of the view that "sodalities *integrate* different residential units; they are not groups exactly, but they have an important relationship to the true groups, i.e. residential groups" (1962 : 14).

Group Functions and Specialisations

Most of the groups have a variety of functions (or purposes). Many anthropologists have noted the following three functions in the analysis of a society or community:

1. **Task function:** A task group is oriented towards producing as well as protecting a product (resource).
2. **Control function:** The orientation of the group towards maintaining its own internal structure (i.e. enculturation group) is called control function.
3. **Expressive function:** In this function, the group satisfies the psychological needs of its members including those needs which result from individual participation in the take and control activities.

The American anthropologist Bock (1969) stated that every human group is oriented towards one or more of above functions, and analysis will, generally, show that all the three functions are present to some degree explicitly or implicitly.

Fission and Segmentation in Social Group

A social group such as a household, a lineage or a clan need not always be sedentary. It may change its form over time due to demographic and economic constraints. Two important processes involved in it are: *fission* and *segmentation*. Fission means that one or more subgroups migrate to a new territory and establish their own groups. Choice of alternatives depends on availability of resources (land, etc.). When fission takes place between parts of a corporate social group (descent group), it is usually called 'segmentation.' Evans-Pritchard has discussed it with reference to the lineage organisation of the Nuer (see Chapter 6).

SOCIAL STRATIFICATION

An important distinction must be made between the concepts of *social inequality* and *social stratification*. Failure to make this crucial distinction has led to much confusion among anthropologists as to whether social stratification is actually a universal feature of social life.

Social inequality refers to the existence of differential degrees of social influence or prestige among individual members of the same society. There are two important facets of this definition. Inequality can and does exist in human societies without any differential degrees of individuals or groups to wealth or to the resources of nature that sustain life. Second, social inequality implies an inequality among individuals, not as members of groups. Thus, social inequality is a universal feature of human societies, for there is no record of a society that fails to make at least some evaluative distinctions among some individuals.

In contrast to social inequality, social stratification involves the existence within a single society of two or more differentially ranked groups, the members of which control unequal amounts of power, privilege and prestige. This definition of stratification closely follows the conception of stratified society developed by the anthropologist Morton Fried. He notes, "A stratified society is one in which members of the same sex and equivalent age status do not have equal access to the basic resources that sustain life" (1967 : 186). The key notion contained in Fried's definition is differential access to resources. This clearly goes beyond the fact of simple inequalities into the realm of fundamental inequities in power and priviledge.

Another crucial characteristic of stratification is that it *involves groups not individuals*. The degree of power, privilege and prestige that individuals have in stratified society depends on their membership in actual social groups, not on their personal characteristics. These differentially ranked groups constitute social strata (stratum, sing.) or layers of the overall sociocultural system, and they have a strongly hereditary character. Hence, in stratified societies, individuals are born into a particular social stratum that gives them a social position and identity regardless of their own personal characteristics. This hereditary quality of stratification clearly sets it apart from inequality. In unstratified societies, the inequalities that emerge (beyond those based on age and sex) are mainly due to individual effort and ability, rather than hereditary social placement.

Stratification is, by no means, a universal characteristic of human societies. While there is no such thing as a society in which all the persons are perfectly equal, there have been many societies lacking stratification. Stratification tends to be found for the first time among those societies that have evolved to an intensive horticultural level of technological development although it is occasionally found below this evolutionary stage. Despite the fact that stratification has not been universal, it has been a common feature of many societies, and it is indeed universal among all the complex societies. (This subject will be taken up in more detail in Chapter 8; see Table 2.1.)

Table 2.1 The Evolution of Social Stratification in Preindustrial Societies

Type of society	*Nature of social stratification*
Hunting and gathering	No stratification, inequalities of privilege generally absent. Mild inequalities exist based on age, sex and personal characteristics such as courage and hunting skill, but they are inequalities of prestige and influence.
Simple horticultural	No stratification, inequalities of privilege generally absent. Inequalities based on age and sex exist.
Intensive horticultural	First emergence of genuine stratification. Common pattern is division of society into three social strata (chiefs, subchiefs, commoners).
Agrarian	Extreme stratification. Bulk of population is a subjugated and exploited peasantry. Rulers and governing classes possess great wealth and power.

Source: Fried, 1967 : 25.

SUGGESTED READING

Many cultural anthropology textbooks have separate chapters on 'culture' and related topics. Below are listed only some specific books on anthropological discussions of the concept.

- Bock, Philip, *Modern Cultural Anthropology*, Knof, N.Y., 1969.
- Clifton, James A. (Ed.), *Introduction to Cultural Anthropology,* Houghton Mifflin, Boston, 1968.
  Eighteen essays are on the scope and methods of science of man by professional anthropologists. For the discussion on culture, Chapter 1 is recommended.

- Fried, Morton H. (Ed.), *Explorations in Anthropology* (Readings in Culture, Man and Nature), Thomas Y. Crowell, New York, 1973.
  This edited volume provides reading materials on various aspects of anthropology; Part IV includes two articles by M.H. Fried and E.B. Lealock on the concept of culture.
  The Evolution of Political Society, Random House, New York, 1967.
- Firth, Raymond, 1951, An Approach to Modern Social Anthropology, *Annual Review of Anthropology*, **4**, 1–24, 1975.
- Goodenough, Ward H., On Cultural Evolution. *Daedalus,* **90**, 521–28, 1961.
  In this short comment, the author proposes an ideational definition of culture. It does work in field situation.
- Geertz, Clifford, The Impact of the Concept of culture on the Concept of Man, *American Anthropologist*, **59**, 20–35, 1957.
- Hammel, E.A. and W.A. Simmons (Eds.), *Man Makes Sense, A Reader in Cultural Anthropology*, Rand McNally Series, 1970.
  Part II provides an extended introduction to the nature of culture.
- Hughes, Charles C. (Ed.), *Make Men of Them,* Introductory Readings for Cultural Anthropology, Rand MC Nally Anthropology Series, 1972.
  This is a very interesting edited book. It provides original writings of a number of prominent anthropologists. Part IV 'The conceptualisation of culture' has 13 articles on nature of culture.
- Kroeber, Alfred L. and Clyde, Kluckhohn (Eds.), *Culture: A Critical Review of Concepts and Definitions*, Paper of the Peabody Museum of American Archaeology and Ethnology, Harvard University, **47,** 1952.
  This is a collection of definitions of culture with comments of their utility for anthropology.
- Linton, Ralph, *The Study of Man*, Appleton–Century, New York, 1936.
- Nadel, S.F., *The Theory of Social Structure*, Free Press, London, 1956.
- Service, Elman, The *Primitive Social Organisation*, Random House, N.Y. 1962.
- Singer, Milton, The Concept of Culture, *International Encyclopedia of the Social Science*. **3**, 527–543, 1968.
  It summarises and compares the completing theories of culture and social structure in anthropology.
- Schusky, E.L. and T.P. Culbert, *Introducing Culture*, Prentice Hall Inc., Englewood, Cliffs, New Jersey, 1967.
  This small book introduces the primary concepts of culture in concise manner.
- White, Lesile A. (with Beth Dillinghan), *The Concept of Culture,* Minneapolis, Burgess, 1973.
- Sociological concepts like society, community, association, institution, group are well dealt in *Society, An Introductory Analysis*, R.M. MacIver and charles H. Page, Macmillan India Edition, Delhi, 1987.

A short discussion of the anthropologist's view of culture is presented by a leading cultural neo-evolutionist. In addition to his own theory of energy system and culture, White traces out history of development of culture, and finally 'How Culture Evolved.'

Chapter 3

Theoretical Interests in Cultural Anthropology

ANTHROPOLOGY, the science of man, was firmly established as an academic discipline in the late nineteenth century in Europe and in the North America. But it does not mean that anthropological contributions made by the man of the ancient period should altogether be ignored. In fact, a connection of anthropological reasoning from Middle Age (the 5th through 13th centuries) through the period of Enlightenment (the 18th century) in Europe can be established well. However, in this chapter, we shall concentrate on the major advances in socio-cultural anthropology of the past 100 years.

This chapter focuses on seven major and other trends that emerged during the period 1870–1970. It also modestly touches upon views of structuralism and its impact on modern cultural anthropology (New anthropology).

SCHOOLS OF ANTHROPOLOGICAL THOUGHT

Realising that anthropological ideas developed by some scholars do not fit into particular 'pigeonholes-conceptual ideas' such as evolutionism, historicism, configurationalism or structural-functionalism, still the following 'schools' are well recognised:

(1) Evolutionism

(2) Diffusionism

(3) Cultural history

(4) Structural-functionalism

(5) Culture and personality

(6) Neo-evolutionism

(7) Structuralism and New anthropology

We will now describe these schools of thought. Contributions of major anthropologists relevant to our discussion are discussed in various chapters of this book.

CULTURAL EVOLUTIONISM

This school is popularly known as *classical evolutionism*. In its most limited sense, the word 'evolution' describes the process of change from one state to another. As popularised by the Western social theorists of the nineteenth century, the word 'Cultural evolution' meant a unilinear cumulative process through which societies get changed from 'lower' to 'higher' stages of development. During this period, the concept to incorporate the idea of progress came, which traced its origin from the social philosophers of the 16th and 17th centuries, such as: Fontenelle (1657–1757), Montesquieu (1689–1755), Turgot (1727–1781) and Condercet (1743–1794) in France; Vico (1668–1744) in Italy; Hobbes (1588–1679), Hume (1711–1776) and Ferguson (1723– 1816) in Great Britain and Kant (1724–1804) and Harder (1744–1803) in Germany.

The classical evolutionary theories of the nineteenth century can be distinguished by their

(a) characterisation of stages of evolution,

(b) description of the trajectories of evolution and

(c) isolation of the causal agents of change.

At a more abstract level, these theories had three common features. Firstly, they tended to be unilinear in that they isolated a single path of evolution that all societies were supposed to pass through. Secondly, the stages were regarded as universal in that the unilinear path began from a similar primeval past and ended with the same destination, usually taken to be similar to the western industrial society. Thirdly, the theories tended to emphasise a single generalised causal agency, which accounted for the evolution of all societies. With these remarks in mind, we will now proceed to look at the specific ideas of some of the key representatives of the evolutionary tradition.

In popular anthropological literature, the idea of cultural progress can be deduced from the writings of scholars such as J. Bachofen, J.F. McLennan, Lewis Morgan, Edward Tylor and James Frazer among others. These writers were not professional anthropologists, rather, they, in the words of Evans-Pritchard, were 'intellectualists'. That is, they imagined themselves as intellectual savages who faced the problem of explaining natural and human events to them. Each had different educational and private life styles. But, inspired by the intellectual feelings of their time, they tried to record the then prevalent ideas. It should be remembered that many early intellectualists believed their own (western) society to be the most evolved or developed.

Edward Burnett Tylor (1832–1917), the English anthropologist argued that there had been a cultural evolution from simple to complex forms. Tylor's most influential work was *Primitive Culture* (1871), in which he used the word 'culture', on the very first page, for the first time in the sense in which anthropologists use it today. In this book Tylor talked at length about the development of culture, i.e. mythology, philosophy, religion, language, art and customs (see Chapter 2). His focus was mainly institutions of primitive men.

Tylor argued that social institutions such as family, marriage, economy and religion are stratified like the layers of the earth, developing through similar stages in different parts of the world. There was, of course, a remarkable degree of similarities, and these similarities were because of *'psychic unity of mankind'*, i.e. the way human mind works under similar conditions. This phrase also means that human beings in various societies when faced with similar problems have come up with similar solutions to them. Tylor also held that the basis of religion is 'the doctrine of supernatural beings' which he called 'animism'. He maintained that primitive beliefs survive as elements of modern civilisation. In Tylor's views, one can reconstruct the earlier stages of institutions by studying 'survivals' or leftovers of the past. Thus, he outlined a developmental scheme for religion as follows:

Monotheism
↑
Polytheism
↑
Animism

Tylor's theory of religion will be dealt with in Chapter 9.

Lewis Henry Morgan (1818–1881) was a lawyer by professional training, but his contribution to social thought falls within the domain of the subject matter of anthropology and sociology. He formulated a theory of social evolution, which has been quite influential in social science, particularly in Marxist social thought.

Morgan regarded technology as the key factor in social evolution. He claimed that since human needs and mental capabilities have been the same across cultures and through time, only technology accounted for the differences in levels of evolution.

Morgan isolated three main stages of evolution: *savagery, barbarism* and *civilisation*. The stages of savagery and barbarism were further subdivided into lower, middle and upper statuses, such that the entire scheme had altogether seven gradations of evolution. Corresponding to each of these stages, there were certain characteristic inventions and modes of subsistence.

Morgan's summary of 'ethnical period', as he termed, is defined by the following sequence of technological innovation:

Lower savagery	Fruit and nut subsistence
Middle savagery	Fish subsistence and fire
Upper savagery	Bow and arrow
Lower barbarism	Pottery
Middle barbarism	Domestication of animals (Old World), cultivation of maize irrigation, abode and stone architecture (New World)
Upper barbarism	Iron tools
Civilisation	Phonetic alphabet and writing

As it is clear from the above points, Morgan conceived the three main stages of evolution as overlapping rather than constituting mutually exclusive categories. He claimed that the three distinct conditions "are connected with each other in a natural as well as necessary sequence of process." This assumption of unilinear and universal stages led him to the methodological error of treating contemporary primitive societies as the mirror image of what technologically advanced societies must have looked like in the past.

The Scheme of Development of Family and Kinship Terminology

In the domain of the family, Morgan recognised the following five successive forms:

(1) The *consanguine,* based on group marriage (marriage of 'brothers and sisters'),

(2) the *punaluan,* based on a form between group marriage in which brothers were forbidden to marry sisters,

(3) the *syndyasmian* or *pairing* family, a transitional form between group marriage and monogamy, in which husband or wife could end the marriage at will as often as he or she wished,

(4) the *patriarchical,* a short-lived variety, mainly associated with the Hebrews and early Romans, in which the supreme authority was vested in the male head (polygamy was a secondary feature, present among Hebrews and absent among Romans) and

(5) the *monogamian,* based on monogamy and female equality, and progressively resembling the modern nuclear unit.

Morgan recognized the following sequence of kinship terminologies:

(1) Malayan,

(2) Turanian-Ganowanian and

(3) Aryan-semitic Uralian.

In modern classifications, the above-mentioned terminologies correspond respectively to the Hawaiian, Iroqois and Eskimo types (quoted in Harris, 1968 : 181).

Many critics do not agree with the Morgan scheme, but, at least, it had the merit of setting forth a plan of evolutionary development. In the sphere of family and kinship organisation, Morgan's ideas were influenced by other 19th century thinkers, viz. Jacob Bachofen, John McLennan, and Edward Tylor. It must, however, be noted that Morgan's *Systems of Consanguinity and Affinity in the Human Family* (1817) have left enduring effects among the American scholars. His *Ancient Society* (1877) was the corner stone of Soviet anthropology influenced by Marx and Engles (1984).

In brief, the Evolutionism of Tylor and Morgan was based on:

(1) The doctrine of *the psychic unity of mankind,* which was first formulated by the German geographer and ethnographer Adolf Bastian (1826–1905). It said that all people, primitive and civilised, had the same basic brain capacity. However, primitive people were less advanced because they had been stunted through less contact with other people or because they somehow got a later start in evolution;

(2) The doctrine of *independent invention,* which assumes that all people are equally creative, that culture has evolved everywhere, and that the same inventions can develop in separate places;

(3) The idea that all cultures evolve through the evolutionary stages.

Sir Henry Maine (1822–1888), in his *Ancient Law* (1864) set forth a patriarchal origin for society on the basis of Roman, Celtic and Germanic laws. His knowledge of Hindu law aided to his career as a judge in India. Maine was a lawyer, a Professor of Jurisprudence at Oxford. He saw the major development of society from a stage in which its law was dominated by status, to a stage in which the law was dominated by contract. This sweeping generalisation has been validated by subsequent research. New evidences began to turn up to counter his evolutionary thesis that societies were originally all organised in patriarchal extended families. He acknowledged that "the observation of savage or extremely barbarous races has brought to light forms of social organisation lacking the beginnings of law.... and possibly in some cases of greater antiquity"—these were reports on matrilineal organised societies, with which Maine dealt in his *Early Law and Custom* (1883). He was prepared to accept new evidences.

THE DIFFUSION SCHOOL

Towards the close of 19th century and early 20th century, some European thinkers developed theories that emphasised the role of *diffusion*. Diffusion is a process whereby cultural elements spread from one society to another. There were two main diffusion schools—one English and the other German and Austrian. The leading proponents of the British school were **G. Elliot Smith** and **William J. Perry.** Both Smith and Perry held that many aspects of higher civilisation first developed in Egypt, and from there, they diffused to other parts of the world. It was their assumption that most of the people are uninventive. Diffusionists also assumed that parallel cultural evolution is rare. The British diffusionists contended that if agriculture, pottery making, weaving, pyramid building and other features were to be found in North America and elsewhere, it was due to the explorations by the Egyptians or the people who had been in contact with Egyptian civilisations. Thus, the British diffusionists explained the conditions of contemporary primitive societies 'as the results of their degeneration from a high estate one conferred upon them by Egypt.'

The other diffusion school is far more important. **Fritz Graebner** (1877–1934) and Father **Wilhelm Schmidt** (1868–1954) represented this among others. Their thinking was moulded by the anthropogeographic tradition of 19th century Germany notably by the work of Friedrich Ratzel. His student Leo Frobenius coined the term *Kulturkreis* to define the spread of a culture tradition. This developed into *Kultur kreislehre* or 'culture-cycle'. school. Both *Graebner* and *Schmidt* developed a theory that reconstructed cultural history of societies.

Unlike the British diffusionists, the German-Austrian scholars postulated diffusion sequence from several centres of origin. At each of these centres, a distinctive cluster of cultural elements evolved. These clusters or circles are called *cutleries*. They held that diffusion of cultural traits may take place over great distances and that they may disperse complexes. In 1906, Graebner applied the culture-circle idea on a worldwide basis. The follower of Graebner was Wilhelm Schmidt. Both formulated two basic rules: 'criterion of form', and 'criterion of quality' for discovering the historical connection between cultural elements and complexes. These rules state that similarities between two cultural elements, which do not arise out of the nature, material or purpose of the traits or subjects, should be interpreted as resulting from diffusion, regardless of distance between these two cutleries. The second rule, criterion of quality, states that the probability of historical relationship between two items increases with the number of additional items showing similarities; (for detail see Harris, 1968 : 382–87). Schmidt suggested the possibility of reconstructing characteristics of 'ethnological oldest' people of the world. Father Schmidt had founded *Anthropos* (1906), a muti-lingual journal in which in major European research papers languages appeared.

Although some field scholars of the classical schools were defunct by the middle of 20th century, some contemporary anthropologists have utilised the notion of diffusion in analysing change process in societies they study; (refer to Chapter 12).

THE CULTURE-HISTORY SCHOOL

Roughly contemporaneous with diffusionists, American anthropologists developed theories in which the study of the history of specific cultural phenomena was emphasised. The key figure in this approach was **Franz Boas** (1858–1942). He made use of his extensive ethnographic knowledge and wrote a series of research papers rejecting evolutionists' search for universal laws. He called into questions and issues and employed assumptions of evolutionists such as use of the cultures of contemporary primitive societies represent early stages of the evolution of culture, and also, assuming that similarities between societies are the independent result of the psychic unity of mankind.

One of the widely read essays of Boas, *The Method of Ethnology* (1920), pointed out the very weak foundation of evolutionism and British diffusionism in clear terms. He clarified his own position brilliantly. To quote a few lines of this essay: "While in natural sciences, we are accustomed to consider a given number of causes and to study their effects; in historical happenings, we are compelled to consider every phenomenon not only as an effect but also as a cause." This position has come to be known as 'historical particularism' which will be described shortly. While the selected works of Boas, together with his contributions to the field of American anthropology, are noted elsewhere, here, it should be noted that he, under the influence of *geographical determinism*, wanted to see to what extent the culture of a society is shaped by its environment. This was possible only by doing fieldwork, which became the academic programme in American anthropology. Boas' own fieldwork among the Eskimo in 1883–84 led him to conclude that the Eskimos did the things not just because of environment but because of their specific unwritten history and tradition. He and his students, of course, were not against diffusion, but they supported the role of spread of culture in a limited and different way.

Under the influence of Boas, a number of anthropologists sought to discover the spatial distribution of individual traits and trait-complexes. They wanted to locate the points of origin of culture-trait-complexes in order to reconstruct the pattern in their diffusion. Clark Wissler, Spier and A.L. Kroeber wrote extensively on the topic of culture-area.

The culture-historical approach has yielded a number of conceptual schemes about as and how to view the natives. The ideas like *world-view, cultural relativism, ethnographic fieldwork, language in culture, race and culture, personality in culture*, etc. emerged during the infancy and maturity period of culture-history school. The leading anthropologists of the Boasian era were Kroeber, Radin, Bunzel, Lowie, Benedict, Edward Sapir, Herskovits, Wissler, Leslie Spier, Mason, Hoebel, Mead and many others who dominated the scene of American cultural anthropology in decades to come.

Historical Particularism

This sub-school, associated with the Boasian period (1900–1930), focuses on a particular culture to explain the regional or geographical distribution of cultural traits. Boas argued that through trait distribution, it might be possible to reconstruct historical and psychological processes of cultural change. This strategy in the American ethnology came to be known as historical particularism, because instead of seeking to discover universal laws governing the processes of cultural change, it called for investigation of the unique histories of individuals or particular cultures.

In short, historical particularism focuses on unique or specific objects, events in time and space. In ethnography, it deals with cultural elements as they have actually existed and they may exist today. Boas insisted on study of 'every phenomenon as the result of historical happenings'.

It is worth noting a statement made by Kroeber on 'determining' factors of cultural phenomena. To him, the direct factors are 'not nature which gives or withholds materials', but 'the general state of knowledge and technological advancement of the group,' in short, historical or cultural influence (Kroeber, 1923 : 182).

STRUCTURAL-FUNCTIONAL SCHOOL

The Impact of French Sociology: Durkheim

The contribution of **Emile Durkheim** (1858–1917) to modern sociology is immense. He is responsible for formulating some of the basic concepts in social theory of the early part of the last century. His notions moved around the questions of social cohesion (in his terminology, *social solidarity*). Percy Cohen, the foremost British sociologist, has rightly remarked that Durkheim wished to understand 'what held societies together'. He concluded that social solidarity was primarily the result of a force arising from participation in a shared system of beliefs and values. These beliefs and values controlled individual behaviour. Durkheim called this system of shared beliefs the *collective conscience*, i.e. shared awareness and understanding.

How did collective conscience originate? According to the Durkheimian theory, collective conscience develops during individual socialisation process, because people are born and raised within a society, and they share collective behaviour. In other words, socialisation determines their values, their beliefs and their behaviours. (Durkheim called them *collective representations*). This makes life possible and meaningful. This collective behaviour is, of course, due to what anthropologists call 'culture', though Durkheim did not use this term in his book. (The beginners are strongly advised to read E.E. Evans-

Pritchard's *Introduction to Social Anthropology*, 1955, the chapter on modern development). Here, we need only to underline a few concepts. In addition to the above-mentioned terms, one more crucial term is *social fact*.

Though Durkheim's original methodological manifesto, *Les Regles de la methode socioloique,* appeared in 1895, its English translation became available only in 1965, (*The Rules of Sociological Method*; now available in Hindi in 1975 by the Rajasthan Hindi Granth Academy, Jaipur).

What is Social Fact?

Durkheim defines sociological data as consisting of 'social facts'. These facts are customary ways of thinking and acting to which each member of society feels compelled to conform.

Personal qualities of individual are irrelevant here. What really matter are those sentiments, thoughts and actions which come automatically in a particular society. (This is because of shared or common socialisation process). Since these 'facts' belong to the group as a whole, they cannot be reduced to the individual in whose conduct they manifest themselves. (Remember, in philosophical doctrine, a *whole* is more than the sum of its parts). By the same token, collective beliefs and behaviour cannot be explained in terms of individual psychology alone. To illustrate this, Evans-Pritchard chooses a language which exists before an individual is born into society which speaks it, and will exist after he is dead. The language is a social fact which can only be understood in relation to other facts of the same order, i.e. as part of social system.

In short, Durkheim insisted that to understand one set of social phenomena, say marriage and kinship, we must see them as a whole in their wider social context, i.e. marriages and kinship are to be understood in spheres of economics, religion and so on. This wholistic approach is the essence of functionalism. According to the present author, it is a kind of 'social determinism'.

The above aspect of the works of French sociologists, mainly Durkheim, formed the basis of the British social anthropologists. Two prominent personalities were **A.R. Radcliffe-Brown** and **Bronislow Malinowski**. Thus, with the coming of 'structural-functional' school in Great Britain, 'modern social anthropology' emerged in the real sense of development. By this time, the students of Malinowski and Radcliffe-Brown had furnished new types of data. Based on observed field-data, both Radcliffe Brown and Malinowski gave a new direction to anthropology influenced by Emile Durkheim.

Functionalists believe in studying a society as an organism of physiologist studies seeing how its various parts are related to one another and how it maintains its continuing existence. How do the members of the society obtain their food? What is the pattern of distribution? How are social conflicts handled and adjusted? What functions do the religious and magical rituals the people perform fulfil? Malinowski and Radcliffe-Brown both had their own version to explain these questions. Malinowski viewed the culture of a society as providing various means for satisfying the needs of its members. He believed that every custom and belief fulfils some function and each custom has some task to accomplish in that society. It is the principal task of anthropologists to discover what these functions are. He directed his attention to the understanding of a culture existing at one time level (*synchronic study*) and not through time period (*diachronic study*). Malinowski, like Franz Boas, independently emphasised on the importance of doing actual fieldwork. This resulted in a series of excellent monographs on primitive cultures of the Pacific, Australia, Africa and Asia by Malinowski and his students. In fact, the trend continued even after mid 20th century.

In order to demolish the theories of his predecessors, Malinowski mobilised his students against them for their utmost failure to understand full complexity of social life. He himself had recorded Trobriander's myths of origin, the full setting of these myths; who told them and who was privileged to tell them, and on what occasions and in relation to what other activities they were recounted. Casual visitors or short-term field workers could not acquire this kind of data. These persons recorded data by questioning through interpreters, instead of observing the process in which human beings co-operated and struggled within a community possessed of a particular culture.

Radcliffe-Brown similarly advocated a synchronic approach, but he did not share Malinowski's notion about cultural institutions satisfying human needs. He shared with Durkheim the emphasis on studying the *conditions* under which social structures are maintained. He believed that laws govern the functioning of societies like natural system and these laws could be discovered through analysis (comparison). The study of *social structure, organisation* and *function* provides such an approach. This is called *structural-functional approach*. For Radcliffe-Brown, the function of a social institution was the contribution it made to the society's structural continuity. He was particularly interested in comparative study of kinship systems—a major field in social anthropology, in which many of his students in England and the United States have since specialised.

Realising well the difference of opinion between Malinowski's functionalism and Radcliffe-Brown's functional approach, their views reached their peak level of influence during the late 1950s. Beginning in the 1960s, their approach commonly called, 'structural functionalism' came to be severely challenged. They entered a period of rapid decline after 1970. The following are the major criticisms against functionalism:

(1) Functionalists tend to overemphasise the degree to which human societies are harmonious, stable and well-integrated systems.

(2) Functionalists tend to neglect or underestimate the degree to which social conflict is a basic feature of most of the societies.

(3) With their exaggeration of social harmony and under-estimation of social conflict, functionalists tend to encourage a conservative bias in the study of social life; that is, they appear to argue for the necessity of preserving whatever social arrangements exist in a society.

(4) Functionalists generally limit themselves to the study of a society at only a single point in time (the present), and thus, disregard a remarkable historical approach to the study of social life.

(5) Since functionalists ignore the historical dimension to social life, they have considerable difficulty in accounting for social change.

Synthesis of Structural Functionalism and Culture History

Both Malinowski and Radcliffe-Brown were a historical on all counts. The latter stood for monothetic analysis, i.e. almost total reliance on ethnographic observations. But, there had been a shift of interest in American cultural anthropology to synthesise structure-functional approach with cultural history. It was Fred Eggan who demonstrated that this could be done by what he called 'controlled comparison'. Here, structure-functional analysis is placed in limited geographical, cultural and historical frameworks.

It is worthwhile to refer to Oscar Lewis' efforts that were searching for comparisons between historically-related societies during 1950-1954 (see Lewis, 1966). Lewis defined historically-related societies as those found within a single community in the same cultural area as nation.

A similar trend was emerging even in Great Britain. Edward E. Evans-Pritchard, like Fred Eggan, was reflecting a view held by many of his colleagues which had become structure-functional unit overtime. Max Gluckman, Aidan Southall and Jonathan Smith were prominent in this kind of analysis; they analysed field data diachronically.

What we get from the above observation is that there is a need of synthesising structure-functional with Boasian cultural history.

CULTURE AND PERSONALITY SCHOOL

During 1920s, some American anthropologists shifted their interest from the study of cultural history to the study of psychological factors involved in culture. By the late 1940s, this interest resulted in several studies related to personality and culture. Thus, a subfield within cultural anthropology started with specific interests involving culture and personality.

Two of Boas' students, *Ruth Benedict* and *Margaret Mead*, were pioneers in the field of culture and personality. In her popular work *Patterns of Culture* (1934), Benedict contrasted three primitive societies, viz. Pueblo, Dobu and Kwakiutl showing that each was characterised by specific *world view* and set of *values* that differed greatly from one society to another. Benedict's approach is also known as *configurationalism* as it emphasised on the tendency of cultures to form internally integrated wholes. According to the cultural configuralists (Sapir, Benedict), cultural traits are not only interrelated, but also organised according to certain dominant characteristics that formed the 'ethos' of the culture. Benedict stressed upon a typological approach to whole cultures, which she thought had distinctive characters like individuals. She viewed cultural anthropology as systems of introverted or extroverted, paranoid, megalomaniac characters.

Margaret Mead (1929) was, however, different. She contrasted the adolescents of Samoan (South Pacific) girls with the tenser 'coming of age' among American teenagers.

Coming of Age in Samoa

The aim of the book is to show that the difficulties of adolescence, particularly those of adolescent girls, which are so common and troublesome a feature of American life, do not occur in Samoa and may, therefore, be regarded as a product of a particular type of social environment. Mead, therefore, sets out to show us in what way Samoan conditions of adolescence are different from those of American adolescence. With this end in view, she tells us everything she observed about the social setting of the Samoan girl—how, in a broad sense, she is educated, what her childhood is like and wider community and her sexual relations with young men. The description is always with particular reference to the problem of the investigation, the moulding of the personality of the growing girl by social conditions and the reactions of this personality to the physiological changes of puberty.

The conclusion of the study is that there are no differences between American girls and Samoan girls in the process of adolescence itself. The difference lies in the response to it. In Samoa, there is no stress or crisis but an orderly development of interests and activities. 'The girls' minds', Mead tells us, "were perplexed by no conflicts, troubled by no philosophical queries, beset by no remote ambitions. To live as a girl with many lovers as long as possible and then to marry in one's own village, near one's own relatives and to have many children, these were uniform and satisfying ambitions."

The American girl at the same time of her life suffers from strains and stresses because of her different social environment. What are the significant differences? Mead is of the opinion that the most important are to be found in the absence of deep personal feelings and of conflicting values in Samoa. The Samoan girls do not care about anyone or anything, and in particular, they do not set high hopes on any one relationship. This is partly due to the fact that they are not brought up in a narrow family circle but in a wider circle of kin, so that both authority and affection are spread over a large number of persons. Even more important is the homogeneous culture of the Samoans. They all have the same standards of behaviour. There is only one set of religious beliefs, and there is only one code of morals. Consequently, in these matters Samoan adolescents do not have to make choices, inevitably affecting their relationships with those around them, They avoid the conflicts. The American adolescent, on the contrary, is confronted in her social environment with so many various and conflicting values that she has to make a choice, and choice is the forerunner of conflict.

Basic and Modal Personalities

In a long collaboration with anthropologists, Ralph Linton and a psychoanalyst, Abram Kardiner, the concept of *basic personality structure* was proposed. This concept refers to the common aspects of personality shared by the members of a particular society. Following Freud, Kardiner viewed that a person's personality is largely shaped by the time he reaches the age of six. To understand the basic personality structure of a particular society, one should study the process of socialization, that is how children are brought up in that society and what their characteristic early experiences are, the structure of the family, length of the period, weaning, nourishing, practice, attitudes towards the sexual behaviour of children and the kinds of discipline imposed. Kardiner's emphasis was on role of primary institutions shaping the personality. Another outstanding study in this field is *The People of Alor* (1944) by Cora DuBois. The idea of *modal personality* was developed in this monograph.

The modal personality of a group is the central tendencies (statistical term: mode) of personality characteristics, obtained mainly through the psychological tests such as the Thematic Apperception test (TAT), Draw a diagram test, Rorscharch or Ink Blot test, found within the population. The modal personality of any group will not be identical to the personality of any of its members. It represents merely a general tendency or pattern. It is useful for comparative purpose only. When based on careful sampling of population, the modal personality may be useful to understand social relations between groups. Some cultural anthropologists (Anthony F.C. Wallace and George Spindler) have identified modal personality type useful in ethnographic field studies.

Briefly stated, from the 1930s onwards, following up Mead, Kardiner-Linton-Du Bois impetus, the anthropological literature on child rearing expanded rapidly. Efforts were made to establish a consistent relation between:

(a) Training in a given cultural setting during early childhood,
(b) type of adult 'characters' vis-à-vis cultural settings and
(c) 'values', 'ethos', 'world view' that are *patterned* in a particular culture.

THE NATIONAL CHARACTER STUDY

During and after World War II, some cultural anthropologists of America started a new dimension in culture and personality studies that came to be known as the study of national character. A question was raised: Could national characteristics of German, French, Russian, Japanese, Chinese and American be identified? Extensive studies, mainly published literature, were made in this direction whose methodologies later on were systematised by Mead and Metraux in a volume entitled *The Study of Culture at a Distance* published in 1953. According to proponents of the study of culture at a distance, *national character is defined as generalised delineation of the worldview, ethos and patterns of behaviour of all the people who share a culture and belong to the same group*.

As discussed above, the anthropological investigation of national cultures was initiated during World War II to facilitate military decisions through better understanding of alien or foreign cultures. Study of national character deals with any population sharing a culture—a nation, region or an ethnic group, such as eastern European Jews. In essence, this genre endeavours to relate the institutions characteristics of the society to the psychological characteristics of the individuals who make up that society. It was influenced by Freudian thought, particularly that portion of Freudian theory which relates the formulation of adult personality to childhood experience. The theoretical basis was set forth in 1953 by Margaret Mead, who stated that national character investigations attempt to trace the way in which a given cultural behaviour is represented in the intrapsychic structure of the individuals in the culture. These studies combine cultural theory and psychological theory—mainly learning theory, Gestalt psychology, Freudian psychology, and child development studies—into a new psycho cultural theory in order to explain 'how human beings embody the culture, learn it, and live in it.'

The first full-length anthropological national character study was Mead's *And Keep Your Powder Dry* 1942, in which she related parental anxiety for status striving not only to the democracy of American institutions and the monetary basis of American social position, but also to the fact that major sectors of the nation are second and third-generation descendants of immigrants, anxious to deny their peasant origins and become a part of the mainstream of American life.

The most influential work of this kind is Ruth Benedict's *The Chrysanthemum and the Sword* (1946), which attempted to show the unity and consistency of Japanese culture and its continuity with the past. Although the book has been criticised for its overgeneralisation and for its many specific errors, it affected American occupation policy during World War II and contributed indirectly to the reconstruction of that nation. It remains the best exemplar of the study of national character. The Columbia university research project in contemporary cultures gathered scholars from different disciplines to study culture 'at a distance,' that is, to investigate societies to which scholars did not have direct access. This involved not only the interviewing of immigrants, refugees and prisoners of war but also the detailed analysis of popular literature, humour, motion pictures and other expressions of the current popular culture. (See also Hsu, 1949; Lowie, 1945; and Gorer, 1949.)

National character studies have been much criticised for their lack of methodological rigour and for their involvement with psychodynamic theory. The study of national character cannot explain the origin of diverse forms of behaviour. But, it can discuss them in an ethnographic sense. The culturally established common modes of handling children, the nature of cultural rewards and punishments, and the affect patterns between parents and children are seen as the mediating and not the causative forces in transmitting and preserving the national character.

NEO-EVOLUTIONISM

Neo-evolutionism is modern version of evolutionism. Soon after World War II, increasing number of anthropologists became involved in reviving the ideas of evolution but in different ways. The prominent among them were Leslie White, Julian Steward, Elman Service, Marshall Sahlins and Gordon Childe. They together with their followers are known as 'neo-evolutionists'. After 1970, Marvin Harris emerged as a proponent of culture-materialist approach in socio-cultural evolution. He too should be included under 'neo-evolutionists'.

Energy Theory of Evolution of Culture

The viewpoint of **Lesile White's** (1900–1975) on universal evolution of culture is also known as 'Energy theory of culture'. White used the term 'culturalogy' to explain his theory. Now this term has become obsolete. Some major points inherent in his theory are:

(1) Culture should be studied in terms of 'symbols' not in terms of biology or individual psychology or environment. 'Culturalogy' is about how cultures behave and not how individuals behave (White, 1975).

(2) The laws of science of culture deal with the way technology-in-environment generate cultural forms: socio-political organisations.

(3) Cultural systems have evolved into higher forms in response to technological advances.

(4) Man's technology has progressed through harnessing and converting energy more efficiently.

Leslie White defined technology as the amount of controlled energy available to a society. Hunting-gathering societies of Paleaolithic period differed remarkably with those of present day industrial societies in the amount of energy directed to human use.

In one of his works, Leslie White (1949) wrote: 'The cultural development of a society is a function of the amount of energy harnessed and the effectiveness of the tools used."

According to White, "the amount of energy harnessed per capita per year is increased or the efficiency of the instrumental means of putting the energy to work increased... Both factors may increase simultaneously, of course,... but this does not mean that the tools and energy factors are of equal weight and significance. The energy factor is primary and basic one; it is the prime mover and active agent. The energy factor may be increased indefinitely. When the efficiency of tools within the limit increases, no further increase in efficiency can make up for a lack of increase in amount of energy. Since increase of energy fosters improvement of tools, one may say that it is the energy that counts the culture process onwards and upwards" (White, 1949 : 369–376).

Leslie White wrote a series of articles in which he criticised Boas ideas and reaffirmed the importance of classical evolutionism. It was conceded that both Tylor and Morgan had made mistakes, but, at least, they had tried to understand the development of cultural evolution. In his latter career, White (1975) propounded a law of evolution which was largely determined by the quality of energy that could be captured and put to work per capita per year. On this basis, one can distinguish one stage of evolution from another. Thus, White argued for both 'form' and 'temporal' sequences in cultural evolution.

It is apparent from the above discussion that White is for 'technological determinism.' Some of the cultural anthropologists, viz. Sahlins, Service and Carneiro, among others have been influenced by this sort of thinking. In recent decades, Marvin Harris has refined the theory of *cultural materialism* which will be dealt with later on incorporating the views of White, Marx and others.

Multilinear Theory of Culture Evolution

Another 'neo-evolutionist' is **Julian Steward** (1902–1972), who has typified himself as a multilinear evolutionist with an interest in finding parallel developments of limited occurrence rather than universals. In other words, his focus was on search for similar sequences of development in different time and space. For example, there seems to have been some regularities or order operating in the Bronze age civilisations of the Old world and the high cultures of Mexico and Peru in the New world, where many similar cultural and social institutions appeared. It is significant to note that multilinear evolution is not a theory but a *methodological strategy* (*Theory of Culture Change*, Steward, 1955). His methodology includes conceptualisation of *culture ecology* and a method of demonstration of variation in single society. (See *Ecological anthropology*, Chapter 12).

According to Steward, the difficulties with classical and other universal evolutionists were that they postulated a single or unilinear set of stages for all societies, whereas several multilinear stages or paths of development could be possible. (Steward, 1968).

Modern researchers who have addressed to the process of cultural evolution include Service, Sahlins, Carneiro, Dumond, Stevenson and Harner. These investigators have used empirical field data; whereas William Sanders and Barbara Price (1969) based their arguments on archaeological data of Meso America. Briefly, their arguments are as follow:

"As a society increases in size, new means of integration must be achieved; kin-based institutions that traditionally regulate disputes and organise explanation of resources cannot do so. Therefore, major changes are seen: informal to formal legal sanctions, dispute settlements and leadership statuses; from self-sufficient economies to specialisation and trade; to equal access basic goods to market inequalities" (Preface).

General and Specific Cultural Evolution

Among the prominent contemporary neo-evolutionists American anthropologist **Marshall Sahlins** comes first. Sahlins (1969) suggested that both biological and cultural evolution move in two directions at the same time. Evolution creates diversity and progress. Diversity in evolution means adaptive changes that evolve new forms out of old forms; progress refers to the fact that evolution creates more complex forms. It is the *general evolution* that provides the basis for evolutionary stages. Sahlins emphasized on *specific evolution* that is the adaptation of a particular culture to its environment in terms of cultural evolution. It stresses upon variability, divergence and convergence. Different results in different settings can be due to *same* kind of influences and processes. Similar pressures may produce similarities between ways of life. In Sahlins' views, adaptation is the key concept, not the evolution.

Thus, in *general evolution*, one can view the tribal societies of Melanesia and Polynesia with horticulture, fishing and polished stone tool technology-as representing a single evolutionary trend. But, how to explain why some Polynesians have elaborated system of social stratification (ranking of lineages) and others do not? Similarly, how to explain some Melanesians have matriliny, others have patriliny and still other possess cognatic descent. These are issues of *specific evolution*. In other words, the diversification of culture is to adapt to environment's stress variability.

Briefly, the reexaminations of evolution has proved to be a valuable theoretical insight. It has allowed scholars like Rubert Adams (1966) and Fried (1967) to compare the development of early civilization in the old and new worlds.

CULTURAL MATERIALISM

The Meaning of Materialist Strategy

'Materialism' is a view that physical matter is the only reality and that all being and processes and phenomena can be explained as manifestations or results of matter. In cultural theory this strategy attempts to explain the basic features of social life in terms of practical and material conditions of human existence. This involves consideration of physical environment, level of technology and organisation of economic system. Materialists see these factors as pre-requisites of human existence. It was **Karl Marx** (1818–1883) and **Fredrich Engles** (1820–1895) who developed what they called 'materialist conception of history'. This has come to be known as 'historical' or 'dialectical' materialism. To them, the economic or social change is materially caused.

Both Marx and Engles divided human societies into two major components. One of the components they referred to as the *infrastructure*, sometimes called the mode of production. The *infrastructure* was, in turn, divided into two categories—the forces of production which consisted of the raw material necessary for a society to engage in economic production, level of technology and the specific nature of natural resources such as the quality of the land. The relations of production referred to the ownership of the forces of production. The other major component of human societies identified by Marx and Engel was the *superstructure.* This component consisted of all those aspects of a society which are not included in the infrastructure such as politics, law, family life, religion and ideas and ideals.

They held that a society's infrastructure and its superstructure were directly related. Although the superstructure could occasionally influence the infrastructure, they argued that the primary direction of causation proceeded from the infrastructure to the superstructure.

Marvin Harris' Materialist Approach to Socio-cultural System and Evolution

Marvin Harris' materialist approach finds its roots in the *materialist conception of history* as propounded by Marx and Engle. Like Marx and Engles, Harris sees material factors such as technology and economy as being among the leading causes of social life. He also expands the notion of material objects to include ecological and demographic variables.

Harris uses two terms, viz. Techno-environmental and Techno-economic 'determinism'. Here, determinism refers to the principles. To quote a few lines from his massive work (1968 : 504):

"This principle holds that similar technologies applied to *similar environments* lent to produce *similar achievements of labour in production and distribution* and that they, in turn, call forth *similar system of values and beliefs*" (emphasis added).

Harris tries to investigate the above strategy of cultural materialism empirically. He agrees strongly for the search for causal relations as an explanation against the 'non-processual ethnography', and he suggests that the search for cause or the independent variable must be among materialistic factors, not idealistic factors. He draws field data from his own research as an example to show 'what is involved in a cultural materialist explanation of the differences between race relations in Brazil and the United States. (See also the Box). He demonstrates that the cultural materialist explanation must incorporate a wide range of "economic, demographic, ecological, political, military and cognition data" (*The Rise of Anthropological Theory,* 1968).

Harris further elaborated the above-mentioned strategy of cultural materialism for general students in his another text book *Culture, Man, and Nature,* 1971, (See also *Cultural Materialism*, 1991).

Harris has been criticised for terms like 'determinism' and 'holistic materialism' he used in developing his research strategy of culture relativism. He has stressed the materialist factors, but has not necessitated considering non-materialist factors. His research strategy lacks 'holistic' view. A research strategy is holistic if it qualifies what social philosophers call *praxis*, i.e. theory and practices. The principle of holism is not simply the search for interrelationships; it is the search for *systematic interrelationships.* Service (1968) designated Harris as a 'monistic determinist' for his over toned 'techno-environmental determinism'.

A Materialist Model: India's Sacred Cow

One of the best-known applications of the materialist evolutionary perspective is Marvin Harris' examination of the origins of religiously based food taboos. Harris has devoted particular attention to explaining why in India the Hindu considers the cow sacred and regards beef as forbidden food item.

It is widely known that a central tenet of Hindu religious ideology is the sanctification of the cow. The cow is regarded as a holy animal, the slaughter and consumption of which is unthinkable. For many westerners, this taboo is a clear case of the irrational mismanagement of resources and responsible for the perpetuation of widespread poverty and misery on the Indian subcontinent. The whole complex of cow worship is thought to be a classic example of the way in which mystical religious practices lead to undesirable and necessary economic results. But Harris (1974, 1977) thinks that this is not the case.

Harris claims that the cow performs vital functions in the context of the Indian ecology and economy. Cows can perform these functions only if they are kept alive. Cow dung is particularly valuable to the Indian farmer. It is used as a fertilizer for the fields, as a source of fuel for cooking and, when mixed with water to form a paste, as an acceptable flooring material for houses. The most useful role played by the cow is that of a traction animal for the ploughing of fields. Since many Indian farmers cannot maintain tractors, the cow is the only mean by which they can plough. Alive cow is far more useful than dead to the average Indian farmer. However, since the temptation to slaughter one's cattle during periods of drought or famine was an ever-recurrent problem to most of the Indian farmers, it was necessary to find a mean of removing this temptation. This mean, Harris claims, was found in the establishment of a religious taboo deifying the cow and marking it an unholy and unthinkable act to kill and consume it.

"Throughout much of Indian history, cattle were regularly eaten, and nothing was considered particularly holy about them... It may not have been until sometime after 700 A.D. that the cow love complex developed into its now familiar form. Regardless of exactly when the cow came to be worshipped in India, we do know that Brahmin priests had been performing the sacrifices and consuming animal flesh for centuries. Under what kind of conditions would these priests have been transformed from ritual sacrifices of cattle into their ritual protectors?" Harris (1977 : 145) concludes: the answer to this question involves increasing population density and declining standard of living (1977 : 146).

In Harris's view, cows were vitally necessary for India's agriculture, and therefore, it came to be sanctified.

STRUCTURALISM

General Meaning of the Term

Any analytical approach in social science and humanity disciplines is structuralism if it is based on the assumption that observed phenomena are specific instances of an underlying generalised principle (structure). Structuralists assume that below the surface of observable appearance there are more (deep) relationships which give rise to the observable. This kind of thinking is very different from structural functional approach discussed earlier under the structural-functional school.

Levi-Strauss in his illuminating paper on 'social structure' published in *Anthropology Today* (Ed., A.L. Kroeber, 1953, pp. 524–53) maintained his line of thinking different from Radcliffe-Brown's social structure. It is here he introduced the ideal on *mechanical and statistical* models' (i.e. relation of the ideal vs. real or normative vs. behaviour pattern).

In cultural theory, structuralism refers to the work of the French anthropologist *Claude Levi-Strauss* (1908–2009) and his followers. This approach has come to be known as '*structuralism in anthropology*'.

The Premises of Structuralism

The objective of structuralism is to gain a general understanding of human thoughts through the analysis of different cultures. It is assumed that human beings have an innate mental capacity to *order* and *classify* the world of experience. The order of the natural world is a product of this mental ordering. Since all human beings have the same capacity of brain, the basic mental organisation is the same for all people. This is what Levi-Strauss wants to convey. It is only the surface expression of the mental structure that varies from one culture to another.

Structuralists assume that people's ability to create categories involves the creation of *binary oppositions*. It should be noted here that the insight generated by the Prague school was that words were built upon contrasts (binary opposition) rather than simply being groups of sounds (for more detail, see Chapter 11). Following linguistic model, Levi-Strauss proposed that human thought also uses binary opposition such as day-night, black-white, hot-cold, etc. We may also recall that Durkheim's distinction between the sacred and profane, right and left were fundamental parts of the collective consciousness (see Levi-Strauss' essay on 'Structural analysis in Linguistics and in Anthropology' published in 1963).

Structuralists conceptualise all behaviour as communication, whether this behaviour is expressed in political, economic, linguistic, literary, kinship or any other mode of human life. It is expected that just as all the diverse speeches can be explained and systematically compared through the reference to the grammatical rules, a grammar of behaviour can be discovered as well that will permit an analysis of patterns of social behaviour. Levi-Strauss was the leader of this theoretical tradition. He himself has attempted to analyse expressive culture-mythology, art, and ritual through the structural method in the hope of obtaining universal formulations applicable to all the manifestations of culture.

Thus, in his major work *The Elementary Structures of Kinship*, first appeared in French in 1949, (Eng. translation, 1967, Chicago University Press). Levi-Strauss used his notion of the binary structure of human thought to analyse kinship, following the work of Marcel Mauss. In *The Gift* (1967, orig. 1925), Mauss tried to demonstrate that exchange in primitive societies was not motivated by economic motives, but by the rule of reciprocity upon which the solidarity of society depended. In his book, Levi-Strauss took Mauss' concept of reciprocity and applied it to marriage in primitive societies, arguing that the women as a commodity could be exchanged. Levi-Strauss contended that one of the first and most important distinctions that a human makes is between 'self' and 'others'. This 'natural' binary distinction, then, leads to the formation of the incest taboo that necessitates choosing spouses from outside of one's family. In this fashion, the binary distinction between kin and non-kin is resolved by the reciprocal-exchange of women and the formation of kin networks in primitive societies. Basing this he developed direct and indirect exchanges of women forming alliances between two groups (see box).

The study of mythologies of primitive people enabled Levi-Strauss to examine the unconscious universal patterning of human thought in its uncontaminated form. To him, the mythology of primitive people is closer to these universal principles than the western beliefs because the training which the latter receives in western society buries the logical structure under layers of 'cultural interference' created by the social environment. In his work on myths, folktales and religion, Levi-Strauss expanded his ideas on the notion that human cognition was structured into contrast and binary oppositions. He proposed that a fundamental characteristic of human thought was the desire to find a midpoint between such oppositions.

Anthropology of Claude Levi-Strauss

Claude Levi-Strauss (b.1908), world's most revered intellectuals, and the father of modern anthropology died at the age of 101 years, in November 2009. Since then several obituaries have appeared in various news papers, journals in almost all leading languages of the world. Most of the notes on him are about his life sketch, academic achievements, awards, publications etc. These are available in web sites. In this brief note our aim is to present the views of Levi-Struass on two focal points, viz., the aims of anthropology and meaning of structuralism.

Aims of Anthropology

It may not be out of place to note that Levi-Strauss was much influenced by Robert H. Lowie's *Primitive Society* (1920, translated in French in 1936). Malinowski too entered into the world of primitives through James Frazer's *Golden Bough (*1911*)*. Levi-Strauss, in a widely circulated paper entitled "The Place of Anthropology in Social Sciences" written especially for *the UNESCO Social Science* volume in 1954 (*reappeared in The Structural Anthropology*, 1963, paperback in 1967, pp. 342–379) has discussed the nature and organization of teaching and researches in Anthropology in European and American universities. Not-with-standing anthropology in other parts of the world including India was organized more or less in the same pattern. It is in this context he referred three aims of anthropology, viz., *objectivity*, *totality* and *meaningfulness*.

According to Levi-Strauss, anthropology must employ objective methods. To quote him, "The observer must not only place himself above the value accepted by his own society or group, but must adopt certain definite methods of thought; he must reason on the basis of concepts which are valid for all possible observers... The anthropologist... creates new mental categories... notion of opposition and contradiction..." (p. 361). Anthropology is more nearer to *semeiological* science whose guiding principle is searching meaning, and is closely related to Linguistics. He stated that "only linguistic knowledge provides the key to a system of logical categories... different from the observer's own..." (p. 366).

The second aim of anthropology is *totality*. By this he meant "all aspects are organically connected. Anthropology, said Levi-Strauss, tries to understand this totality by creating "model" which is "common to the various manifestations of social life". Note that here he is referring to the idea of "structure" underlying social phenomena. This will be dealt with shortly.

The third aim of anthropology is searching *meaningfulness* in anthropological research. In Levi-Strauss' view, this aim of anthropology is more difficult compared to the first two noted above. Anthropology began with the studies on the "non-civilized societies, without the system of writing, and pre or non-industrial in types... its small size is known as primitive generally permits personal or concrete relationship... based on direct relationship" (p. 363).

Meaning of Structure

Levi-Strauss does not define structure in explicit terms. By this he means the system, or model, hidden in the object of the study. It is the task of researchers to analyze the data to deduce what kind of pattern does exist. This pattern is known as structural pattern. Interested readers may see his essay on *Language and Kinship* (1967, 29–96). According to him, some kind of relationship does exist between social phenomena on certain level, and "our main task is to determine what these things are and what these levels are" (p. 83). The way it is carried on is structural analysis or structuralism. It will be more clear by quoting a passage of Edmund Leach, a British functionalist and an expert on Levi-Strauss. He states:

If a piece of music, originally in the form of printed notes, is played on a piano, recorded on a phonogram, transmitted over the radio, and finally played back to an audience, the music pass through a whole series of transformations—it appears as printed notes, as a patterns of finger movements, as sound waves, and so on. However, something is common to all these manifestations. That common something is their "structure".

Let us take Levi-Strauss' famous paper aptly titled 'The Bear and The Barber' (published in *Journal of Royal Anthropological Institute*, vol. 93, 1–11). The terms (symbols) bear and the barber correspond to the Australian horde groups and the Hindu system, respectively. All the points under the left and right as noted below are structurally and functionally interdependent; *but their structure is the same.*

The Bear	**The Barber**
1. Social unit is horde which is exogamous	Social unit is jati (sub caste) which is endogamous
2. Horde is totemic group (category of nature)	Jati are occupational (cultural category)
3. Activities are group oriented	Activities are individual
4. Totemic groups exchange food and women	Such exchange is forbidden
5. Horde groups are equal	Jati are unequal

We may add more points of contrast, but the hidden principle remains the same, and this is rule of transformation as in linguistics. It is also known as rule of contrast or binary opposition. I have deliberately avoided the details, but the point is clear: structure is latent at deep level, different from the structure at surface level. Deep and surface structures are again from linguistics. Levi-Strauss wants to unveil *the structure* of structure. This is structuralism.

Alliance Marriage

Perhaps among all publications of Levi-Strauss, it is *The Elementary Structures of Kinship* (1949, 1969) which has attracted cultural anthropologists the most. This book is all about the "preferential marriage". A brief note on this is as follow:

"Elementary structures of marriage are those which... prescribe marriage with a certain type of relative, or, alternatively, those members of society are categorized as possible spouses and possible prohibited spouses" (*Preface*, 1969, p. xxiii). The preferred cross cousin marriage (CCM) basically rests on reciprocity and alliance. This reciprocity is not simply about give and take but one is obliged to give female to one who has *right* to receive the female over generation. The latter reciprocates in the same spirit. The unit of exchange may be family, band, phratry, clan, lineage or group as a whole. They must enter into exchange and form alliance maintaining through the time. This is known as preferential marriage. This is what Levi-Strauss meant by elementary structure of kinship. Anthropologists have called this the positive marriage rule. It is called positive because people specify not only whom one may not marry but also whom one should marry. (A negative rule operative in complex societies would be whom one should not marry, but there is no rule of choice of partner). This is called alliance marriage because such exchange (direct or indirect) binds the segments of the society with women as link between them. (For more detail see Chapter 6)

Where is the structure located in the above system? This is a question relevant in all cultural systems, but ultimately these are lying in human mind: Levi-Strauss quest is to discover not much collective consciousness (in Durkheimian sense), rather the *collective unconsciousness of human mind*. This requires further explanations.

(Relevant portions are extracted from A.R.N. Srivastava's paper "Remembering Levi-Strauss", The Asian Man (an International Journal), 5:1(2011), pp. 93–96.)

In Levi-Strauss' view, the elements of myth, like the phonemes of language, acquire meaning only when arranged according to certain structural relations. Consequently, the structuralists examine the rules that govern the relationships between the elements of myths. The task of structural analysis is to break the myth into its constituent elements and uncover the unconscious meaning found in the binary relationships between them. Uncovering this hidden structural code will reveal the essential elements of human thought. What Levi-Strauss wants to convey is that cultural elements are graded according to specific attributes that either included or excluded from it.

NEW ETHNOGRAPHY AND NEW ANTHROPOLOGY

Structuralism had a profound effect on American anthropology. Indirectly, it influenced a group of cultural anthropologists who under various banners (such as formal analysis, componential analysis, ethno science, ethno semantics, socio linguistics, emic-etic and so on) wrote numerous articles especially during the period 1962–1972. It may also be noted that some of these anthropologists were greatly influenced by Thomas Kuhn's '*The Structure of Scientific Revolution*', 1962. Kuhn proposed that paradigms (the models used to describe the natural world) changes when scientific explanations no longer account accurately for data.

Stephen Tyler, in the introductory chapter of his edited volume *Cognitive Anthropology* (1969) explicitly noted that such a paradigm shift was happening in anthropology. In this volume, nearly all the published articles under various captions discussed above are included; he appropriately titled it 'Cognitive Anthropology'.

What is Cognitive Anthropology?

The term 'cognition' is a broad one that encompasses all the various ways of knowing. It includes, in general usage, perception, judgement, reasoning, remembering, thinking and imagining.

Much of the current work in anthropology distinguishes between cognition and other modes of perception, usually considered to be more emotional. Thus cognitive anthropological research emphasises on an intellectual approach to the interpretation of culture, usually defined in terms of the categories and to convey messages among those who share the culture. In a cognitive approach to kinship, for example, the focus is on the intellectual meanings that kinship relations have to the informants, rather than on their emotional meaning.

Following the above strategy, the cognitive ethnographers spend much time to the accurate description of culture; what people think and communicate away themselves in day-to-day activities. One of cognitive anthropologists–Charles Frake, claimed that a record of communication would yield record of cognitive system as a whole.

Cognitive anthropologists are concerned with the problems of classification of cultural data. It would be recalled that the traditional ethnographers usually classified the field data according to their own systems to the societies they studied. Therefore, a new approach is to be followed—People's way of classification. Though it is subjective, it promises to yield 'a method of analysis of society that provide results that could be replicated'. This movement in cultural anthropology is called '*New ethnography*' (New anthropology).

We now briefly deal with conceptual schemes mentioned above.

Ethnoscience

Study of folk conceptual system of classification (folk taxonomy) is called ethnoscience. The basic assumption of ethnoscience is that the things and events in a people's conceptual world will be reflected in their linguistic categories. Stephen Tyler, Charles Frake, R. Berlin, Ward Goodenough are among a few anthropologists who have used this kind of strategy in understanding culture and society. Ethnoscience is sometimes called ethno semantics.

In some respects, the goals of Levi-Strauss and ethnoscientists are the same. Both are interested in the underlying logical structures of human organisation; both draw heavily on linguistic models to analyse cultures. Differences between these two approaches lie in their scope.

The major task of the ethnoscientists is to seek explanation rather than interpretation of facts. Ethnoscience has made a contribution by putting importance on explanation of the native informant (the *emic* approach), as opposed to investigator's interpretation (the *etic* approach).

Ethnosemantics

Ethnosemantics is the study of meanings attached to specific classes or terms used by members of a group. The prefix *ethno* refers to the fact that a study of a segment of reality from the perspective of the people is being studied. The suffix *semantics* refers to meaning. Thus, ethnosemantics concentrates on the meaning of categories of reality and folk taxonomies to the people who use them as their basis of action. The underlying assumption of ethnosemantics is that the categories designated by a language adequately reflect the entire range of things important to a people within a socio-cultural system. This assumption is far from universally accepted fact.

Componential Analysis

It is primarily a technique employed in the analysis of kinship terminology system. Ward Goodenough has used it extensively for understanding American kin terminologies. A componential analysis would first involve defining the universe of kin terms (*denotata*) and attempting to discover their meaning (*significata*). Each term is mapped on to it, called *designata* (genealogical kinship categories, e.g. MB, MZH, FB, FZ, etc.). After the 'core term' or 'kernel' for each of the ranges has been decided, all of the terms are defined by isolating, in each case, the smallest number of distinctive features which put an individual term apart from the rest to the set. These features or criteria are 'components' which distinguish each kin term from every other and which, when 'bundled together' in an individual definition, identify each term and define its place on the domain. There may be more than one way of doing this, and the choice of component to be used depends on the analyst's preference and his intuitive understanding of the informants' cognitive map.

Revitalisation

Some anthropologists have been more concerned with phenomenon of vital changes in the native religions. This change usually, not necessarily always, occurs when natives come into contact with dominant cultures. Several terms are used by the ethnographers to denote this type of situation, viz. nativistic movement, messianic movement, cargo cult, millenarian cult, etc. Anthony F.C. Wallace has proposed a term *'revitalisation'* to accommodate these terms. Revitalisation implies an attempt to create a new or reanimative mode of existence that would be preferable to the current state of affairs. He defines it as a deliberate and organised movement by some of the members of a society to create a more satisfying culture. These movements occur under extreme stress social disruption and cultural disintegration. Such conditions may be caused by forced acculturation, by natural disasters or by any other factor which create rapid change (Wallace, 1956).

As already noted, a revitalisation movement may be of a special category such as 'millenarian' or 'messianic' concerning around a cult of a savior (*Messiah*) who is believed to be present or about to appear. Such movements occur under conditions of extreme social stress or crisis in periods of rapid social change when people are uprooted from their traditional patterns of life (see Chapter 9).

EMIC-ETIC AS A LINGUISTIC MODELS IN ANTHROPOLOGY

General Use of Emic-Etic

Unlike other social scientists, cultural anthropologists have been confronted with the problem of translating the cultural world of the natives into the idiom of professionals.

The problem of translation occurs at both ends of one's research—learning about the people one is investigating and then, communicating what one thinks about these people to one's professional colleagues. Confronting these, some anthropologists wish to keep 'perspectives' and 'world views' separately: the perspective of the people being investigated is called *emics* and the perspective of social science in general (and anthropology in particular) is called *etics*. The task of keeping these 'folk' and 'analytical' perspectives separate, whether one is engaged in field research or the subsequent analysis of data, is very difficult. In short, 'emic' is inside or native view; while 'etic' is the view of anthropologists or social scientists. Derived from linguistics after *'phoneme'* and *'phonetic'*, (see below) have viewed this as an objective in contrast to subjective view. But, a closer examination of use of this concept reveals totally different thing (M. Durbin 1975 : 384–386).

Specific Use of Emic and Etic Model

The terms of *emic* and *etic*, first developed in the context of phonology (*phonetics, phonemics*) and subsequently extended to morphology (*morphemics*) and syntax, is used by Pike (1954) as a mode of analysis for nonverbal human behaviour. Pike's proposal was to develop two conceptually separate strategies, analogous to phonetics and phonemics in linguistics for analysing other cultural behaviour. Thus, the *emic-etic* model in anthropology to human behaviour involves the intersection of various cultural subsystems as evidences, for example, in the *The Nature of Cultural Things* (Harris, 1964), *The Silent Language* (Hall, 1959). These attempts rarely dealt with cultural analysis *per se*. Non-productive results of these attempts can be attributed to two factors. On one hand, cultural anthropologists heavily underrated the intricacies of the linguistic model; while on the other hand, linguists underestimated the complex nature of the cultural data. In addition to this, some anthropologists did not properly understand the models used, as manifested in *The Rise of Anthropological Theory* (Harris, 1968 : 568–604). Harris confounded the nature of the model by interpreting the *emic-etic* approach solely as classificatory *vs.* non-classificatory and by ignoring other characteristics.

Mridula Durbin, one of the specialists of Anthropological linguistics has remarked: "A close look at phonetics and phonemics reveals that it is not correct to consider phonetics solely as a non-classificatory frame since sounds (phones-etics) are classified according to their natural (articulatory, acoustic) inherent properties. Furthermore, in phonemics, even though sound is classified as structurally same (i.e. same phoneme) *vs.* structurally different (i.e. different phonemes) on the basis of their role in distinguishing meanings of utterances (i.e. discriminatory functions), the significant feature of the phonemic model is that the functional criterion of classification is operationally shifted to distributional criteria. This is a crucial shift in phonological methodology in particular and in the linguistic model in general...

"... Harris' propositions that (a) kinship systems are mixed domains of etic and emic (578–79), and (b) emic cultural categories cannot be transmuted into etic simply because they are found cross-culturally (577–78), are anomalous in the model described above. It must be noted that the elements of kinship (or of any cultural system) viewed from their inherent properties form etic categories, and when classified from the standpoint of contrastive relationships, form emic categories. Further, emic categories are based on the configurations of relationships between an element (e.g. sound) and the rest of the elements of the system, and since no two systems share exactly identical configurations, it is meaningless to consider any element cross-culturally emic. Even if two systems are identical, the emic status of a category in both systems does not prevent its conception as an etic element when viewed as a pre-analysed element" (Durbin, 1975 : 390).

To recapitulate section on 'new development in anthropology' or 'new anthropology', it may be said that avid researchers in new anthropology must take precautions in using these concepts; unless knowing the conceptual background in which these concepts were developed, one must not blindly follow them. It would blink the explanatory power. Long ago, in the context of cattle milk and distribution of dry(milk) powder among the natives, Edmund Leach had remarked: "We (anthropologists) should not view a 'gender' a 'goose' merely at surface level that both look alike."

Hocus-focus and God's Truth Views

What do we get out of above review of anthropological discourses developed over a period of 150 years?

The readers may arrive at different conclusions depending on nature of topical theme they wish to approach. By way of concluding this Chapter, we may refer to two ways of viewing the ultimate goal of socio-cultural anthropology. Usually in 'social science theory construction' these opposite views are discussed under 'Hocus-focus' and 'God's truth' discourse. The former view amounts to saying that a variety of theories about human culture and society are equally acceptable; any theory is all right as long as it works. The other view assumes that there is a single ultimate truth that is looked for. Evidences may be cited in support of these views. In the eyes of the author of the present book, the ultimate truth about societies and culture will be discovered only through a successful blend of what the philosopher of social sciences have coined *induction* and *deduction*. The former, in simple words, means data lead to theory; while the latter tends to invent theory first and then, to test them against observable facts (see, Srivastava, 1976 : 109–116).

SUGGESTED READING

Since contents of this chapter have direct bearing on some major intellectuals and professional anthropologists of repute, their major publications are noted under Appendix II (Pioneers of Anthropology) of the present book. Below are given some specific titles useful to general readers.

- Adams, Robert M., *The Evolution of Urban Society,* Aldine, Chicago, 1966.
- Bohannan, Paul J. and Glaza Mark (Eds.), *High Points in Anthropology*, Alfred A. Knof, New York, 1973.
  A collection of excerpts from some of the major works of the leading contributors (Tylor, Morgan, Durkheim, Radcliffe-Brown, Malinowski, Levi-Strauss, White, Steward, Sahlins, Kroeber) also valuable for its historical summaries and introductions to each contribution.

- Brace, Gerald, *History of Anthropology,* Burgess, Minneapolis, 1973. This is a very short overview of the history of anthropological theory and is helpful to the readers who seek a limited discussion on this area.
- Brew, J.O., *One Hundred Years of Anthropoly*, Cambridge, Harvard, 1968.
- Cassagrande, Josheph, *In the Company of Man,* Harper New York, 1964.
- Durbin, M., Linguistic Models in Anthropology, *Annual Review of Anthropology*, Polo Alto, California, 1975.
- Durkheim, E, *Les Règles de la Mèthode Sociologique,* Paris, Aleon, 1895. Translated by S.A. Solovay and J.H. Mueller as *The Rules of Sociological Method.* The Free Press, Glencoe, Illinois, 1938. See Chapters on Social facts and comparative method.
- Evans-Pritchard, E.E., *History of Anthropological Thought*, London, 1981. 25 thinkers (mostly of 19th century) including Maine, Tylor, Frazer, Durkheim, Malinowksi, Radcliffe-Brown, White are dealt with. Useful for advanced students.
- Fried, Morton H., *The Evolution of Political Society: An essay in political anthropology*. Random House, New York 1967.
- Gorer, G., (1) *The American People: a study in national character,* London, 1948. (2) *The People of Great Russia: a psychological study*, Norton, New York, 1949.
- Graebner, F., *Methode der Ethnologie,* C. Winter, Heidelberg, 1911.
- Harris, Marvin, *The Rise of Anthropological Theory,* Alfred A. Knof, New York, 1968. It deals with history of science of anthropology in depth and biographical accounts of nineteenth century anthropologists at work.
- Honigmann, J.J. (Ed.), *The Handbook of Social and Cultural Anthropology*, Rand McNally Chicago, 1974.
- Hsu, Francis L.K., *Under the Ancestors Shadow, Chinese Culture and Personality*, The Cresset Press, London, 1949.
- Kardiner, A. and Preble, E. (Eds.), *They Studied Man*, Penguin series, 1961. The volume contains essays on Darwin, Herbert Spencer, Tylor, Frazer, Durkheim, Boas, Malinowski, Kroeber, Benedict, and Freud.
- Keith, I., *Age and Anthropological Theory*, University Press, Ithaca, 1980.
- Kroeber, Alfred L., *Anthropology,* Brace, Harcourt, 1923, Revised 1948, Indian print 1975.
- Kroeber, Alfred L. (Ed.), *Anthropology Today: An Encyclopedic Inventory*, University Press, Chicago, 1953.
  Several thematic papers relate to the development of theories in anthropology are written by the noted anthropologists of 20th century.
- Lane, M. (Ed.), *Structuralism: A Reader*, London, 1970. See also (1) *Description and Comparison in Cultural Anthropology* by Ward Goodenough, Aldine, Chicago (2) *Anthropology: Its Achievements and Future* by C. Levi-Strauss Winner Gren, N.Y. and (3) *Current Anthropology,* 124–127.

- Lowie, R.H., (1) *The History of Ethnological Theory*, Farrar and Rinehart, New York 1937. (2) *The German People: A social portrait to 1914*, Rinehart. One of the earliest textbooks on anthropological theories; should be used to fill in on the British and Austrian diffusion schools.
- Malefijt, Annemarie De Wall, *Images of Man: A History of Anthropological Thought*, Alfred, A. Knof, New York, 1974. It is a survey of anthropological theory, written for the beginners (Reprints 1978, Calcutta).
- Main, Sir Henry James Sumner, *Ancient Law; Its connection with early history of society, and its relation to modern ideas,* Charles Scribner, New York, 1964.
- Mead, M. (1) And keep your Powder Dry: An anthropologist looks at America. Morrow, New York (New edition in 1942). (2) "National Character" In A.L. Kroeber's edited volume, 1953: 642–67. See also Mead's National Character and Science of Anthropology, 1961:15–26.
- McGee, R. Jon and Richard L. Warms (Eds.), *An Introductory History of Anthropological Theory*, Magfield Publishing Company, California, 1996. In this volume, the editors have colated 38 critical essays by some of the most important thinkers in anthropology, (1880–1980). For each essay, commentaries are provided at appropriate places.
- Naroll, Raoul and Narol Frada (Eds.), *Main Currents in Cultural Anthropology*, Appleton-Century-Crofts, New York, 1973. A more advanced discussion of the major areas of anthropological theory, with chapters written by experts in their fields.
- Penniman, T.K. (Ed.), *A Hundred Years of Anthropology*, (This is available in paperback edition), Morrow, New York, 1935, 1965 (Revised), 1974. This book is valuable for its treatment of the development of archaeology and physical anthropology. A short account of social anthropology is also included. The volume should be consulted by those who are engaged in researches in anthropology irrespective of specialisation.
- Sahlins, M. and E. Service, *Evolution and Culture*, University of Michigan Press, Ann Abor, 1960.
- Sanders, W.T. and B.J. Price, *Meso America: The Evolution of a Civilisation*, Random House, New York, 1969. This book is based on the theory of civilisation. It deals with the processes of growth that shaped history in Mexico and Guatemala.
- Spier, Leslie, *The Distribution of Kinship Systems in North America.* University of Washington Publications in Anthropology, 1925. (Also The Sun Dance of the Plains Indians, its Diffusion, 1921.)
- Srivastava, A.R.N., *Ethnography and Ethnology,* The relationship of the given to the godly *Man in India*, **56** (2), 1092–116, 1976.
- Steward, Julian H. *Theory of Culture Change; the Methodology of Multinear Evolution,* University Illinois Press, Urbana, 1955. (Originally published in 1951, paperback in 1968.)

- Tyler, Stephen (Ed.), *Concepts and Assumptions in Contemporary Anthropology*, Univiersity Press, Georgia, 1971. Also his edited volumes on *Cognitive Anthropology* published by Winston, Rinenart, New York, 1971.
- Voget, Fred W., *The History of Cultural Anthropology,* Rand McNally Publisher, N.Y. 1974. Chapter I of *The Handbook of Social and Cultural Anthropology,* edited by John. J. Honigmann, Rand McNally Publisher, 1–88.
  This is a concise treatment of the subject and contains more than 550 books and research articles on aspects of cultural anthropology.
- Wallace, Anthony, F.C., Revitalisation Movement, *American Anthropologist,* **58**, 264–281, 1956. (See also his book *Culture and Personality,* Random House, New York, 1971.)
- White, Leslie, *The Science of Culture,* Grove Press, New York, 1949; *The Evolution of Culture,* McGraw-Hill, New York, 1959; *The Concept of Culture,* Burgress, Minneapalis, 1975.
  This booklet is based on White's recent lectures on his culturalogy and methods.
- *Anthropology: Annual Review*, published from Pal Alto, California, 1978.
  Two chapters on 'Structuralism in Anthropology' and 'Linguistic models in cultural anthropology' are worth reading. These articles are referred in the main text.

Some textbooks and articles on the anthropological theory written by the Indian anthropologists.

(1) Gopal Saran: *Comparison in Anthropology and Contributions of Radcliffe-Brown and other British Anthropologists,* Lucknow, 1970.

(2) Surjeet Sinha: *Evolutionism:* Reconsidered. *Man in India* vol. 40, 1960.

(3) Makhan Jha, *An Introduction to Anthropological Thought,* Vikas Publisher, Delhi, 1982.

(4) Behura N.K., *Anthropological Theories,* Institute of Applied Anthropology, Bidisa, Midnapur, 1990.

(5) Upadhayay, V.S. and Pandey, *A History of Anthropological Thought* Concept, Delhi, 1995.

Sinha, Sarna and Behura have cited references correctly and have expressed their views clearly; Jha and Upadhayay have not indicated the sources of the passages though they have extracted them from the original texts word by word. Jha and Upadhayay have heavily drawn materials from *The Images of Man* and *The Rise of Anthropological Theory*. (See above for full reference).

Chapter 4

Anthropological Field Researches

Anthropology developed as a distinct subject because of its fieldwork pursuit. Spending time with the people of an unknown/unfamiliar culture, observing them and collecting first hand information are essential elements of a fieldwork enterprise. Therefore, it has become an agenda in all branches of anthropology. Fieldwork for cultural anthropology is an ethnographic exercise carried out among the living people. It is usually held that social-cultural anthropologists study pre-literate/small scale/primitive societies. But, this is not true. Several anthropologists in the past did study western industrial societies, traditional complex societies such as the Hindu castes, urban-industrial societies and have written excellent ethnographies. In this chapter, we shall briefly outline how do the contemporary anthropologists carry out fieldwork. This chapter is not intended to present historical account of field tradition in cultural anthropology. Much has been reviewed in Chapter 3.

FIELDWORK TRADITION IN ANTHROPOLOGY

Franz Boas in America and Bronislaw Malinowski in Great Britain set up fieldwork tradition in anthropology among the primitive cultures towards the beginning of twentieth century. In the process of becoming a professional/academic anthropologist, it is required that he/she must do fieldwork in an alien culture and write a report on the people (Ethnography). Whether the setting is a forest or a desert, a hut or an isolated village or in modern time, a city or town, a work factory or a slum, the mode of anthropological fieldwork is nearly the same. It entails through going into the life of the people living in 'any convenient locality of suitable size' (Radcliffe-Brown, 1952 : 193).

Anthropologists seldom work on large samples of people. They focus on a small group of people/society/community. Robert Redfield referred to this small community as *microcosm of the whole*.

In order to produce a balanced all-round picture of people in preliterate/tribal societies anthropologists must be in the field. "They must go out into the villages," declared Malinowski, "and see the natives at work in gardens, on the beach, in the jungle; he must sail with them to distant sandbanks and to foreign tribes and observe them in fishing trading and ceremonial overseas expeditions. Information must come to him full-flavoured from his own observations of native life and not to be squeezed out of reluctant informants as a trickle of talk. Fieldwork can be done first-or second half even among the savages, in the middle of pile-dwellings, not far from actual cannibalism and headhunting. Open-air anthropology, as opposed to hearsay note taking, is hard work, but it is also great fun. Only such anthropology can give us the all-round vision of primitive man and of primitive culture. Such anthropology shows us, as regards myth, that far from being an idle mental pursuit, it is a vital ingredient of practical relation to the environment" (Malinowski, 1922 : 17).

Anthropological Model of Fieldwork

The terms 'model' refers to structure of ideas. Unlike in other social sciences, fieldwork in anthropology characteristically involves a long stay among the people being studied in order to get a more nearly total view of that society. A general model of research is usually formulated before the fieldwork begins. Here, the ethnographer goes through all the literature about the society under study if available.

This stage is also marked by the ethnographer's own preparation. What to carry along with other items? Some of the most important items are note-books, pencils, pens and if possible, audio-visual equipments (camera, tape recorders), sleeping bag, water bottle and medicine.

The Field Entry

This phase is the most difficult part of the research, for serious problems may crop up during the first few weeks in the field. Meeting the members of the community creates the problems of initial impression, especially when the research appears as a potential threat to the group. Investigators tackle this problem by more than one ways. Anthropologists learn the language and their way of life by doing participant observation. They live with the people and view their patterns of life over weeks and months.

Ethnographic enterprises involve the problem of health of the researchers. Usually, a researcher works relatively in an area away from doctors and hospitals. Some medical supplies such as antibiotics, sulpha drugs, vitamin and pain relievers, etc. do much help to investigations. During the fieldwork, precautions are to be taken at occasion when local people come for medical aids and gifts.

Culture Shock

During the early stages of fieldwork, the anthropologists may experience a situation facing depression and frustration resulting from the confrontation of a way of life very different from that of the researcher. This is known as culture shock. Malinowski's field dairy written during 1914–15 revealed the problems of fieldwork and of adjustment to long period of isolation in foreign surroundings. Given below are a few statements (Quoted in Malefijt, 1974 : 199–200):

"The old man began to lie about burials. I became enraged."

"The stanch, smoke, noise of people, dogs and pigs greatly irritated me."

"Sick, fever and a violent toothache."

"I was fed up with the niggers and with my work."

The contributing factors to culture shock are loneliness, language/communication barrier, living and food patterns and above all, people's attitude towards the researcher. McKim Marriott mentions that he was politely thrown out of three villages in which he attempted to work in eastern India before he was allowed to settle in one village (1957:423). One can very well imagine what would happen to a North American fieldworker who visits rural area in south India (see Beals, 1974).

The return from the fieldwork sometimes causes another type of culture shock. American anthropologist Allan Beals wrote about his experience in India: "Where in Gopalpur there was a feeling of stability, timelessness and adaptation to nature,... United States seemed to express instability, sterility and a land of opposition of nature."

For a fuller picture a detailed account of fieldwork experience including culture shock narrated by Napoleon Chagnon is as follow:

Studying Yanomamo, a south American Indian tribe of Venezuela

"We arrived at the village... It was hot and muggy, and my clothing was soaked with perspiration. The small biting gnats were out in astronomical numbers, for it was the beginning of the dry season. My face and hands were swollen from the venom of their numerous stings. In just a few moments, I was to meet by first Yanomamo, my first primitive man.

I looked up and gasped when I saw a dozen burly, naked, filthy, hideous men staring at us down the shaft of their drawn arrows! Immense wads of green tobacco were stuck between their lower teeth and lips making them look even more hideous, and strands of dark green slime dripped or hung from their noses. My next discovery was that there were a dozen or so vicious, underfed dogs snapping at my legs, circling me as if I were going to be their next meal. I just stood there holding my notebook, helpless and pathetic. They put their weapons down when they recognised Barker [a missionary] and returned to there chanting, keeping a nervous eye on the village entrances.

I had not eaten all day, I was soaking wet from perspiration the gnats were biting me, and I was covered with red pigment. The Indians would blow their noses into their hands, flick as much of the mucus off that would separate in a snap of the wrist, wipe the residue into their hair, and then carefully examine my face, arms, legs, hair and the contents of my pockets...

Eating three meals a day was out of the question. I solved the problem by eating a single meal that could be prepared in a single container or at most, in two containers, washed my dishes only when there were no clean ones left, using cold river water, and wore each change of clothing at least a week to cut down on my laundry problem, a courageous undertaking in the tropics. I was also less concerned about sharing my provisions with the rats, insects, Indians, and the elements, thereby eliminating the need for my complicated storage process. Frequently, my single meal was no more complicated than a can of sardines and a package of crackers. But at least two or three times a week I would do something sophisticated, like make oatmeal or boil rice and add a can of tuna fish or tomato paste to it...

"Meals were a problem in another way. Food sharing is important to the Yanomamo in the context of displaying friendship. 'I am hungry', is almost a form of greeting with them. I could not possibly have brought enough food with me to feed the entire village, yet they seemed not to understand this.

"Despite the fact that most of them knew I would not share my food with them at their request, some of them always showed up at my hut during mealtime. I gradually became accustomed to this and learned to ignore their persistent demands while ate.

"The thing that bothered me the most was the incessant, impassioned, and aggressive demands the natives made. It would become so unbearable that I would have to lock myself in my hut every once in a while just to escape from it: privacy is one of Western culture's greatest achievements. But I did not want privacy for its own sake; rather, I simply had to get from the begging. Day and night for the entire time I lived with Yanomamo I was plagued by such demands as: "Give me a knife, I am poor!" "If you don't take me with you on your next trip to Widokaiya-teri I'll chop a hole in your canoe!...

"I soon learned that I had to become very much like the Yanomamo to be able get along with them on their terms: sly, aggressive and intimidating.

"Had I failed to adjust in this fashion I would have lost six months of supplies to them in a single day or would have spent most of my time ferrying them around in my canoe or hunting for them. More importantly, had I failed to demonstrate that I could not be pushed around beyond a certain point, I would have been the subject of far more ridicule, theft and practical jokes than was the actual case. I had to acquire a certain proficiency in their kind of interpersonal consequence might follow if they did such and such to me." (Chagnon 1968 : 4–9).

Problem of Understanding Local Language and Role of Informants

The most difficult part of ethnographic fieldwork is working with people through local languages. It is always good to learn the local (native) language but the average anthropologists cannot speak the language of the people they study. Here, role of interpreter becomes crucial. An interpreter is one who acts in a two-way process. He knows anthropologist's language (English, Hindi, etc.; at the same time he is well verse in native language. He is, thus, capable of translating each other's conversations. Total dependence on interpreters is, however, not recommended.

Reliability of Informants

For many years, ethnographers working in tribal societies collected their information from a single key informant—a man who was knowledgeable about his community. It was assumed that the tribal society was so homogeneous that one person's information would be the same as that of others. However, when more attention was given to the woman informants, it was discovered that their responses were often different from those of male informants. Gerald Berreman noted that there are people who deviate from the norm (1968). The ethnographers have also discovered that some informants have specialised knowledge (i.e. the diviners, priests) which is not shared by the other members of the group. This problem becomes more crucial in complex societies.

Ethnographers should remember that the accuracy of information provided by the informants of different backgrounds should be checked properly. This is also related to the *validity* of response. Validity means the degree to which observations actually measure what they attempt to measure.

TECHNIQUES OF DATA COLLECTION

A complete account of all the techniques used by the field anthropologists cannot be presented here. We may, however, refer to those popular ways by which the anthropologists collect information. These techniques are also called Ethnographic techniques or tools.

Participant Observation

Two terms—'participation' and 'observation' are crucial. 'Participation' simply means living with the people as one study. It implies understanding people *subjectively*—what people do, why people feel while doing so. 'Observation', on the other hand, implies some degree of objectivity. Inherent in participation is certain amount of biasness while 'observation' minimises biasness and detachment. In anthropological fieldwork, these two terms are combined. Thus, it is a technique involving the direct, first-hand observation of a group's way of life. Through participant-observation, information on the material culture, ritual and economic behaviour are collected and the researcher participates in the group's daily affairs as much as possible. Audio-visual aids are used frequently while documenting these data. In any study, full participant-observation is not possible since the elements of participation depend on people and researcher and a lot depends on personal interaction with the people.

Anthropologists have realised that participant-observation is a valuable tool for undertaking people and their behaviour; in particular, publicly shown activities. The process involving participant-observation includes talking to the people, taking notes, preparing relevant questions (schedule) asked and answer obtained among others. Participant-observation alone cannot yield all the information ethnographers want to know; therefore, it is always combined with some other techniques of data collection.

Interview

Many types of interviewing techniques are used by the ethnographer including structural and in-depth interview types. Informal interview, which involves some types of schedule (not questionnaire, which is more prevalent in sociology), is the popular mode of collecting data. Formal interview or structured interview, if followed in anthropology, is often directed on the basis of sampling procedures. It is valuable for quantifying certain types of data. 'In-depth' informal interview is used more frequently in ethnographic fieldwork because the anthropologists are not familiar with the culture being studied. Sociologists, working in their own society, can make certain implicit assumptions about the responses of their informants. They know that which questions are meaningful in their own society. But, ethnographers cannot make assumptions about the society. They study until they become familiar with the culture. They must ask open-end questions, which allow the informants to discuss the things they consider important. Eventually, through the extended in-depth interviewing, the anthropologists will begin to learn about the society's way of life. At this point, she or he may switch to a more structured interview. In-depth interview is often conducted with key-informants. A key informant is a knowledgeable person of the society being studied.

Preparation of Genealogies

The collection of genealogies has been regarded as the most significant part of the anthropological fieldwork. Usually, ethnographers follow the procedure of asking an informant in some form of *lingua franca* or through an interpreter such questions as "What is your name? How many brother-sisters do you have? What do you call your mother's brother?" Because of the complexities involved in kinship structure of a society, this led to endless confusion. The modern method is to write down the names of relatives first, and then, ask what kinship terms are applied to them. This procedure is known as the *genealogical method* and was first introduced by W.H.R. Rivers (1903) in his study of the Marqueses of Melanesia and then, the Todas, a pastoral tribal group in south India.

Rivers' procedure with some modifications is still practised by modern ethnographers. This may be illustrated by reference to a hypothetical genealogy given below. First, we must note some conventional notations.

(1)

(a) For male: △ (Triangle)

(b) For female: ○ (Circle)

(c) Sex not specified: □ (Square)

(d) For marriage: = (Equal)

(e) For decent | (Vertical)

(f) Sibling ties: — (Horizontal)

(g) Illicit child ¦ (Broken vertical)

(h) Divorce: ≠

(i) Member died ⊘ ⧄

(j) Twins: 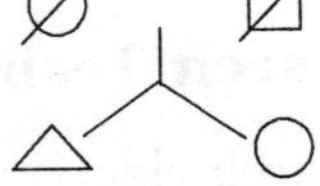

(2) In genealogies, it is useful to take one individual (called Ego) as a point of reference for defining kinship relation.

(3) In describing relationship, it is suggested that one should always define the relationship exactly. Thus, we should not use the term 'brother-in-law' but either wife's brother (W B) or sister's husband (Si H), as the case may be. In many ethnographies, Z is used for sister.

(4) To minimise the detail information, particulars of a person such as rank, place of residence, membership of a clan, age, etc. may be entered below the name of each individual, as required.

(5) Order of birth of children and order of marriage of spouse may be indicated by the order in which they appear in a genealogy, preferably from left to right.

(6) Some symbols, such as an asterisk in brackets, etc. are often devised by the researcher. For example, MM means Ego's mother's mother or FFF refers to Ego's father's fathers, i.e. great grandfather and so on.

(7) Researchers frequently encounter problem of space while preparing genealogy of a large group such as lineage or kindred. In such cases, separate sheets of paper may be used and compiled later on.

Some examples are provided in Chapter 6 of the present book.

Life History

Some members of a society under study prove to be more helpful and knowledgeable (key informants). When someone is unusually interesting, we tempted to collect his/her history. This is merely a reconstruction of lifetime experience of informants. Life histories provide how people look at and react to certain social phenomena in changing circumstances. Diversities within a society/culture are reflected in life histories. Some ethnographers keep life histories of informants in their field diaries. This is used at later stages.

Other Techniques

Field data are collected through a number of other different means, viz. census, map, case study, audio-visual aids, etc. Photography is rapidly becoming an integral part of anthropological research. Generally 35 mm still camera is used to record aspect of the society and people. Tape recorders are used to collect information on the language of the people and their music. Surveying is carried out to map the area being studied. Projective tests and Draw a figure, if required, are administered to collect data on personality. Wherever possible, archival data are examined in order to view the people under studied from a historical perspective. In some cases, newspapers, posters and other published data can be utilised.

Combining Sociological Research Techniques

Recent trends in ethnographic research clearly point out a growing tendency towards using sociological techniques; often ethnographers use structured interview while working in heterogeneous societies (such as an Indian village/town/city). It involves defining universe, using questionnaires, sampling, socio-psychological social distance scales, etc. A few ethnographers, whenever opportunities arise, employ these techniques even working among the homogeneous communities. In other words, ethnographic method is combined with survey method.

Importance of Field Diaries

Keeping a field diary is an integral part of any fieldwork programme. The ethnographer keeps an account of day-to-day work for some important events in his/her diary.

Anytime an informant tells anything to the researcher, anthropologist may collect it as 'personal documentation' in the form of a diary. Some of the well-known anthropologists' collection of diaries have appeared in the form of autobiographical essays, see for example, Mead (1972) and Malinowski (1967).

A Few Tips

As ethnographic fieldwork involves living in close contact with people under study who are usually 'other' than the researcher, a few tips might be useful here.

It is always good to begin the work with preparing community map. Here, the researcher asks the people about prominent places, ritual shrines, and locate them. Collecting genealogy is other convenient way to know about the people; collecting folklore and material objects help establishing rapport. The local people, young and old, enjoy telling their oral traditions. Playing with the local children may help researcher to build up confidence and love and affection towards the people.

Writing an Ethnography

Perhaps, the most difficult aspect of fieldwork is the analysis of data. During the field study, data are analysed each day randomly to discern patterns and to determine what information should be collected next day. Evans-Pritchard, the celebrated British social anthropologist, is of the opinion that detailed analysis must wait till the ethnographers return home.

The ethnographers must analyse the significance of his field data before he presents them in written forms. Anthropologists usually write about the primitive societies in *ethnographic present* tense which is the 'present' that the sources describe, no matter how long ago or how recently ethnography is written (see Appendix II).

As mentioned above, the analysis actually begins during the course of observations. The prevalent mode of writing ethnography during Malinowski era was to write down everything in a systematic way and end up with some general statements. These statements certainly helped generating theoretical options about a society. In other words, in the tradition set up by Malinowski and Radcliffe-Brown, field data did generate theoretical insights such as structural-functional analysis of institutions. Evans Pritchard wrote:

"The anthropologist must study the whole of the social life. It is impossible to understand clearly and comprehensively any part of people's social life except in the full context of their social life as a whole. He may not publish every detail he has recorded... He may decide to write on people's law, religion or on their economics, describing one aspect of their life and neglecting the rest, he does so always against the background of their entire social activities and in terms of their whole social structure" (Evans-Pritchard, 1952 : 80).

The latest edition of *Notes and Queries in Anthropology* states, "It is important that not even the slightest expression of amazement or disapproval should ever be displayed at the description of ridiculous, impossible or disgusting features in customs, cult or legend" (1967 : 32).

Testing Evidence and Explanation

Ethnographers' ultimate aim is not only *to describe* the facts but also *to explain* them. In other words, ethnographers want *to understand* why people have certain customs or beliefs, not just to observe that they *do* have them and why questions deal with explanation. "An explanation is an answer to a why question", maintain the philosophers of social sciences. There are several types of explanations, some of which are more satisfying than others.

After 1950s, a tradition in anthropology developed that the researcher first develops some theoretical insight before he enters the field and determines findings that would be made by directing attention towards certain phenomena. In this process, selective observations are more useful for it is believed that it is impossible to observe everything. Therefore, ethnographers use 'models' as devices for looking at a society. It is to be noted that this kind of analysis does not really yield *pattern of the society* but *pattern for the ethnography*. A scientific ethnographer combines both patterns.

Some anthropologists have discussed at length the relevance of model building in anthropology. To them, accurate models are derived from more adequate theories of culture; therefore, modern researchers must search for a dual goal of ethnographic investigation. The results of each study help refine reasoning (models) to be used in further studies. Ethnography is, therefore, a social enterprise; results are cumulative and every study is strengthened by what has been learned in various studies.

Difference between Ethnographic Research and Survey Research

A number of social researchers especially sociologists, economists, health scientists and political scientists follow survey research strategy. This involves testing hypotheses, sampling, identifying *universe*, using formal questionnaires, tabulation and analysis of data by means of statistical procedures. Usually, a survey research is directed on large population (town, city or industrial belt). The basic idea behind the survey research is to generate information from sample and to make correct inferences about the population being studied. In ethnographic research (described above) the community is studied as a whole (Srivastava, 1979).

In ethnographic research, small-scale societies are studied. In this situation, researches (i.e. anthropologists) get to know most of the members (informants). In survey research, the person who reply to queries is called respondent.

Survey-researchers may hire people for assistance in filling-in questionnaires. It is usually not done in ethnographic research.

It is often alleged that the position of anthropologists, following the ethnographic research strategies, described here become weak; for they generalise about entire culture on the basis of studying just one community. But, there are some ways to overcome biasness (see Epstein, 1967).

Ethnographer's Bias

One cannot be completely objective in any undertaking. The question then arises—to what extent is the ethnographic report a projection of the ethnographer's personality and to what extent is it a reflection of external 'reality'? More than one ethnographer may have studied same society. Sometimes, the results have been quite divergent. For example, Robert Redfield (1930) and Oscar Lewis (1951) both studied the Mexican village of Tepoztlan within a gap of twenty years. While the former described it as well-integrated, peaceful, homogeneous and populated with contented people; the latter described it as faction-ridden, tense and populated largely by frustrated, fearful, envious and distrustful people (cf. Redfield 1955 : 132–148)

Ralph Piddington (1957 : 546), with reference to two classic ethnographic studies, *We, The Tikopia* by Raymond Firth and on the Trobriand Islanders by Malinowski, had noted that "the Trobriand Islanders are very like Malinowski and the Tikopia very like Professor Raymond Firth."

"A human", Berreman writes, "is a cultural animal, and since ethnographers are men, such problems are inevitable. Objectivity in any absolute sense is impossible in the study of human beings. To deny bias is to mask the problem rather than to eliminate it. Perhaps, the best advice for the ethnographer is to attempt to recognise his/her biases, compensate for them insofar as possible, and in any event, to make them as explicit as possible so that the readers will be able to take account of them in evaluating the ethnography. Obviously, even the most conscientious effort will fall short since no one is fully self-aware, but this, like explicating the research methods and the bases for inference, is a direction in which ethnography must go in the pursuit of increasing scientific validity, and it constitutes no thereat to humanistic insight" (Berreman 1970 : 370).

Ethics and Responsibility

Berreman has raised the problems of ethics and responsibilities in the following way: What is researcher's responsibility to his informants with reference to the information they divulge and entrust to him? How much should he let them know of his intentions? How much should he reveal of his methods? When does research efficiency defer to moral responsibility, and what is moral responsibility in research? How much should the ethnographer reveal of his subjects' secrets in his published report? If they engage in illegal activities, should he report the fact or not? If so, how can he protect them or should he? Social researchers have long been faced with these problems. In this context, it must be remembered that ethnography, like all social researches, is a human undertaking. It carries with it the responsibilities of all human undertakings—neither less nor more. These responsibilities must be realised by the individual researcher and must be translated in human terms. Sometimes, he/she will find that the use of pseudonyms will suffice to protect his/her informants; sometimes, information will have to be suppressed. Sometimes, he/she will intervene as a result of moral commitment; sometimes he/she will remain aloof. He/she will always balance the human values of his/her subjects and himself/herself. He/she can do no more ethnographers have maintained a level of responsibility which has made it possible in most of the areas of the world, for subsequent ethnographers to be welcomed back.

Community Study

Redfield's definition of community is no longer fully acceptable by the ethnographer anthropologist (Redfield, 1955 : 4). For our immediate purpose, we may define a community, in simpler terms, as a group of persons having common interests, organisations or living in the same area under the same social rules and regulations. Drawing insights from Chapters 2 and 4, a guideline is presented below for planning a community study (see Box).

Ethnographic Profile of a Community

I. Name and area of the community for study

1. Name of the community, its synonyms and etymology.
2. Present-day distribution.
3. What is the language/dialect spoken?
4. What are the other language/dialects spoken?

II. Entering the community

1. Permission of the local govt. officers.
2. Cooperation of community elders.
3. General persons: key informants

III. Ethnographic details

1. *Food habit:* Staple food–drinks, smoking etc.
2. *Social:* What are the major social divisions/groupings and their hierarchical order, if any, in the community? What are the chief functions of the subdivisions?
3. *Institution of marriage:* What are the marriage rules? Age at marriage. Bride price/dowry. Rules of residence after marriage. Rules regarding divorce.
4. *Family pattern:* Type/forms of family. rules of inheritance in family. Succession pattern. Inter-family linkages in and outside the community.
5. *Life cycle rituals:* What are the major rituals observed on the occasion/state of (a) birth (and how names are given), (b) adolescence, (c) marriage, (d) death and (e) any other function. Any significant change reported lately in the ritual performances.
6. *Economic activities:* What are the major economic resources? Occupation of the community—(a) traditional, (b) primary, and (c) subsidiary. The market system, forms of trade, barter, exchange, etc. Patron-client relationship (*jajmani* system) or any other form of socio-economic interdependence changes that have come about after independence in various economic pursuits.
7. *Mechanism of social control:* What are the traditional and statutory councils and regional associations (*sabha*) in the community? Composition and function of such councils/regional associations. Forms of punishment and reward.
8. *Religious attributes:* mention religion/s the community professes. What are the main family, clan, village and regional deities? What are the major sacred centres/shrines/pilgrimages? Role of ritual specialists. What are the major festivals and the significance associated with them? Changes in religious organisation of the community.

9. *Inter-community linkages:* Traditional linkages. Modern linkages.
10. *Impact of development programmes:* Literacy and education. Health. Drinking water. Employment and self-employment. Communication. Electricity. Any other parameter.

IV. Any other observation of importance concerning life and culture of the community.

V. Writing the report

The following points should be taken up appropriately in a report:

- Title and sub-title
- Statement of problem
- Objective/purpose/aims
- Description of studies related to the problem
- Methodology–Area group selection, sampling, if any, specific hypotheses, if developed and techniques used
- Organisation of data–Description and analysis and presentation of quantitative data in table, graphs, photographs, etc.
- Conclusions
- References of texts
- Appendix

SUGGESTED READING

A number of publications related to field-work are available. Some are general, a few are specific and the rest are on personal problems encountered by the ethnographers. Only selected titles are presented below which are useful both for beginners and advanced students.

- Beals, Alan R. (Ed.), *Village Life in South India*, Aldine, Chicago, 1974. First chapter of the book contains a vivid account of anthropological field expedition in a peasant village of southern India.
- Beattie, John, *Understanding an African Kingdom: Bunyoro*. H-R-W-Series, New York, 1965.
  A review of the methods used in fieldwork among the Bunyoro.
- Berreman, Gerald D., *Behind Many Masks*, Society for Applied Anthropology Monograph, No. 4, Washington, D.C., 1962. Also appeared in revised form in James Clifton's edited volume *An Introduction to Cultural Anthropology*, Houghton, Boston, 1968. A through discussion of author's field-work in Garhwal region of Uttarakhand (India).
- Bowen, Elenore Smith, *Return to Laughter*, Random House, 1954, N.Y. Paper back. A novel by a woman anthropologist academically known as Laura Bohanan based on her study of the Tiv, African society. A delightful fieldwork narration.
- Chagnon, Napoleon E., *The Yanomamo: the Fierce People*, Holt, Rinehart and Winston series, N.Y., 1968.

This is a lively and readable ethnography. It depicts the adverse conditions under which Napoleon worked in Venezuela. Chagnon has also contributed to method of studying Yanomamo (H-R-W series, 1972).

- Casagrande, J.B. (Ed.), *In the Company of Man*, Harper, N.Y. 1960.
  Twenty distinguished anthropologists each offer a profile of the one key informant who has been central to his or her own anthropological fieldwork. In doing so, they convey the human aspect of teamwork between the scientist and his 'subjects' in a way that is highly empathic.
- David, Mayberry-Lewis, *The Savage and the Innocent,* London, 1965.
  This is a fascinating account of the personal trials of an anthropologist and his wife doing fieldwork in a remote area in South America. Ethnographic Research published by the *Association of Social Anthropology*, London, 1980, is a thorough treatment on cultural anthropology researches. It is almost an encyclopedia of anthropological research and researchers.
- Epstein, A.L. (Ed.), *The Craft of Social Anthropology*, Tavistock Publications, London, 1967.
  A number of problem-oriented essays are written by British anthropologists.
- Evans-Pritchard, E.E., *Social Anthropology and Other Essays*, Oxford University Press, Oxford, 1952.
  Chapters IV and V are crucial. Development of fieldwork in social anthropology has been described well.
- Foster, George M., *Long-term Field Research in Social Anthropology*, Academic Press, New York, 1979.
- Freilich, Morries (Ed.), *Marginal Natives: Anthropologists at Work*, Harper and Row, New York, 1970.
- Hughes, Charles C. (Ed.), Introductory Readings for Cultural Anthropology, *Make Men of Them,* California 1972.
  Part II of this volume has four valuable essays concerning field-work in cultural anthropology by Casagrande, E.S. Bowen, B. Malinowski and on urban ethnography by Elliot Liebow.
- Jongmans, D.G. and Gutkind, P.C.W. (Eds.), *Anthropologists in the Field*, Assen: Van Gorcun, 1967.
- Langess, L.L., *The Life History in Anthropological Science,* H-R-W series, N.Y. 1965.
  This is a manual on the utility of life-history material. It contains excellent bibliographic sources as the 'personal documentations' in Anthropology.
- Levi-Strauss, C., *Tristes Tropiques,* Translated by John Russell, Basic Books, N.Y. 1961.
  One of the leading anthropologists discusses in a philosophical way what it means to do participant observation field-work.
- Murdock, G.P. (Ed.), *Outline of Cultural Materials*, Yale University, Yale, 1971.
  This is the revised edition of a well-known and handy checklist for fieldwork.

- Malinowski, Bronislaw, *A Diary in the Strict Sense of the Term*, Harcourt, New York, 1967.
  Private notes of Malinowski written during his field expedition among the Trobrianders published after his death. The problem of 'culture stock' is mentioned in the diary. Malinowski's *Argonauts of the Western Pacific* (1922) is about the Trobrianders. A thorough description of participant observation is presented in it.
- Mead, Margaret, *Male and Female*: A study of the sexes in a changing world, Dell publication, New York, 1968 (First published in 1949).
  This book is an outcome of many field trips to the South Pacific, Bali, Samoa, New Guinea and the Admirality Island to show sex-roles in different cultures.
- Mead, Margaret, *Blackberry Winter: My Earlier Experiences*, Dell Publication, New York, 1972.
  This is autobiography of M. Mead, one of the leading anthropologists of the 20th century. It is a lengthy description of her field-experience in a variety of cultural settings.
- Newman, Philip, *Knowing the Gururumba*, H-R-W series, N.Y. 1965.
  This is a short ethnography which contains very good materials on the initial stage fieldwork.
- Pelto, Peritti J., *The Structure of Inquiry, Anthropological Research,* Harper and Row, N.Y. 1970.
  A well-rounded textbook that treats the various aspects of field-Work and their theoretical foundations.
- Powdermaker, Hortense, *Stranger and Friend: The way of an Anthropologist*, New York, 1966.
  As the title suggests, it is a personal account of the researcher in four societies and different approaches he adopts in each.
- Redfield, Robert, *Chan Kom: A. Mayan Village*, Camelie Institution of Washington, 1934.
  One of the pioneering studies in the anthropological approach to community study. It is a classic ethnography.
- Rivers, W.H.R., The Genealogical Method of Anthropological Inquiry, *The Sociological Bulletin,* **3**, 12, 1903.
  Also appeared in Nelson Graburn's edited volume *Reading in Kinship and Social Organisation,* Harper and Row, 1971.
- Royal Anthropological Institute, *Notes and Queries in Anthropology*, RAIGI, London, 1951. (6th edition, 1967).
  This is the best known single anthropological field manual.
- Spindler, George D. (Ed.), *Being on Anthropologist: Fieldwork in Eleven Cultures*. Holt, Rinehart and Winston series in Anthropology, 1972.
  Eleven anthropologists present their experiences in conduction research in other cultures.

- Spradley, James P., *The Ethnographic Interview*, Holt, Rinehart and Winston series in Anthropology, 1979.
  Detailed description of interviewing technique as used in anthropological field research. Spradley has also written Participant Observation (H-R-W series, 1980) that surveys on the problem and research methods in participant observation in Anthropology.
- Srivastava, A.R.N, Sampling in Social Anthropology Researches, Journal of *Social Research,* **32** (1), 96–105, 1979.
- Thomas, Elizabeth Marshall (Ed.), *The Harmless People*, Vintage, New York, 1959.
  An entertaining ethnographic account of the Bushman of the Kalahari, provides many insights into their day-to-day activities.
- Vidyarthy, L.P., *The Maler: The Nature Man-Spirit Complex* in a Hill Tribe of Rajmahal Hills, Bookland, Calcutta, 1963.
  The author describes how he had undergone problems and also solved the problems. Appendix contains several case studies.
- Williams, Thomas Rhys, *Field Methods in the Study of Culture,* H-R-W-series in Anthropology, 1967.
  This is a concise guide to field methods, focusing on the author's personal experiences among the Dusun of Borneo.

Chapter 5

The Domestic Sphere of Culture

The conventional way to describe the domestic life of simpler societies is in terms of family or household types, marriage and the relational patterns of the members of the group, i.e. kinship. Very often, these are described under social organisation (defined in Chapter 2). In this chapter, our task is to present some relevant findings of the domestic domain of societies as reflected in ethnographies. Societies of all over the world have domestic unit of one or other kind. Activities of this unit include preparation and consumption of food; cleaning, grooming and enculturating the young; sleeping and adult sexual intercourse. (There are a few societies, in which sexual tasks are performed away from their dwelling places!) Cultural anthropologists try to understand the very organisation and functions of social groups structured around a domestic unit.

THE NATURE OF DOMESTIC GROUP

Study of social forms is centrally important in socio-cultural anthropology. Anthropologists have been analysing them for more than a century. It is easy to describe the range of social forms in terms of 'family', 'marriage', 'residence', and 'kinship' but when we look at them on a grand comparative scale, confusions do arise. The basic issue posed here is how to look at the social form. Many texts begin with either a definition of the family or a proposition that the family is universal. Murdock, for example, opens his discussion in *Social Structure* (1949) by stating:

"The family is a social group characterised by common residence, economic cooperation and reproduction. It includes adults of both sexes, at least two of whom maintain a socially approved sexual relationship and one or more children, own or adopted, of the sexually cohabiting adults" (1949 : 1).

Since Murdock, anthropologists have focused their discussions mainly on three topics—the presence or absence of nuclear of elementary family, typologies of family and the development cycle in family. In his cross-cultural studies, Murdock argued that the nuclear family (defined above) was found in every human society (1949 : 1). Talcott Parsons (1955) also claimed that the small conjugal family provided the most satisfactory framework for socialising children.

In recent decades, however, cultural anthropologists have been critical of this line of thinking. Studies by Gough (1959), Spiro (1954), Fox (1966) and Goodenough (1970) among others, have shown that the nuclear or conjugal family is not necessarily the core of a society. These studies, however, do not preclude the existence of small domestic units. Rather, they show how erroneous are terms like 'elementary' or 'extended' family when the boundaries for these social groupings have not been defined, and when it has not been well established, how these social units operate within the context.

FAMILY, HOUSEHOLD AND DOMESTIC GROUP: CONCEPTUAL ISSUES

It would be profitable if we first clarify the meaning of the terms *family*, *household* and *domestic group*. Anthropological usages of these terms have been ambiguous because each of these concepts may carry more than one meaning at a time, and the users of these terms seldom specify the context in which they are used. Many times, the terms family, household and domestic group are viewed as synonymous even when it appears that the household and domestic groups are not based on the family.

The frequently cited works on *Taravad* of the Nayar and on *Okka* of the Coorgs of south India offer excellent examples (Gough, 1961, Srinivas, 1960).

Meaning of Family and Household

Some scholars have delineated systematic distinctions between family and household. The generally accepted meaning of the term 'family' has already been discussed. A 'household' is composed of people who unlike family, though not necessarily related, live in the same house or compound. Bohannan (1963, 1968) uses the term 'household' for this kind of arrangement. He defines the family in terms of kinship and marriage; and the household in terms of residence and propinquity. He uses household as a synonym for domestic group. He states: "A family is a kinship group, marked by kinship (genealogical) relationships. A household is a 'local' or spatial group, marked by propinquity. A family need not live together as a household. A household need not be made up solely, or even primarily, of members of the family. Thus, the family and the household must not be confused (even though such is a norm in most of the societies)" (Bohannan, 1963 : 78).

Household is a group of people who live together and form a functioning domestic unit. Bohannan cautions that 'the members of a household' may and may not constitute a family; and even if they do so, it may or may not be a simple nuclear family.

Household is an unfortunate term because it carries more than one meaning. In common parlance, it means a 'house' or a 'hut' or a dwelling place where people live together. The 'living together' implies residing under the same roof. It does not deal with the question of whether or not the members form a common consumption unit (hearth), a production (economic) unit and a resource-holding unit. Nor does it refer to who are the members. For a western (industrial) society, the household is treated as the same unit as that of a family. In many non-western societies, the situation is less clear-cut. For this reason, many ethnographers describe a non-western society without making appropriate qualification in their use of these terms. This should be avoided.

In specific sense, the term household refers to a number of activities common to a group of person. At least three, such activities are commonly recognized—residence, food consumption and production. To put it differently, a statement concerning the household organisation of a society implies that some people (not necessarily related to one another) live together (under the same roof, or in adjacent buildings or huts forming a common compound.), sharing and contributing to a common hearth. Here, sharing and contributing to a hearth means that these members hold a common resource/fund/budget and their consumption needs in part are met by this fund. The variations in household criteria are of particular concern to census enumerators who, while taking a household census, must decide what criteria should be followed. When not specified in explicit terms, confusion arises and the analysis becomes dubious.

The Meaning of Domestic Group

Some scholars, among whom Meyer Fortes (the British social anthropologist) appears to be the forerunner, have encouraged ethnographers to emphasise on 'domestic group' rather than on 'family'. Because of paucity of space, it is not possible here to examine relevant ethnographic works reflecting this trend. It suffices to say that the investigators are now much concerned with defining the criteria of the domestic group and separating it from the family and household. A detailed list of related ethnographies are given at the end of this chapter. Fortes defines domestic group in the following words:

"The domestic group is essentially a householding and housekeeping unit organised to provide the material and cultural resources needed to maintain and bring up its members" (1958:8)

Fortes further remarked that in the realm of domestic group "kinship, descent and other bonds enter into the constitution of the group, whereas the nucleus is formed purely by the direct bond of marriage, filiations and siblingship" (1958 : 8). Thus, he maintains that the family and the domestic group are analytically distinct, although actual composition of the two may be identical. The major features of the domestic group are co residence, production-consumption of food and participation in day-to-day affairs in the domestic life. It is the task of the ethnographers not to use these terms synonymously if the situations are different. Jack Goody (1958, 1972) has supported these criteria in the light of ethnographies.

To state briefly, a domestic group refers to a group of people related by marriage, filiations and siblingship, who concurrently form a residential, reproductive, consumption, production and a resource-holding unit. This statement needs further clarification. *Related by marriage* means the relationship among the members by the bond of marriage (to be described fully in Chapter 5). *Filiation* refers to the relationship between the parents (father, mother) and the children. If relation extends over two generations, then father or mother is usually regarded ancestor or ancestress and this is called descent. *Siblingship* refers to the relationship between brothers and sisters of the same parents.

The people forming above-mentioned unit may not actually live under the same roof; there may be a cluster of huts forming a large compound. Further, it may not be the case that the members would cooperate in all these ways. Ethnographers find one or more reproductive/consumption/production units in a society upon a given moment of time. In a society, domestic group containing more than one reproductive/consumption/ production unit represents the phases of development which will be described shortly under 'processual analysis'.

DIVERSE FORMS OF DOMESTIC GROUP

Typological Approach

In anthropological textbooks, chapter on the 'institution of family and marriage' are full of statements concerning types of families. Some anthropologists consider the number of persons including the number of mates as the basis of classification, others stress the degree of genealogical relations (primary or secondary, etc.), the relative importance of kinship versus conjugal ties (affinal, congenial, etc.), and still others consider the activities of members for classification (orientation, procreation). In fact, the categorisation of family (household/domestic group) is culture specific. We must not forget that a particular group enters into another type along with changes in the individuals and their role-behaviour. In other words, some other variables are affecting the organisation of a social group. However, it has become a tradition to depict the social life in popular typological terms. The following are some varieties and sub-varieties of the social life:

I. Conjugal/nuclear variety

II. Consanguineal

III. Composite conjugal
- (a) Polygynous
- (b) Polyandrous

IV. Composite unilineal/extended
- (a) Patrilineal
- (b) Matrilineal
- (c) Joint

The above varieties and sub-varieties are illustrated through the genealogical diagrams (see diagrams illustrated in Fig. 5.1).

Forms of Domestic Group

What emerges from the above description is the nature of composition of society in concrete social unit. Thus, in many societies, the living arrangement is around a co-resident husband and the wife and their dependent unmarried children. This is called *nuclear family*. It is to be noted that the core of the family, in comparative perspective, is the unit of mother-plus-dependent children. When a male (husband) joins to this unit, the resultant group is nuclear family. But, his roles are as spouse-cum-sexual partner, begetter of children, bread provider, legal guardian is not always subsumed. Consider the following example:

The existence of *matrifocal family* among many societies of the Caribbean, British Guinea, Puerto Rico and elsewhere clearly emphasises on 'mother-children unit'

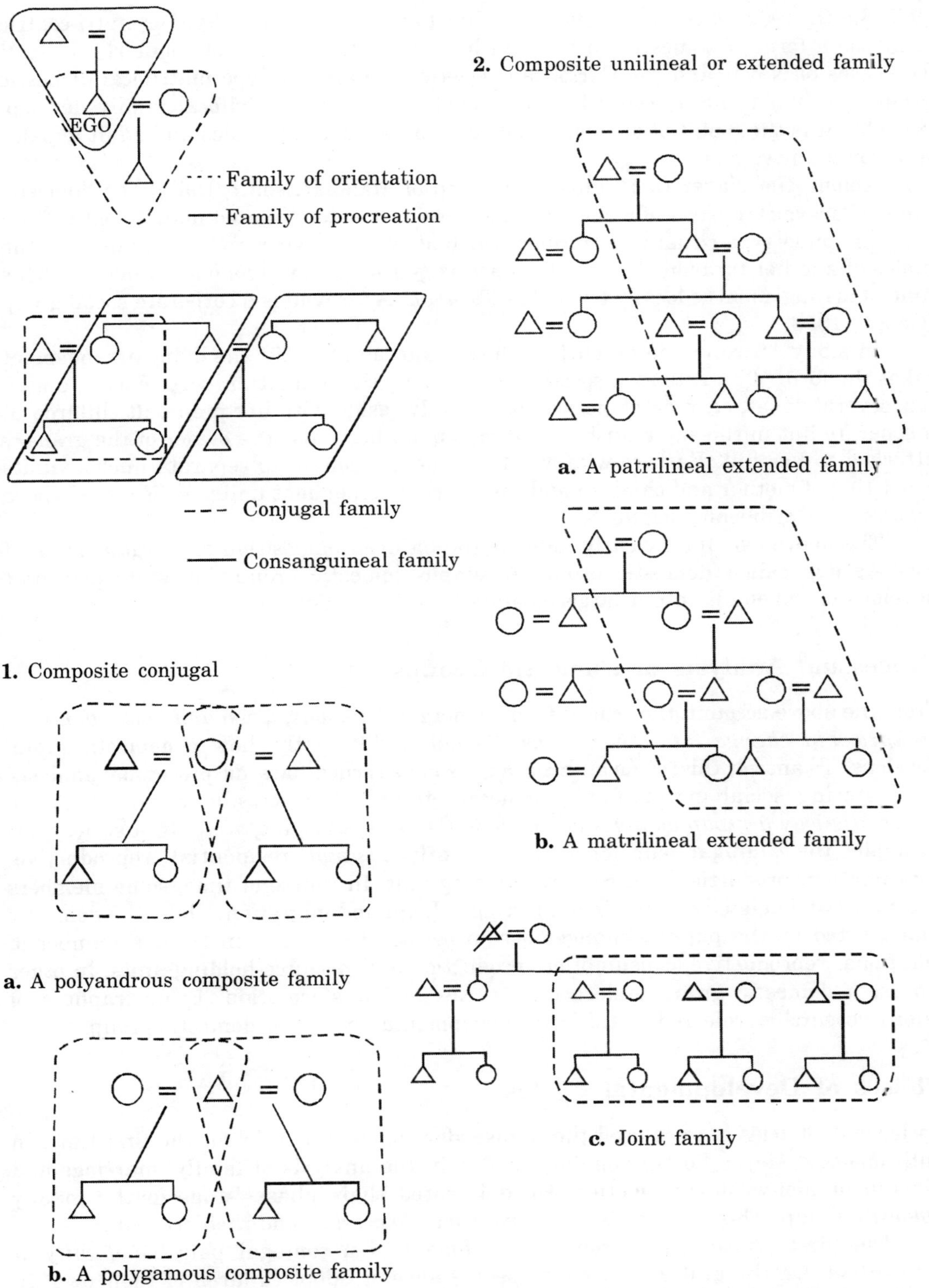

Fig. 5.1 Diverse forms of domestic groups. (Dotted lines indicate conjugal family segments)

(R.T. Smith, 1962; M.G. Smith, 1965 and Kunstadten, 1963). Matrifocal or matri-centric family is a form of domestic unit in which husband (father) is not regularly present. The cases of Nayar and the Caribbean societies are archaic type matrifocal domestic groups. Although our purpose is not to explain how did matrifocal family develop; probably it is the result of division of labour separating adult males and adult females in a community.

Among the Nayar (a Hindu caste group of Malabar, south India) the domestic group (Taravad) consists of a cluster of brothers and sisters related matrilineally. Soon after the puberty, a ritual is performed which allows the sisters to bear children by the males of another taravad. The brothers act as guardians and economic providers. This kind of arrangement is locally termed as *Taravad*. A taravad is a corporate social group (Gough, 1958).

In many African societies such as the Ashanti and the Tiv, the living arrangement takes the form of an extended social group. Among the Ashanti, reports Fortes, a man has several wives, each of whom would normally reside with her pre-adult children in a separate hut in the same husband's compound. She is also the owner of the granary attached to her hut. Each co-wife and her children constitute separate nuclear units consisting of mother and children and thus, form independent units as discussed above among the Caribbean societies.

The above examples clearly indicate the nature, composition and organisation of social group called domestic group. A simple domestic group, i.e. a nuclear unit develops or expounds into a larger composite unit through time.

Processual Analysis of Domestic Groups

From the above account, the crucial points emerging are: *why, when and how a domestic group would change into other forms*. To put it differently, how a domestic group develops? To answer this, some anthropologists have turned towards 'processual analysis' of clustering social group (family/domestic group). *A processual approach is the systematic way a group changes or develops through passage of time*. In a society, for example, the conjugal pair forms concurrently a single residential, reproductive, consumption, production and resource-holding unit. In course of time, some members are added and deleted due to birth, marriage, death and migration. Thus, the domestic unit started by the parents changes over a period of time and includes a number of additional reproductive, consumption, production and resource-holding units. In other words, a domestic group undergoes a series of transformation. Ethnographers of family-researches referred to this as 'developmental cycles' in domestic group.

Phases of Developmental Cycles

Sociologist Charles Loomis used the phrase 'developmental cycle' for the first time. In anthropology, Meyer Fortes popularised this in the analysis of family, marriage and kinship of non-western societies. He delineated their phases/stages/paths in any domestic group. They are: *phases of expansion, dispersion* and *displacement*.

The first phase starts from establishment of a conjugal pair, i.e. *family of procreation*, i.e. the unit within which people have or adopt children of their own. In others words, the expansion of the original group continues till the birth of the last child to the couple. The phase of dispersion is marked by the first marriages of all the children. In this situation, some or all of the married children are coresidents of the parents' unit. The death of the parents' and establishment of family of orientation by the offspring characterise the third phase of replacement. Family of orientation refers to the unit into which people are born and receive socialisation.

To the processualists, one phase is a *dynamic part* of the original unit; to the typologists, one particular 'type' or 'form' is present at a given moment of time. Processualists are more interested in carving out all possible phases through which a group passes. They suggest that every society has characteristic demographic properties; and that these properties manifest in conjunction with economic variable in the functioning of domestic group. In short, pattering and development (phases/paths/cyclings) are reflected through the distribution of surviving sons, their relative ages, their ages relative to their father/mother, marriage age, age at the birth of the first and the last sons, spacing of birth, distribution of economic resources such as land and forest, among others (For detail, see Srivastava, 1979, 1994; Shah, 1974; Goody, 1958, 1969; Wilk, 1989).

Developmental Cycles, Residence Patterns and Inheritance Customs

We have discussed above the three popular stages in developmental cycles, viz. expansion, dispersion and replacement. At any point of time, the current phase of domestic group may influence its residential patterns. For example, in societies like the Korwa of North-central India, if one of the spouses is the last child remaining in the group after the others have married and left, he/she stays on as prospective heir.

The pattern of residential decision may depend on factors like residence customs and succession (Netting, 1984). In some societies, the oldest child inherits the property. This is known as *primogeniture.* In other societies, the youngest' hold remains in the domestic group and inherits the property. This is referred to as *ultimogeniture.* In the latter case, the child begins a new family cycle after his father.

Thus, the processual analysis may hope understanding the *changes* in the social structure, which is beyond the scope of typological description of a social group. The domestic group is not static; it follows a series of stages—expansion, dispersion and replacement. These patterns are *outcome* of a number of variables—demographic, economic and cultural norms such as inheritance customs. A consideration of these variables is absolutely essential if we are to go beyond structural description of social structure.

SUGGESTED READING

- Bender, Donald R., A Refinement of the Concept of Household, Families, Co-residence, and Domestic Functions, *American Anthropologist,* **69**, 493–504, 1967.
- Bohannan, Paul, *Social Anthropology*, Holt, Rinehart and Winston Inc., New York, 1963.

Bohannan, Paul and Middleton, John (Eds.), *Marriage, Family and Residence*, 126–131. The Natural History Press, New York, 1968.

- Buchler, I.R. and H.A. Selby, *Kinship and Social Organisation: An Introduction to Method and Theory,* Macmillan Company, New York, 1968.
- Coale, Ansley J., Estimates of Average Size of Household, *Aspects of the Analysis of the Family Structure*, M.J. Levy and Others (Eds.), New Jersey, Prentice Hall Inc, 64–68, 1965.
- Davenport, William, The Family System of Jamaica, *Social and Economic Studies*, 20–454, 1961.
- Fortes, Mayer, (a) *The Web of Kinship Among the Tallensi,* The Second Part of An Analysis of the Social Structure of a TransVolta Tribe, London, Oxford University Press, 1949.
  (b) Time and Social Structure; an Ashanti Case Study, *Social Structure Studies Presented to A.R. Radcliffe-Brown*, Meyer Fortes, (Ed.), Russell and Russell, New York, 1949.
  (c) Introduction, *The Developmental Cycle in Domestic Groups*, Jack Goody, (Ed.), The Cambridge University Press, Cambridge, 1–14, 1958.
- Freeman, J.D., The Family System of the Iban of Borneo, *The Development Cycle in Domestic Groups*, Jack Goody (Ed.), The Cambridge University Press, Cambridge, 1958.
- Goodenough, Ward H., *Description And Comparison in Cultural Anthropology*, Chicago, Aldine Publishing Company, 1970.
- Goody, Jack, (Ed.), (a) *The Developmental Cycle in Domestic Groups*, Cambridge, The Cambridge University Press, 1958.
  (b) *Production and Reproduction: A Comparative Study of Domestic Domain.* Cambridge, London, 1958.
- Gould, Harold A., Time-Dimension and Structural Change in an Indian Kinship System, A Problem of Conceptual Refinement, *Structure and Change in Indian Society*, Milton Singer and Bernard Cohn, (Eds.), Chicago, Aldine, 413–22, Robert F. Gray and P.H. Gulliver, (Eds.), 1968.
- Gulliver, P.H., A. study of Two Pastoral Tribes in Central Africa, The Jie and Turkana, *The Family Herds*, London Routledge and Kegan Paul, 1955.
  The Arusha Family, Studies in the Role of Property in Family Structure and Lineage Continuity, *Family Estate in Africa*, Routledge and Kegan Paul, London, 197–229, 1964.
- Hammel, E.A., The Family Cycle in Coastal Peruvian Slum and Village, *American Anthropologist*, **63**, 986–1005, 1961.
- Harris, Alfred and Grace Harris, Property and the Cycle of Domestic Groups in Taita, *Family Estate in Africa–Studies in the Role of Property in Family Structure and Lineage Continuity,* Robert F. Gray and P.H. Gulliver (Eds.), London, Routledge and Kegan Paul, 117–155, 1964.

- Kolenda, Pauline, Region, Caste and Family Structure, A Comparative Study of the Indian 'Joint' Family, *Structure and Change in Indian Society*, Milton Singer and Bernard Cohn (Eds.), Chicago Aldine, 339–96, 1968.
- Kopytoff, Igor. The Family and Lineage among the Suku of the Congo, *Family Estate in Africa–Studies in the Role of Property in Family Structure and Lineage Continuity*, Robert F. Gray and P.H. Gulliver, (Eds.) London Routledge and Kegan Paul, 83–116, 1964.
- Levine, Robert A., The Gussi Family, *The Family Estate in Africa*, Robert F. Gray and P.H. Gulliver, (Eds.), London Routledge and Kegan Paul, 63–82, 1964.
- Levi-Strauss, C., The Family. *Man, Culture and Society,* H.L. Shapiro (Ed.) The Oxford University Press, Oxford, 1956.
- Lasslet, Peter, Household and Family in Past Time, A Comapartive Studies in the Size and Structure of the Domestic Group Over in Last Three Centuries (In England, France, Serbia, Japan and colonial North America with further materials from Western Europe), *The Evolution of Family*, pp. 103–124, Peter Lasslett, (Ed.), The Cambridge University Press. 103–124, Cambridge, 1972.
- Loomis, Charles, The Cross Section vs The Historical Method, *Family Life Cycle Analysis*, East Lansing State Collage Book Store, 1945.
- Malinowski, B., 1913, *The Family among the Australian Aborigines*; A Sociological Study, New York, 1963.
- Mc Netting, R., R.R. Wills and E.J. Arnold (Eds.), *Household: Comparative and Historical Studies of the Domestic Group.* The University Press, Berkeley, 1984.
- Martin, John F., (a) On the Estimation of the Size of Local Groups in an Hunting/Gathering Environment, *American Anthropologist,* **75** 1448–1468, 1973. (b) Changing Sex Ratios among the Hava Supai Indians, *Current Anthropology,* **35** (4), 402–422, 1994.
- Murdock, George Peter, *Social Structure*, The Macmillan Company, New York, 1949.
- Metting, R. Mc. C., Wilk, R.R., Arnold, E. (Eds.), *Households: Comparative and Historical Studies of Domestic Groups.* Berkeley University Press, 1984 (see article of R.R. Wilk, and also Wilk 1989).
- Otterbein, Keith F., The Development Cycle of the Andros Household, a Diachronic Analysis, *American Anthropologist,* **72**, 1412–1419, 1960.
- Shah, A.M., *The Household Dimension of the Family in India*, A Field Study in a Gujarat Village and a Review of other Studies. The University of California Press, Barkeley, 1974.
- Smith M.G., *West Indian Family Structure*, Washington University Press, Seattle University, 1962.
- Smith, Raymond T., *The Negro Family in British Guiana*, Routledge and Kegan Paul (Eds.), London 1956.

- Solien, Nancy L., Household and Family in the Caribbean: Some Definitions and Concepts, *Social and Economic Studies,* **10,** 101–106, 1960.
- Spiro, Melford E., Is the Family Universal, *American Anthropologist,* **56,** 839–849, 1954.
- Srivastava, A.R.N., *(a) The Development Dimension of Domestic group in India,* (An Anthropological Analysis of Demography and Economy of a Tribe of Central India) Book Today, New Delhi, 1979.
  (b) Household Dimension of the Family in India: A Review Article. *Indian Anthropologist,* **6**, 21–29, 1976.
  (c) On Social Structure and Demography, *Current Anthropology*, 35, No. 5, 456–57, 1994.
- Symes, David, A Study of Twentieth Century Changes in Ballyferriter, Farm Household and Farm Performance, Southwest Ireland. *Ethnology* **11**, 25–38, 1972.
- Weiss, Kenneth M., Demographic Models for Anthropology. *Memoirs of the Society for American Archaeology*, Number 27, Washington D.C., 1973
- Wilk, R.R., *The Household Economy: A Reconsideration of Domestic Mode of Production*, Boulder, Co. Westview Press, 23–24, 1989.

Chapter 6

Social Sphere of Culture
Marriage and Kinship

A study of kinship involves domestic organisation and marriage as described in the preceding and present chapters. Domestic group, marriage, kinship and descent—all comprise together to make 'a total kinship system'. Individual anthropologists differ in interpretation with respect to a particular system because of their emphasis on 'built-in-theory'.

THE NATURE OF MARRIAGE

According to Malinowski, marriage is the 'fountainhead of kinship'. Marriage is a complex institution. It is complex because its so many qualities vary tremendously across the cultures. The proposition that the nuclear family is not a universal institution creates a further problem of defining marriage. If the institution of marriage is defined as a recognised relationship between male and female, which is expected to result in the establishment of a domestic unit consisting of both the parents and their children, then obviously, this domestic unit is not the same everywhere. Modern cultural anthropologists have reported diverse pattern of mating including the case of the Nayars discussed in the last chapter. Therefore, the definition of marriage has to be set out in broader terms. This is possible only if we define marriage in terms of its *regulative functions*.

Every society has rules concerning sexual relations, pregnancy, birth and child rearing. These rules, in turn, determine duties and privileges of the members of a social group. Thinking in this way, Edmund Leach (1968) proposed the functions of marriage as follows:

(1) It establishes the legal father of a woman's children.
(2) It establishes the legal mother of a man's children.
(3) It gives the husband or his extended family control over the wife's sexual services.
(4) It gives the wife or her extended family control over the husband's sexual services.
(5) It gives the husband or his extended family control over the wife's economic power.

(6) It gives the wife or her extended family control over the husband's economic power.
(7) It gives the husband or his extended family control over the wife's property.
(8) It gives the wife or her extended family control over the husband's property.
(9) It establishes a joint fund of property for the benefit of children.
(10) It establishes a socially significant relationship between the domestic groups of the husband and the wife.

Leach has also observed that "in no single society can marriage serve to establish all of the above types of rights simultaneously, nor is there any one of these rights which is invariably established by marriage in every known society" (1968 : 83).

Basis of Classification of Marriage

Kingsley Davis, the American sociologist, in his popular textbook *Human Society* (1948) has presented a nine-fold classification of marriage on the basis of 'attributes of marriage'. They are:

(1) Number of mates (e.g. monogamy, polygamy)
(2) Degree of authority (patriarchal, matriarchal...)
(3) Residence after marriage (patrilocal, matrilocal, neolocal...)
(4) Choice of mate:
 (a) Who determines choice? Free selection by the young people, controlled selection by the parents.
 (b) Bases of choice: kinship, caste, class, religion
(5) Exchange at marriage (bride-wealth, groom-price)
(6) Age at marriage (early or child marriage, late)
(7) Strength of the bond (temporary, easy divorce, unbreakable with no divorce)
(8) Possibility of remarriage (no marriage after death, permissive remarriage, mandatory remarriage)
(9) Kinds of mate (marriage, concubinage)

Paul Bohannan (1963) has rightly pointed out that some of the above-mentioned variables are not really 'marriage', rather they are related to other matters associated with marriage. For example, in 'patrilocal marriage' what is patrilocal is not the marriage, but is the household that emerges from it. Likewise, the word 'polygamous' refers not to marriage alone, but more importantly, to the family and the household. Thus, *"marriage is a relationship, a family is a kinship group and a household is a local group"*.

Domestic Group and Avoidance of Incest

Marriage between members of the same domestic group is widely prohibited. In other words, sexual mates must come from separate domestic groups. Sexual relations among the close relatives (incest) must be avoided. This is known as *incest taboo,* and it is universally practised. Therefore, the members of a domestic group must marry exogamously, that is outside one's group. They cannot marry endogamously.

While defining *exogamy* and *endogamy*, the contextual groups must be defined. Many societies have kinship groups larger than the family, which are exogamous, e.g. clans. The *effect* of exogamy is to link the mates of opposite sex to one another. Marriage between offspring of the siblings of the domestic groups (family, lineage) is strictly forbidden. Beyond this, there is much relaxation.

The Somali nomads of East Africa, for example, prohibit marriage between closely related kin because they consider it disruptive. Those who infringe this rule are subject to fines. They deliberately marry their daughters to men of distant lineages to establish alliances with distant or hostile groups.

Some Muslim communities follow a form of endogamy, strongly favouring marriage between the sons and daughters of brothers (patrilateral parallel cross-cousin). They do not consider it incestuous marriage. The rule of incest is relaxed among them.

Implications of Endogamy and Exogamy

What can we say about the general effects and implications of endogamy and exogamy? According to some theorists, for example, Lewis—endogamy can bring people together (as in the case of Somali) or separate them; it can unite a group and disassociate them from others (1985). Schapera (1950) had remarked in his ethnographic account of the Tswana: "Child of my father's younger brother marries one so that the cattle may return to our kraal."

However, from a defined perspective, exogamy and endogamy may produce similar results. Either can emphasise on group identity and exclusiveness. Lewis remarks: "The exogamic motto declares in effect: We are those who do not marry each other–this is distraction. The endogamic manifesto proclaims: We are those who do not marry among themselves. Each statement has the same effect: it defines the limits of group solidarity in terms of marriage" (1985 : 240).

Causes of Incest Prohibition and Exogamy

The prevention of conflict within closely-knit groups appears to be the primary function of the rules prohibiting incest and those of exogamy. These rules also play a positive part in social life. They ensure that the smaller social units shall be bound to one another by ties of affinal kinship, and so conducive to the integration of wider social groups.

The rules of endogamy are not only less common than those of exogamy, but are also, in general, less rigidly defined. Sometimes, as in Indian caste system, the group within which a man must marry is circumscribed.

Marriage Regulations

One of the functions of exogamy is to protect the interest of the corporate social groups (see Chapter 2). Therefore, some societies practise what anthropologically is called *preferential marriages*. In this, there is a requirement that one marries a certain kind of relative. A person may marry his cross cousin, i.e. one related to him through siblings of the opposite sex. Marriage between offsprings of siblings of the same sex (parallel-cousin) is infrequently practised. Some of the tribal societies, such as the Gonds of middle India, practise maternal cross-cousin marriage (see Fig. 6.1). Cross-cousin marriage is a way of uniting two lineages and may have important consequence in community life.

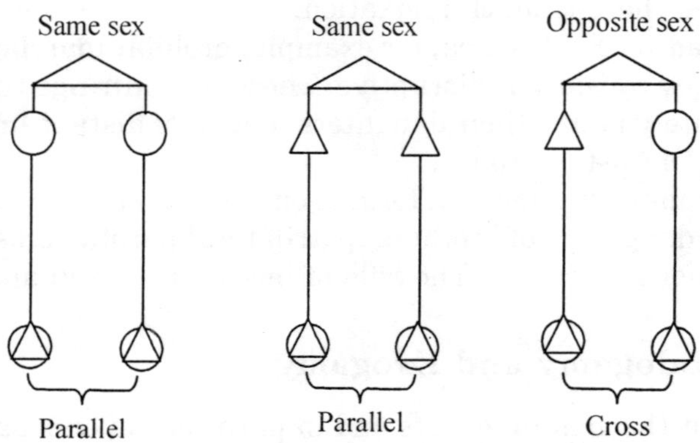

Fig. 6.1 Parallel and Cross cousin.

Another way to protect the interest of corporate domestic unit is the practice of *sororate* and *levirate*. The former is a situation where a man, after the death of his wife, marries one of her sisters; Levirate is a practice when a woman, after the death of her husband, marries one of his brothers. In this way preferential (levirate and sororate) marriages help continuing the union between the same set of relatives of two domestic groups.

The corporate nature of marriage is further reflected in the practice of *bride-wealth* or *bride price* and sister-exchange. In the bride-price marriage, the bride's domestic group receives valuable items from the husband's domestic group. In other words, the groom pays the price of the bride to the relatives of bride's group. This would be paid not only in compensation for the loss of the female but also for the loss of the children she will bear. It is to be noted that this institution of bride-price marriage is widely prevalent in Asian and African agricultural group, and it fulfils one of the functions of marriage mentioned above (see Appendix-1).

Dowry

In some of the textbooks, the term 'dowry' is used, as opposite to 'bride price' as a form of marriage transaction formerly practised in India, Sri Lanka and parts of the Mediterranean. Dowry is a kind of 'groom-price'. It aids to frequently an advance settlement or allotment of a daughter's hereditary portion from her father's estate.

In Hindu caste system, ambitious families endeavour to marry their daughters to grooms who have higher status by paying cash and other kind of dowry. Bride matrimonies are regularly advertised in the local newspapers in attractive terms (moneys!) that go with him. In spite of the recent Dowry Prohibition Act, there is a phenomenon rise of bride burning cases due to non-payment of dowries. Many poor families cannot afford to pay worthwhile dowries demanded by the groom family, and therefore, cannot secure matrimony.

Popular Ways of Acquiring Mates

Finding a mate is important in the life of the higher animals including the primates. However, in human beings, it is culturally determined. In popular textbooks of sociology and anthropology, Hoebel's eight-fold classification of modes of courtship (i.e. acquiring mate) is usually cited. They are:

(1) Marriage by purchase (Bride-wealth)
(2) Suitor service
(3) Exchange marriage
(4) Marriage by capture
(5) Inheritance of wives
(6) Adoptive marriage
(7) Fictive marriage
(8) Elopement

A brief note on each of the above modes of acquiring mate in the Indian tribal context is to be found in Majumdar and Madan (1955). (see Table 6.1). A brief note on *Fictive marriage* is, however, required here. It is seen in some societies including the Kwakiut/Indians of North-west coast of America and the Nuer of Northern Sudan. Among the former the interitance from a titled man to his grandsun through his sun-in-law, the grandson's father. Among the Nuer, the woman of post-child bearing age use the cohle of her dead husband to set up a marriage between a man and a woman whose children are held as children of dead man. They call it ghost marriage.

Table 6.1 Distribution of Percentage of Marriage–transaction Among Societies that have them

Bride price	*Bride service*	*Gift exchange*	*Dowry*	*Indirect dowry*	*Exchange of female*
44	19	11	8	12	6

Source: American Anthropologist (1988, 291–309).

Alliance Marriage

The term 'alliance', as employed in anthropology, refers to a system whereby descent groups or other non-corporate groups are linked by a rule of *prescriptive* marriage so that the groups remain in an affinal (marriage) relationship to one another across the generations. In simple words, *alliance is a social contract between two parties.* Examples of alliance marriages are to be found in widely scattered societies in south- East Asia, Australia and South America.

System of affinal exchange

French anthropologist C. Levi-Strauss (1908–2009), in the light of published ethnographies, set forth a thesis that system of marital exchange was an ancient one, therefore a valid explanation for kinship system should be based on 'exchange marriage'. This thesis was first set elaborately in *The Elementary Structures of Kinship* (1949). According to him, "Elementary structures of marriage are those in which ... prescribe marriage with a certain type of relative, or, alternatively, those members of the society..., (Categorised as) possible spouses and possible prohibited spouses" (1969: Preface). The alliance theory assumes a rule of band/group exogamy to be the basic in human societies. It would be worthwhile to note some fundamental points of alliance theory. First, we note the major modes or forms of alliance (see also relevant matter on Structuralism described in Chapter 3).

Symmetrical Alliance

This involves the direct exchange of women between the men of two local groups (band, lineage, clan, phratry, moiety, lineage or any other kin-group). Men of group I marry women of Group II, and men of latter marry women of Group I. Now, consider an exogamous moiety (patrilineal or matrilineal). How important is to understand that this system conceptually divides the person's relatives into two classes—'our class' and 'your class'. Such division is technically called a 'two-section system'. Numerous cases of section-marriage have been reported from South Asia, North and South America and the South Pacific.

A more complex form of alliance system occurs among the Australian aborigines, (e.g. the Kariera, a hunting gathering). Levi-Strauss interprets this in terms of *four-section* systems.

It is to be noted that the four-section marriage system has been interpreted in various ways. Specialists have also mapped out a compounded version of four section as *eight-section system* for the Aranda of Australia.

How did symmetrical alliance develop? To alliance theorists, systematic *sister-exchange* between two groups over generations is the basis of symmetrical alliance. Consider the following diagram (Fig. 6.2):

The outcome of the above direct sister exchange results in 'cross-cousin marriage'. That is, a male person is marrying the daughter of his mother's brother; a female is marrying the son of her father's sister (see Fig. 6.2, generations 2 and 3).

Levi-Strauss has called the above type of marital exchange *'restricted exchange'*. Thus the terms symmetrical and restricted exchange refer to the same entity. It is to be noted that the reciprocal exchange is between two exogamous groups. The moment of women is in opposite direction; it is symmetrical in the sense that the exchange is direct and balanced (1969: 128–30).

Asymmetrical Alliance

A system of *indirect exchange* of women occurs in some parts of southeast Asia. Levi-Strauss called it 'asymmetrical alliance,' in which a Group A that gives women to another

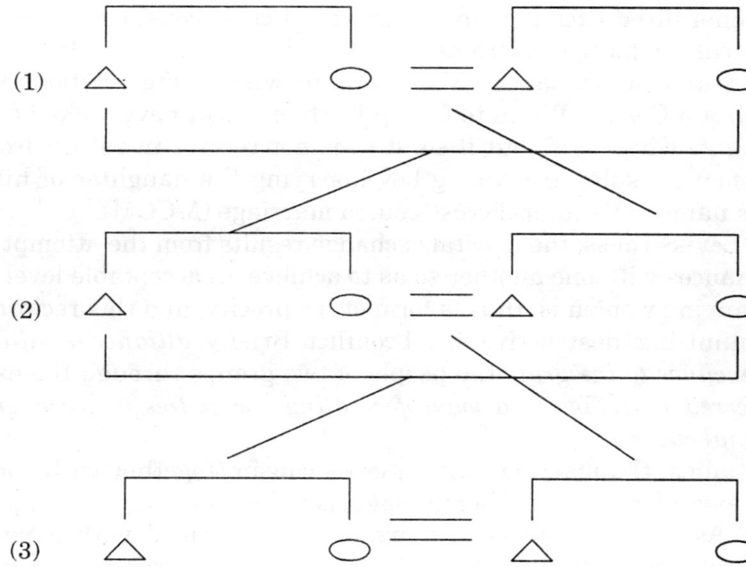

Fig. 6.2 Sister–exchange marriage.

group B does not take women from that group. It takes women from the third Group C So, exchange of women is indirect as well as in circle. It is also known as 'marriage in a circle' (*connubium*). In other words, the alliance is formed asymmetrically. The basic notion is that the group which gives wives to another group does not receive wives from that group i.e. affinal alliance is not symmetrical (see Fig. 6.3). Of this being the case where is the exchange hidden? Consider the following diagram. A gives to B, B to C, and C to A. Think of group B takes woman from A, it must gives to C. Here is exchange involved, but hidden. A frequently example is the study of Kachin of Burma by Leach (1967).

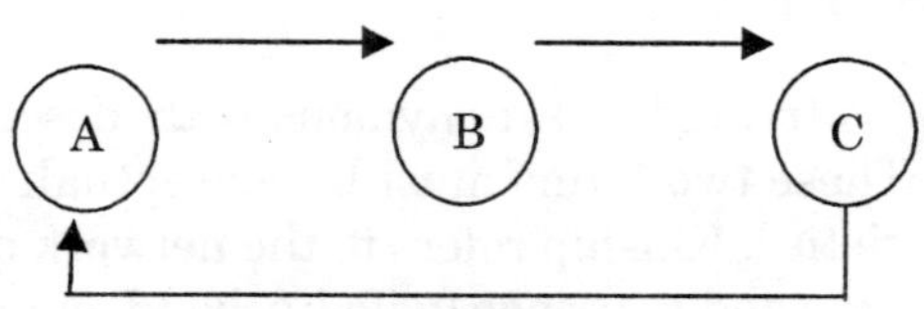

Fig. 6.3 Indirect exchange.

The above type of asymmetrical marital exchange is also known as *generalised exchange*. Levi-Strauss has referred to its two subtypes—*short-cycle generalised exchange* and *long-cycle generalised exchange*. The former is also known as patrilateral cross-cousin marriage. It occurs when the descent groups involve in exchange and then skip a generation in returning women to other groups. Thus, if Group A gives women to Group B in one generation then B would not give women to A until the following generation. Both A and B are exchanging women mutually, but unlike restricted exchange, the relationship alternates between generations. This form of exchange, is called patrilateral cross-cousin marriage (PCCM), because it logically results in a young boy marrying the daughter of his father's sister. Ethnographic cases of PCCM are rare; therefore, it should be held as a theoretical model.

Long-cycle generalised exchange (or matrilateral cross-cousin marriage) involves highly asymmetrical exchange relations between descent groups. In this form of exchange, groups stand in permanent wife-giving or wife-taking relations with other groups. Thus, if Group C gives Wives to Group D, then it will never take back from D. Likewise, D may give wives to F, but if so, it does not receive in return from F. This marriage arrangement results in a young boy marrying the daughter of his mother's brother, hence the name matrilateral cross-cousin marriage (MCCM).

According to Levi-Strauss, the marital exchange results from the attempt of kinship groups to form alliances with one another so as to achieve an acceptable level of societal integration. Exchanging women is, thus, a form of reciprocity, and this reciprocity helps preventing (or minimising) destructive social conflict. Briefly, *alliance is called alliance because it opens avenues to integrate* the people of two groups through the exchange of women. *The preferred marriage is a way of creating social ties between groups and individuals who makeup society.*

In kinship studies, the marriage with a cross cousin (together with sororate and levirate classified as preferential cousin marriage) is referred to *preferential prescriptive marriage pattern*. As the term denotes, marriage is prescribed with a partner of a particular kinship category. When we look at the cross-cousin marriage, especially where it is required that the mate must come from a particular class of kin, any girl of wife-giving lineage is thought to be the daughter of the mother's brother. There are many cases in which the Ego does not marry his/her own cross cousin rather any one who hails from eligible category. Anthropologists have debated over the issue of 'preferential' and 'prescriptive' terminologies (see Needham, 1962). They have also raised the question that why is there opposite rule of asymmetrical alliance (father's sister daughter marriage, see Schneidar, 1965; Korn, 1973)? Very recently, a book by Robert Deliege has come out in which the subject of alliance marriage has been elaborately presented (2011, see also Srivastava, 2011).

KINSHIP AND DESCENT

In some textbooks, 'kinship' is treated as synonymous with 'descent', or kinship is thought to be the result of descent. These two terms must be conceptualised in such a way so as to make sense of worldwide societies. Kinship refers to the network of relationships *created* by genealogical (parents-child, etc.) and marriage (wife-husband, etc.) ties or the both. "Kinship is a relation where mutual moral obligation prevails" (Keesing, 1975 : 14). Individual identifies his/her position in a social world through the ties of kinship.

'Descent' refers to a principle (rule) arising out of a series of 'affiliations,' i.e. parents-child links known as *filiations*. It is to be noted that in descent-oriented society, the individual links his/her relationship with reference to an ancestor, not with a living person. As discussed above, there exist definite rules on how to reckon descent. In the tribal world, the following ways are recognised:

1. *Patrilineal (or agnatic) descent rule*: from an ancestor down through a series of male links, i.e. through the ancestor's son, his son's sons and so on.
2. *Matrilineal (or uterine) descent rule*: from an ancestor down through a series of female links, i.e. through daughter's daughters; and so on.

3. *Cognatic descent rule*: from an ancestor or ancestors through a series of links that can be male or female, or combination of the two. (Note that use of term father and mother may mislead the situation!).

(See Figs. 6.4, 6.5 and 6.7)

Since each patrilineal and matrilineal descent traces one sex-linked chain, the members are classified together as unilineal and non-uninlineal descendants. The existence of unilineal descent groups within a society should not be construed to mean that individuals have kinship ties only with other individuals who are related through males or strictly through females. In other words, it is not the case that in patrilineal societies, all of the relatives of a person are traced through males. What the principle of unilineal descent establishes is a set of *primary* kinship ties.

The existence of secondary relationships through one's mother in a patrilineal society as well as secondary relationships through one's father in a matrilineal society, is generally known as *complementary filiation* (Fox, 1967). It is interesting to note how secondary relationships are structured. In patrilineal societies, one's patrilineal relatives are generally regarded in stern and formal ways, while relationships through one's mother are often warm and relaxed; conversely, in matrilineal societies, it is the matrilineal relatives who are frequently treated in stern and formal ways, while relationships through one's father are those that are warm and easygoing.

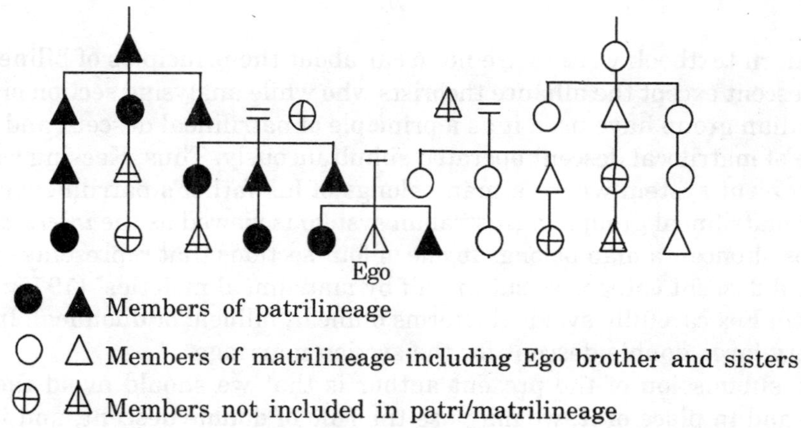

Fig. 6.4 The unilineal principle.

'Double descent' is another term used in descent classification. This is a system whereby a set of two social groups exists in the same society; each set is for a different purpose. One set is based on patrilineal descent, another on matrilineal descent. Note that the existence of two kinds of descent groups qualifies 'double descent'. In this situation, an individual belongs to his/her father's (patri) lineage as well as mother's (matri) lineage. The Yako of Nigeria is frequently cited as a well-documented example of double descent system (Forde, 1939, 1964).

Bilineal or Duolineal

In some textbooks, the term bilineal/bilinear or duolineal is used to denote a system in which every individual belongs *simultaneously* to a matrilineal and to a patrilineal groups. Obviously, it is a double system as illustrated in Fig. 6.5.

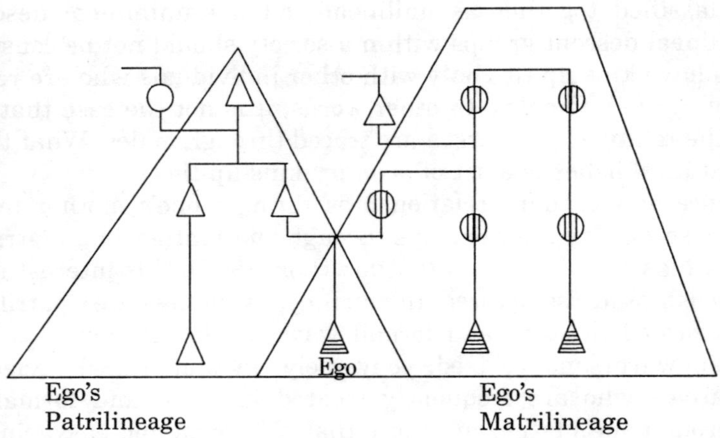

Fig. 6.5 Double descent. Ego is not related to his father's matrilineage or his mother's patrilineage.

Modern textbook writers are not clear about the principles of bilinear descent and double descent except the alliance theorists who while analysing section or class marriage of Australian group have used it as a principle of patrilineal descent and a cross-cutting principle of matrilocal descent operated simultaneously. Thus, Keesing writes: "Unlike a double descent system where a man belongs of his father's patrilineage group and his mother's matrilineal group, an Australian system is viewed as the *intersection* of both the principles at once—a man belongs to one of four sections that represents either of the two patrilineal descent categories cut in half by matrilineal moieties" (1975 : 76).

Robin Fox carefully avoids the terms bilinear, bilineal or duolineal. Instead, he talks about very large double descent for the section marriage.

The submission of the present author is that we should avoid the term bilinear descent, and in place of it, we may use the rule of double descent; and it must be used in the proper context.

Bilateral Kinship, Not Bilateral Descent

In every kinship system, relationship is traced through both father and mother. Everywhere, father's brother and mother's brother are a person's relatives and so are their children. In other words, kinship reckoning is always 'two sided', i.e. *bilateral*; some are matrilateral kins (mother's side relatives), the remaining are patrilateral kins. But, a potential confusion arises when the above situation is described as bilateral descent. In fact, as we have seen above, a descent is traced unilineally not unilaterally. (See Fig. 6.6)

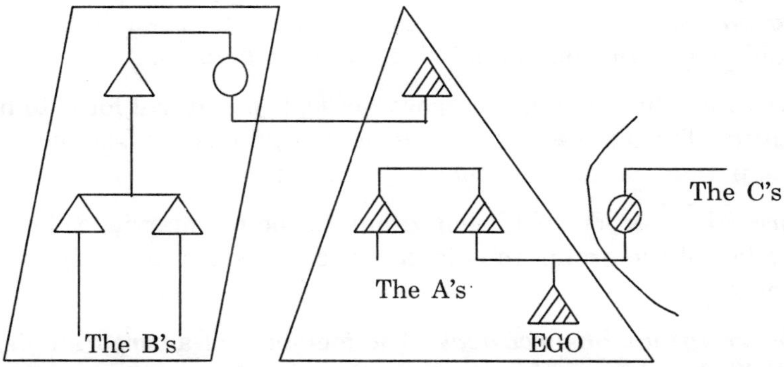

B's are Ego patrilateral kin because he is related to them through his father. But, A's are his patrilineal kin, while the B's are not. The C's are matrilateral.

Fig. 6.6 Patrilateral and patrilineal.

Difference between Patriliny and Matriliny

1. Under the patriliny, females can be severed from membership in their natal descent group and fully absorbed into the descent group of their husband. But, under the matriliny, no such severance can take place, and both men and women remain members of their natal descent group for life.
2. With patriliny, the roles of both husband and father are of crucial importance. But, with matriliny, such roles are not even necessary for the maintenance of the group.
3. The establishment of strong husband-wife bonds is not compatible with matrilineal descent. With patrilineal descent, however, such bonds are both compatible and desirable.
4. In patrilineal systems, no special mechanisms are needed to deal with in-marrying affines. But, in matrilineal systems, in marrying affine is a threat to the descent group, and special mechanisms are needed to deal with such threats.
5. In matrilineal societies, the bonds that may develop between a child and his biological father tend to be in direct competition with the bond between the child and his mother.

KIN GROUPS BASED ON UNILINEAL DESCENT

While all societies display strong or weak descent rules, the nature of the kinship groups or categories formed by these rules differs significantly from one society to another. In the majority of the world's societies, the descent rule is of *ancestor-focus* type (Fox, 1967). This situation creates what is termed *corporate descent groups*. These are the individuals who trace descent from a common ancestor (real or mythical) who is believed to have been the founder of the group. Membership in a corporate descent group defines individuals, rights and obligations they have in regard to the other members of their group. *Corporate descent groups, generally, have the following characteristics*:

1. ***Corporateness:*** The group possesses a unity in the sense that the entire group may act as a single legal unit on behalf of any of its members.

2. ***A name:*** Since the group has corporateness, it is natural for it to have a name to signify its identity. The names of corporate descent groups are frequently taken from founding persons, plants, animals or other natural phenomena.

3. ***Exogamy:*** Most corporate descent groups forbid the marriage of their members to any other member of the group, thus forcing them to select marriage partners from other descent groups.

4. ***Common religious observances:*** The members of a corporate descent group frequently symbolise their identity through the enactment of common ritual and ceremony.

5. ***Corporate property ownership:*** The members of a corporate descent group commonly hold collective title to land and other property. Individuals may, therefore, own land only as members of the group. This is, perhaps, the most crucial feature of a corporate descent group.

6. ***Obligations of mutual aid and hospitality:*** Members of a corporate descent group are frequently called upon to render assistance to one another in times of need.

Corporate descent groups vary greatly in terms of size and complexity. They range from as small as a dozen (lineage) members in some cases to as large as a thousand members in other (the latter, for example, in the case of the traditional Chinese clan). On an average, they contain from a few dozen to a few hundred members.

Some societies, however, use *ego-focus criteria* as a basis for forming kin-groups. When it occurs, kinship is traced from the point of view of *any given living individual*, rather than from some putative common ancestor (Fox, 1967). An ego-focus group gives rise to small-scale personal kin groups known as *kindreds*. These groups are not corporate.

Unilineal descent is one of the most common principles used in the formation of social groups. Four such basic groups are *lineages, clans, phratries* and *moieties*. These groups are briefly discussed below.

Lineage

Technically, a lineage consists of two or more generations of persons consanguineously related through one sex. Thus, a man and his children, or a woman and her children form a lineage. In all of the unilineal descent-oriented societies, such a group is purely operational. In other words, the specific tasks are carried on by this group. This is called a *minimal lineage.*

A minimal lineage expands over generations. When it occurs, major segments may develop; finally, when a number of major segments unite together the form of lineage is known as *maximal lineage.* The use of classification such as maximal or simply minimal and maximal depends largely upon how people organise themselves.

Characteristics of Lineage

A lineage has several important features. First, regardless of its size, the lineage within a society serves as a powerful *mechanism of solidarity*. A lineage of 20 persons is equivalent to a 200-member lineage. Secondly, a lineage is a *localised descent group*, and it operates as a corporate groups as defined earlier. That is the individual members have legal and political status only as a member of the group. It serves the basis of political organisation.

Thirdly, a lineage is *characterised by perpetuity*. It exists as long as its members survive. Anthropologists such as Fortes and Evans-Pritchard have extensively written on how perpetuity is maintained.

Fourthly, each lineage is changed with certain rights and obligations, and its members ensure that these *rights and obligations* will not be lost to their lineage.

Fifthly, a lineage unites many persons across generations. It may even incorporate dead ancestors. *Ancestor worship*, for example, is a popular form of religion of many descent-oriented societies.

Clan

A clan is simply a grouping of two or more (maximal) lineages (in American usages, it is called *sib, 'gens' in Morgan's terminology*). A clan is a kin-based group but the ties of kinship cannot be traced explicitly. Its members either account for a common ancestor or some mythological ancestor. Like lineage, a clan is also an exogamous group since 'feelings' of consanguineous relations among the members prevail in a clan.

Unlike the lineage that is a localised descent group, members of a clan are distributed over a large territory. Like the lineage, a clan may also have characteristics of corporate groups. The clan continues after the death of its member. Besides this, it has a name, often a symbol (*totem*) and special norms.

Differences between Extended Domestic Group (Family) and Clan

Extended domestic group or the extended family must be distinguished carefully from the clan, which is often confused. The following are the important differences between the extended family and the clan:

Extended family	*Clan*
Always an economic unit.	Frequently an economic unit, but not always so.
Always a local group.	Members may be scattered over a wide area.
Includes affinal kin.	Does not include affinal kin.
Genealogical relationships can be traced among all the members.	Genealogical relationships between the members are not necessarily definable.

Phratry and Moiety

These are large groups based on unilineal descent. A phratry is defined as any grouping of two or more clans provided there are three or more such groups within a society. Where two or more clans are linked forming only two major groups, they are called moieties. Activities such as ritual, economic and political are carried on through the organisation of phratry and moieties.

Anthropologists have written a great deal about the functions of each of the above-mentioned unilineal descent groups. Commonly, descent groups perform four major functions—regulation of marriage, mutual aid, ceremonial ritual and political functions.

KIN GROUPS BASED ON COGNATIC DESCENT AND BILATERAL KINSHIP

As discussed earlier, the principles of cognatic descent insist that all of the descendants (patrilineal or otherwise) are entitled to membership of a group. But, there is disagreement on whether or not this group is to be regarded a true descent group.

Murdock (1960) has reviewed the conceptual and terminological preferences prevalent among the investigators. He has strengthened the confusion by applying the term 'cognatic' as used by Radcliffle-Brown and others, to refer to social forms that do not have unilineal descent. Two kinds of cognatic structure are recognised:

Ego-based Sets of Kin and Ancestor-based Sets of Kin

A kindred is an example of the ego-based sets of kin while a ramage is of the ancestor-based (see glossary, Appendix I).

The kindred can be defined, in the words of Robin Fox, as "ego's relatives up to a certain fixed degree". The degree need not be defined cognatically or bilaterally as noted in kinship literature. *The essence of kindred is that all recognised relatives of ego have some duties towards him.* The relatives do have some claims on him as well.

A ramage is a grouping of two or more lineages, but unlike the unilineal descent, the descent is traced through either a male or a female. Here, choice is involved. It is a common feature of many Polynesian societies. Since the ramage is descent group but not like that of unilineal descent group, Murdock proposed *ambilnieal* descent group. Specialists of societies having cognatic descent have observed that the rights, duties and privileges must be examined closely to understand the manner in which 'ambilineal descent' operates (see Fig. 6.7).

Some kinship theorists have argued that the 'kindred' and 'ramages' involve choice of the individual. To them, privilege and choice cannot be transmitted by descent. Therefore, cognatic form of descent offers a weak organisation, not to be equated with double descent (compare Figs. 6.6 and 6.7).

Bohannan has used a term '*omnilineal*' to refer to the form of cognatic descent. He defines it as 'kinship groups including all of the descendants of an ancestor or ancestress or else they include all of the kinmen, on all sides, of a contemporary ego, limited only by degree of kinship' (1963 : 127).

In short, *omnilateral* group (the cognatic group) based on a contemporary ego is rare. But, another variety of cognatic group is 'omnilineal descent group' computed from an ancestral ego. It was Goodenough (1955) who first discovered functioning of this type

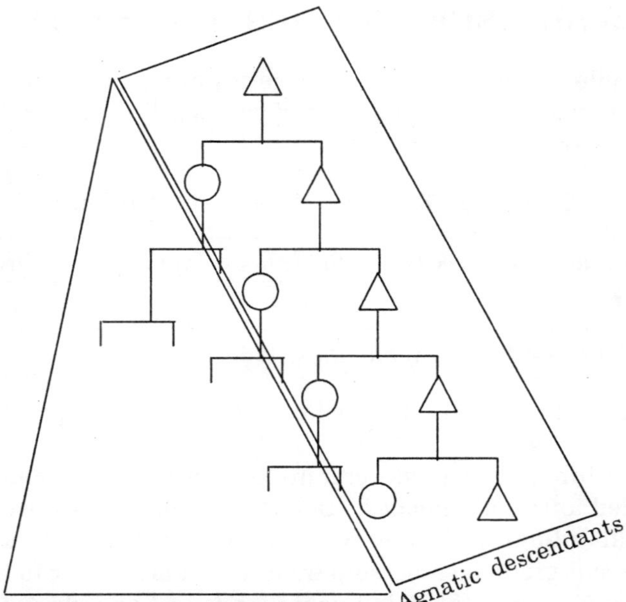

Fig. 6.7 Cognatic descent.

Note: The agnatic (patrilineal) form is also shown.

of cognatic descent group in the Gilbert Islands. It is to be kept in mind that this is different from the unilineal descent groups. Goodenough has mentioned three types of cognatic descent groups.

First of the three groups is the 'unlimited descent group' from any ancestor, which the Glibertese called an *ooi*. This group is an entity and functions in relation to the property that was owned by the founder. This group can be limited by the application of a non-kinship criterion of eligibility, when the inheritance of certain seats in the community house is considered. The second group is of the eligible holders of certain lands, and such a group is called a *bwoti* by the Gilbertese. The third group is the *kainga* which is made up of those members of an *ooi* that form a residential or local unit. Thus, the primary criterion of all three of these groups is descent. Secondary criterion of a non-kinship nature limits the membership of two of the groups. The *ooi* contains all the people who have a right to inherit land from a single ancestor or ancestress, whether or not they have actually taken it up. Thus, the *ooi* is a group determined by land rights, and it is also an unrestricted descent group.

The *bwoti* is quite a different group, it differs from the *ooi* in the sense that the latter is an unlimited descent group all of whom may inherit, and the *bwoti* is a limited descent group—limited to those members who have actually inherited. *Bwoti,* thus, has two criteria of membership—one the membership in the *ooi* and other actual inheritance of land that belonged to the ancestor of the *ooi*.

The third type of descent group is the *kainga*, which is a residence group. When a man and a woman marry each other, they move into the area in which they will inherit land. Since either is entitled to inherit land, they will probably move into that area in which the larger holdings will be available.

MARRIAGE RESIDENCE AND DESCENT SYSTEM

As the following table reveals, patrilineal societies are overwhelmingly patrilocal. The great majority of patrilineal societies, therefore, neatly combine both residence and descent in the hands of males.

Table 6.2 Residence Practices in Percentage

Partrilocal	*Matrilocal*	*Bilocal*	*Avunulocal*	*Neolocal*
67	15	7	4	5

Source: Murdock *Ethnographic Atlas*, 1965.

The following examples will serve to illustrate the actual operation of patriliny and patrilocality.

In traditional China, descent was organised in terms of exogamous patrilineages. A lineage was divided into sublineages, and these sublineages were often dispersed throughout several villages. Residence was patrilocal. Upon marriage, a woman transferred her descent group membership from that of her father to that of her husband; she severed ties from her natal patrilineage and was absorbed completely into her husband's group.

A patrilineal system of a somewhat different nature exists among the Tallensi of northern Ghana. Residence among the Tallensi, who raise cattle as well as cultivate fields, is patrilocal. Descent groups exist in the form of patriclans, which are further divided into patrilineages. The rule of exogamy applies to the clan as well as the lineage. While women move in with their husbands, they never move far away, and therefore, it is easy for them to retain close ties with their natal patrilineage. In this regard, the Tallensi contrast strikingly with traditional China. Whereas in China, women were completely lost to their natal patrilineages, among the Tallensi, women continue to play an important role in the descent group of their fathers and brothers.

Since most of the patrilineal societies are patrilocal, descent and residence are neatly tied together. Things are not so neat among the matrilineal people. Matrilineal societies display a wide range of residence rules. The most common residence rule associated with matriliny is matrilocality. Matrilineal societies are almost as likely to adopt avunculocality as matrilocality. A well-known matrilineal society practising avunculocal residence is the Trobriand Islanders of Melanesia.

Bilateral descent is found mainly among the hunters and gatherers, it is very frequently associated with patrilocal residence. Matrilocality and bilocality, however, are also found to some extent in these societies. Among bilaterally organised industrial societies, residence is normally neolocal. The combination of residence rule and descent rule is also known as *compromise kinship* which will be described shortly.

The Causes of Residence and Descent Systems

As Robin Fox (1967) has pointed out, many scholars have talked about residence and descent systems as if they simply dropped from the sky upon the people practising them.

Such a view is likely to provide much illumination about the dynamics of these systems. A better approach would be to examine residence and descent systems as adaptive consequences of the practical conditions of local social life (Keesing, 1975; Harris, 1979; Goody, 1976).

The first essential premise holds that *residence systems are logically prior to descent systems*. This means that the members of a society must first organise themselves in workable domestic arrangements before organising their descent patterns. From this point of view, descent systems largely reflect and serve to validate the kinds of domestic arrangements already established. .

KINSHIP TERMINOLOGIES

Every society has a special variety of terms or lebels for designating 'types' of relatives. The lebels are called 'Kinship terms' and the rules for using them constitute 'kin terminology system' of that society. According to the prevailing system of kin terminology, some people may differentiate their relatives on the basis of sex; others lump relatives of both sexes under the same term. In some societies, a person uses one term to refer to an older relative and a different term for a younger relative of the same kind. Some societies have separate terms for the older and younger brother. The kin terms also vary according to the sex of a speaker. In other words, a male child may use a particular term for his father, whereas a female child uses another term for her father. It is also relevant to note that terms are different for the same society if the person referred to is alive or dead. In brief, a number of criteria are taken into consideration. There are enormous anthropological studies on kin terminology system. On comparative perspective, anthropologists have generated some common principles that help understanding the behaviour of the people of a defined social group. Paraphrasing Kroeber (1909), we may briefly deal with the following principles:

1. *Generation:* Most of the kinship terms employ the criteria of generation. In Europe-American societies, 'father', 'mother', 'uncle', and 'aunt', belong to the parental generation, 'brother' and 'sister' belong to Ego's (speaker's) generation, while 'son', 'daughter', 'nephew', and 'niece' belong to the generation below Ego.

2. *Relative age:* Distinctions may be made in age levels within the same generation, with different terms being used for one older and younger siblings or for the older and younger siblings of one's father or mother.

3. *Lineality versus collaterality:* Lineal kins are related in a single line of descent as grandfather-father-son. Collateral relatives are those relatives who are not in the single line; they are related indirectly through a linking relative, such as father's brother or mother's brother. In some kinship systems, distinctions are not made between lineal and collateral relatives. This is known as 'merging'. Cousins may be equated with siblings. As such relatives they are addressed by the same term. Similarly, father's brothers may be addressed by the term for father and mother's sisters by the term for mother. Other systems have different terms for these relatives.

4. *Sex of relative:* The Euro-American term 'mother' and 'father', 'brother' and 'sister', 'uncle' and 'aunt', 'nephew' and 'niece' make distinctions with regard to the sex, but the term 'cousin' does not.

5. *Sex of speaker:* In some societies, male and female use different terminologies.

6. ***Sex of linking relative:*** Distinctions among collateral relatives may be made on the basis of the sex of the connecting relative. As such, a distinction is made between cross-cousins and parallel-cousins. Both have different terms.

7. ***Consanguine versus affinal kin:*** Usually, a distinction is made between kinship based on descent and kinship resulting from marriage. Persons of the latter category are referred to as 'in-laws'. This term is affixed to 'mother', 'father', 'brother' and 'sister' who are Ego's consanguines.

8. ***Status or life condition:*** Distinctions may be made between relatives on the basis of whether a linking relative is alive or dead, married or single.

Some kinship systems distinguish between lineal and collateral relatives, having different terms of father and father's brother, mother and mother's sister; while other kinship systems merge these relatives. Some systems emphasise generational differences, merging all the relatives within a given generation, so that the same kinship terms is applicable to father, father's brother and mother's brother. It is very common form of the kinship system to merge father and father's brother while distinguishing them from mother's brother and to merge mother and mother's sister while distinguishing them from father's sister. This system is known as *bifurcate-merging*.

CLASSIFICATION OF KINSHIP TERMINOLOGIES

Classificatory vs. Descriptive Terms

One of the most successful works in anthropology done on kinship was by L.H. Morgan. During the study of two groups of the American Indians—the Iroquois and the Ojibwa-Morgan realised that both of these groups classify their kins in the same way. On the basis of hundred of facts generated by the questionnaire, he discerned two types of terms—*descriptive* and *classificatory*. The former are 'isolation' terms and refer to only one kinship category such as 'mother', 'father'. The latter are 'lumping' terms, that is a single term is used for two or more categories. Let us consider the following diagram (Fig. 6.8):

In the above diagram, lineal kins are kept distinct from all of the collateral relatives. Lineal relatives are not lumped with collateral. All the collateral relatives of Ego are labeled with terms that are distinct from the labels of lineal relatives. In Morgan's classificatory system, some collateral relatives are lumped with lineal relatives.

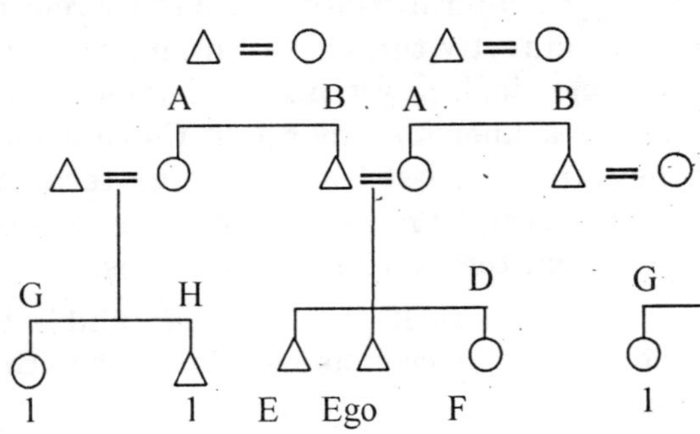

Fig. 6.8 Descriptive system.

Robert Lowie's Categories of Kin Terms

Morgan's two-way scheme of classification of kin terms is well known. But, the problem with this scheme is that many societies do employ both classificatory and descriptive terms concurrently. Anthropologists of post-Morgan era do not stand by handful types of categories. The most important criteria used by the ethnographers for general classification are of two orders: (1) the degree of merging and bifurcation of lineal and collateral kin in the parental generation, and (2) the degree of merging and bifurcation of collateral kin ego's own generation. It is to be noted that first was formulated by Lowie in 1931, while the second was duly formalized by Murdock (1949: 223–259).

Lowie's classification by grouping terminological systems into four categories are as follow:

1. *Generational:* In this system, the distinction of sex and generation are considered. For a particular generation, there are only two terms—A & B.

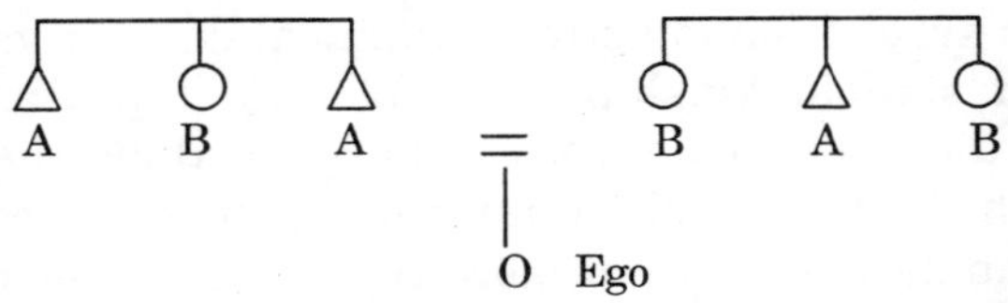

2. *Lineal:* Here, the distinction of lineal and collateral is added. Thus, there are four terms for one generation, e.g. Euro-American societies.

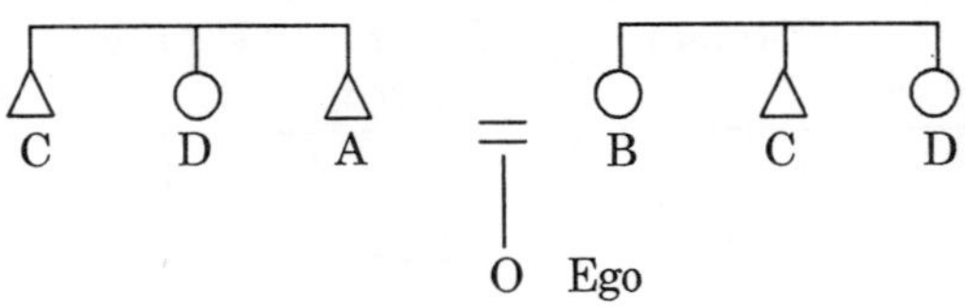

3. *Bifurcate collateral:* In this system, additional distinction is added. Here, sex of the individual who stands between Ego and his collaterals, that is the siblings of Ego's F is differentiated from that of the siblings of Ego's M. Thus, there are six terms for one generation.

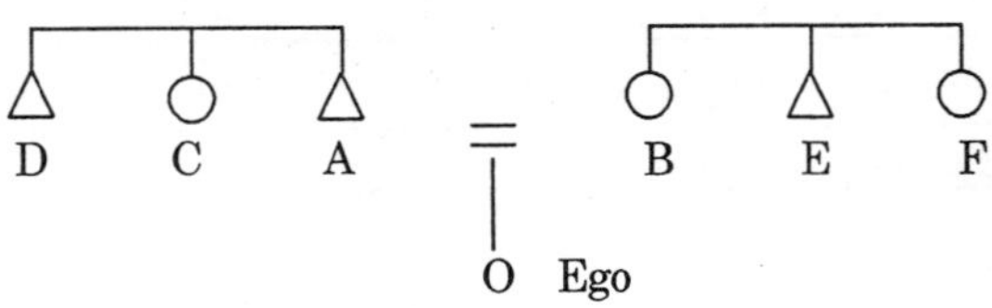

4. *Bifurcate merging:* Here, all of the above principles are maintained except that a parents' siblings of the same sex is lumped with the parents. This generates four terms for members of one generation.

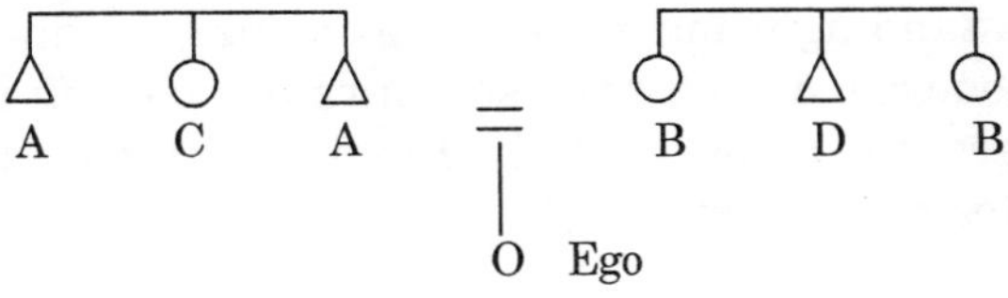

Murdock's Scheme of Kin Classification

In 1949, Murdock presented a more refined classification of kinship terminologies. It is to be noted that his scheme was based on the terms of *Ego's own generation* rather than on terminology for the parental generation formulated by Lowie.

Thus, in *Eskimo system* (named after a group, i.e. Eskimo) parallel and cross- cousins are lumped but are distinguished from siblings. In *Iroquois* system, cross-cousins are distinguished from siblings and parallel-cousins. In the *Hawaiian* system, no distinctions are noted, i.e. siblings and cousins are lumped under the same term. The *Sudanese* have terms distinguished between all of the categories of Ego's generation.

In the *Crow* (matrilineal) and *Omaha* (patrilineal) matrilateral, cross-cousins are differentiated from patrilateral cross-cousins. Parallel-cousins on both sides are lumped together. In senior generation terms, matrilateral cross-cousins tend to be lumped with the junior generation terms. In the Omaha, the system is reversed. It is found that the Omaha group of American indians, merging of cross-cousins terms across generation lines occurs in kinship system having strong unilineal descent groups.

Above-mentioned six-fold kinship terminological types are empirically based. However, it is possible that a particular society may not exhibit the characteristics of one of these types. As such, it is the task of anthropologists to discover how a particular society follows the combination of two or more types. (See Table 6.3).

Table 6.3 Numerical Distribution of Terminological Types

Types	*Africa*	*Eurasia*	*North America*	*Oceania*	*South America*	*Total*
Eskimo	1	7	6	1	3	18
Hawaiian	3	1	24	11	6	45
Iroquois	7	3	8	15	–	33
Crow	7	–	13	8	2	30
Omaha	10	6	5	3	1	25
Sudanese	8	2	–	2	1	13
Mixed Type	29	15	14	10	8	86
Total	65	34	70	60	21	250

Source: Murdock, G.P. (1949 : 249).

SOME SUGGESTED EXPLANATIONS OF TERMINOLOGICAL SYSTEM

A.R. Radcliffe-Brown (1955), in a series of articles, has shown the importance of kinship terminologies in understanding primitive societies having unilineal descent groups. He has also indicated that one can demonstrate statistically *a good fit* between kin terms and kin-grouping if one selects the cases carefully. Empirical studies directed on the kinship system in recent decades do support this.

G.P. Murdock suggests the statistical interpretation of kin terms. In other words, if one looks at the classification of closest relatives and kin terms in statistical correctional terms, he can explain the variations up to a desired level of significance. But, its value may be limited because of inadequate samples.

Rodney Needham (1962) and Edmund Leach (1958) have presented *adhoc* explanations of structural relationship between the particular features of one society and details of its kinship terminologies. In this sense, it does not mean anything to the people whether they *genealogically* link their own siblings with FsiD and MBD, rather they include them under one class because they view classifying kin universe *structurally*.

Ward Goodenough, F. Lounsbury, H. Scheffler, Roger Keesing and Robin Fox are among the anthropologists who look at the kin terms at global scale and have classified the system in many finer details.

In short, kinship terminological systems do make sense functionally, if the cultural contexts in which they operate are systematically explored and understood. *It must however be noted that a people's cultural ideas do not necessarily reflect the objective reality.*

DESCENT AND ALLIANCE COMPARED

Both descent and alliance theorists look at the kinship differently. It is worth noting some of their conceptual points. Levi-Strauss, alliance marriage underlines the structural analysis based on the binary principle, i.e. my group vs. yours group; consanguines are opposite to affines, wife givers are opposite to wife receiver. Descent theorists, on the other hand, argue on the principle of descent. The comparison between descent and alliance is given as follow:

Descent	*Alliance*
(1) Defined with reference to an ancestor (ess). Status of descent is absolute.	(1) Status of affines is absolute.
(2) Clear distinction between consanguine and affines, e.g. affines are not the members of a lineage.	(2) There is no distinction between kin and affine, or kin and non-kin.
(3) Non-involvement reciprocity	(3) Involvement of direct reciprocity between two groups.
(4) Marriage is simply a 'residue of exogamy'.	(4) Structural importance of marriage; marriage is a part of structure of the system.
(5) Kinship system is seen as mechanisms for the formation of recruitment of property-owing groups, residential groups, political units, etc.	(5) Kinship system as mechanisms for distributing women between groups.

SOME RELATED CONCEPTS TO KINSHIP

Compromise Kin Group

According to Murdock (1949), some kinship groups compromise the descent principle with marriage residence. The resultant group is known as compromise group. One kind of compromise group consists of a core of men (such as male siblings) who are patrilineally related to one another, unmarried women who are patrilineally related to these men and to one another, and those women who, according to the patrilocal residence rule, are married to the men in the group in question. Conversely, compromising matrilineal descent group and matrilocal with patrilineal may occur.

Another compromise arrangement results from the compromise of matrilineal descent and avunculocal residence, whereby a married couple goes with his maternal uncle? The resultant group consists of matrilineally related males and their wives and unmarried children.

Murdock suggests that the functions of the compromise kinship group tend to differ from those of the pure or original unilineal descent group. The compromise group is more important in the economic, recreational, political and military aspects of life. Being a residence group, it is the everyday, face-to-face socio-economic group. The members of this unit work together in the production of food and fibre and, accordingly, they own land and other forms of tangible property. When anthropologists refer to 'localised' unilineal descent groups, they are probably talking about what Murdock calls the compromise kinship group.

Ritual Kinship/Functional Fictive Kinship

This term refers to one of the various means by which an individual may extend his personal network by extending kin-like relationships to nonkin-like. This relationship is usually conceived of as the social status of the partners (dyadic contact) in the relationship. Such relationship is established for mutual support and socio-economic status. Institution of ritual kinship also occurs in Africa, Harry Tegnaeus has presented an account of "blood-brotherhood" in the northwest Africa in which participants "mix and shallow each others blood" (*Blood-Brothers: An Ethno-sociological Study,* New York, 1952). One of the excellent examples, and also much researched topic is *compadrazgo* (parent-godparent relationship), an institution prevalent in Spanish speaking region, viz. Mexico and in some parts of Latin America and Spain.

Compadrazgo refers to the relationship between the parents and grandparents of the child. This is what Durkheim had meant ritualised function to solidify social relationships.

KINSHIP BEHAVIOUR AND USAGES

Joking and Avoidance Relationship

Usually, two types of standardised kinship behaviour found in tribal societies are avoidance and joking relationships. The rule of avoidance means that the individual who stands in a particular relationship must, as far as possible, ignore each other's existence and must refrain from establishing social intercourse. They may not speak to each other, and if they meet on a path, then one must stand aside or make a different route. Sometimes, they may not even mention each other's names. The most common relationship in which avoidance is enjoined is the between a man and wife's mother commonly called 'mother-in-law avoidance'.

The joking relationship may be observed with other kinsfolk also, particularly other affinal kins, and between sibling brothers and sisters of the same parents. Avoidance has been explained as a mechanism for the prevention of sexual relation between kins. This is at best a partial explanation, for it does not account for cases of avoidance between relatives of the same sex, for example, between a man and his wife's father.

The joking relationship refers to the custom whereby specific relatives may or must joke with or tease each other when they meet. The joking relationship is commonly found between affinal kins. As with avoidance, there is a great range of variation in the actual usages described by the term. Sometimes, joking is obligatory, sometimes optional. It may be symmetrical; both the parties making jokes at each other's expense, or one party may be expected to make the jokes of the other in good part without retaliating.

The two contrasting customs of the avoidance and the joking relationship appear, at least in certain cases, to be capable of similar explanation. All of the kinship relationships entail expressions of goodwill and mutual services between the members concerned. But, in many of them, particularly between affinal kin, this is tinged by a feeling of tension and even by the possible hostility that may arise from the failure of one party to honour his or her obligations.

The structuralists use terms like 'solidarity' and 'opposition' to describe these contrasting aspects of kinship relationships. Radcliffe-Brown has suggested the terms *conjunction* and *disjunction*. The psychological term *ambivalent* might be used to describe relationships in which both of these contrasting aspects occur.

The joking relationship minimises or even avoids tension between kinsfolk by enabling them to express both the aspects of their ambivalent relationship at the same time.

Teknonymy

We have already described that in some societies, two terms for a single type of relationship—term of reference and term of address—are used while speaking to a relative and while speaking to them. In some primitive kinships, there is a practice whereby he is habitually referred to and addressed as 'Father of x', x being the name of an infant. Similarly, the mother may be called 'Mother of x'. This custom is known as *teknonymy*.

Couvade

Though this custom is ancient, its relic is still operative in some of the societies. In this custom, when a child is about to born, the father goes to the bed and lies there as if bearing pains and delivering the child, cares for it and submits himself to fasting, purification or taboos. In modern medical maternity ward one can watch the activities of the husbands of expectant mothers; they move back and forth anxiously around the delivery cabin of parturient females.

FUNCTIONAL IMPORTANCE OF KINSHIP

The study of kinship is significant in understanding society in several ways:

1. Kinship practices are useful in making historical reconstruction. Both Tylor and Morgan used kinship (marriage, descent and residence) practices for reconstruction of human societies.
2. Analysis of kinship behaviour enhances interpretation of theory of society. Radcliffe-Brown and his associates found kinship model very useful in social structure and social organisation. Cultural anthropologists differentiate between ideal and actual behaviours. Kinship behaviour of a particular society helps understanding this distinction.
3. Analysis of meaning of terms has led to new thoughts on how people view the world or at least how do they classify the things around them. Stephen Tyler and other have tried to understand the cognitive behaviour of the people by means of kin terms.
4. The importance of kinship in structural linguistics cannot be overlooked. C. Levi-Strauss and Edmund Leach among others, are prominent personalities who have emphasised the method of kinship study analogous to the method of structural linguistics.
5. Lastly, the knowledge of kinship is invaluable during anthropological fieldworks. The initial task of a fieldworker is to record how people are related to each other. Diagramming kinship chart (genealogies) in the presence of informants help researchers establishing confidence and rapport as these matters are not verbally discussed by the informants. In this way, kinship study aids anthropological fieldwork even though the research project is not directed to kinship as such. In short, a thorough grounding in kinship is valuable for cultural anthropology.

SUGGESTED READING

- Bohannan, Paul, *Social Anthropology*, Holt, Rinehart and Winston, New York, 1963. This is a basic introductory textbook containing excellent sections on kinship and marriage.
- Bock, Philip, *Modern Cultural Anthropology*, Knof, Chicago 1969. Part III of the book is useful for kinship diagrams.
- Bohannan Paul and John Middleton (Eds.), 1. *Kinship and Social Organisation,* Natural History Press, Washington, D.C. 1968.
  This volume contains twenty articles by anthropologists on themes related to family, marriage and kinship. Many of them are not easily traced out since they originally appeared in scholarly journals. Some of the crucial articles are by Robert Lowie (*Relationship terms*), Drayll Forde (*Double descent*), G.P. Murdock (*Cognatic forms of social organisation*), J.D. Freeman (*Kindred*) and John Middleton (*Lineage system*).
  2. *Marriage, Family and Residence*, Natural History Press, Garden City N.Y., 1968.

This is another volume edited by the same persons. It has 20 articles divided into six parts, viz. *Incest-exogamy, marriage, marriage forms, family, residence* and *household and special problems*. Dumont's *Marriage Alliance*, Kathleen Gough's *Definition of Marriage*, Spiro's *Is Family Universal* are among others.

- Deliege, Robert., *Anthropology of Family and Kinship* (Translated from French by Latha Anantharaman), PHI Learning Private Limited, New Delhi, 2011 (second edition).
- Forde, D., *The Yako of Nigeria*, London 1964 and "Kinship in Umor-Double Unilateral Organization in a Semi Bantu Society," *American Anthropologist,* 41(4), 523–54, 1939.
- Fortes, Meyer, *The Structure of Unilineal Descent Groups*, Oxford University Press London, 1953 and *Kinship and Social Order,* Chicago Aldine, 1975.
- Fox, Robin, *Kinship and Marriage,* An anthropological perspective, Baltimore, Pelican, 1967.
  A more advance analysis, dealing in greater detail with the major aspect of kinship and marriage. Hindi version of this book has been published by the M.P. Grantha Academy, Bhopal (1978). Fox presents alliance views more elaborately with arguments.
- Goodenough, Ward H., *Description and Comparison in Anthropology*, Aldine, Chicago, 1975.
  The author rethinks on definition of family, marriage and kinship. Useful for advanced students.
- Gough, Kathleen, Definition of Marriage, 1961. See above *Bohannan and Middleton*, 1968.
- Grabner, Nelson (Ed.), *Readings in Kinship and Social Structure*, Harper and Row, New York, 1971.
  This volume is divided into six parts; each part contains essays on aspects of social structure and kinship. Altogether, there are 59 essays. Practically all the important scholars from Henry Maine and Lewis Morgan to David Schneider and Raymond Firth are represented here. Each part of the book contains suggested readings for further studies. The essays of the authors—Meyer, Fortes, Fred Eggan, Raymond Firth, Raiph Linton, George Murdock, Louis Dumont and A.R. Radcliffe-Brown—are crucial.
- Keesing, Roger M, *Kinship and Social Structure*, Holt, Rinehart and Winston, New York, 1975.
  A useful discussion through illustrations on kinship. Alliance theory is illustrated through genealogical charts.
- Korn, S. 1973: see Keesing, 1975.
- Krober, A.L., Classificatory systems of relationship. JRAI Great Britain and Ireland. (39) 77–84.
- Leach, Edmund R., Polyandry, Inheritance and the definition of Marriage, *Marriage, Family and Residence*. Paul Bohannan and J. Middleton (Eds.), Natural History Press, Garden City, N.Y., 73–83, 1968.

This is a very important article on the regulative functions of the institutions of marriage.

- Lewis, L.M., *Social Antropology in Perspective*, Cambridge, London, 1985.
- Leicthter, H.J. and W.E. Mitchell, 'Kinship Concepts', included in M.H. Fried's edited volume, *Explorations in Anthropology,* 304–320, Knopf, 1973.
  This essay discusses the utility of kinship studies both in non-industrial and industrial societies.
- Levi-Strauss, C., *The Elementary Structures of Kinship,* Chicago, University Press. First published in 1949, English Edition in 1969. This is a revised edition by Levi-Strauss translated by Needham and others. It contains a long Introductions by the authors and Needham.
- Lowie, R.H. "Kinship", Encly of the Social Sciences, V. 3, 568–72, 1931.
  This article is a must reading as it contains elements of Kinship explicitly.
- Murdock, George P, *Social Structure,* Free Press, New York, 1949.
  This is a basic textbook now classic in social anthropology. Analysis of institutions, viz. family, marriage and kinship is based on 250 reported societies.
- Radcliffe-Brown, A.R., *Structure and Function in Primitive Societies,* Oxford University Press, London 1952. Collection of articles by Radcliffe-Brown written over two decades. He places kinship in social structure and social organisation of primitive societies.
- Radcliffe-Brown, A.R. and D. Forde (Editors), *African Systems of Kinship and Marriage,* London, Oxford University Press, 1950, See "Introduction" by A.R. Radcliffe-Brown.
- Schusky, E.L., *Manual for Kinship Analysis.*, Holt, Rinehart and Winston, New York, 1965.

  A diagrammatic analysis of the materials related to kinship. Useful for undergraduates.
- Schneidar, David, *American Kinship*, Princeton university, New Jersey, 1965.
- Srivastava, A.R.N., Rethinking Descent and Alliance, *South Asian Anthropologist,* **3**, 31–41, 1981.
- Srivastava, A.R.N., Rise of Kinship and Marriage studies in South Asia, *International Journal of Asian Studies,* UNESCO, **4** (1) 106–123, 1984.
- Srivastava, A.R.N. Anthropology of the Kinship, a critique, *Indian Anthropologist*, 41 (1), 77–84.

Chapter 7

The Economic Sphere of Culture

The older generation of the American cultural anthropologists viewed 'economy' as an aspect of culture; the British social anthropologists studied the economic behaviour as an institution of the society. While these views still continue, modern social—cultural anthropologists have explored this aspect/institution in details, and have written so much that a new sub-field has emerged within the general anthropology. This is *economic anthropology*. (A brief historical development of this sub-field has been well documented in Schneider and Mc Clair, 1970; Cook, 1974).

Economic anthropologists study systems of production, and distribution and consumption patterns of non-industrial societies cross-culturally. They have defined the field and have conceptualised the following problems:

(i) The meaning of economy, economic and economising;

(ii) The relationship between Economics and Anthropology; and

(iii) The formal and substantive contexts of economic anthropology.

TERMS DEFINED

It would be profitable to note meanings of the above terms. Briefly, the term *economy* of a society consists of the social relationships that organise and regulate the production, distribution and exchange of goods and services. *Production* is the concrete set of activities concerning creation of goods of services; clearly the *technology* (physical tools and cultural knowledge) is an important ingredient to production. *Distribution* is the process of allocating the goals and services to members of a social group. *Exchange*, in simple terms, is the process whereby people transfer goods and services among one another. Experienced ethnographers have presented a vivid account of economy of a society in terms of subsistence, environment, technology and demographic condition of the people. One such scholar is Raymond Firth (1929).

The Relationship between Economics and Anthropology

Economics in comparison to Anthropology is one of the oldest and theoretically sophisticated discipline. In their long tradition, economists have developed a number of technical terms such as resources (capital), distribution, production, principles of market, demand-supply, surplus, profit, income, etc. In recent decades, 'fewer' cultural anthropologists have borrowed some general ideas from economics; others strongly feel that it would be irrelevant to explain the economic behaviour of societies in formal economic terms, which were developed for the industrial societies. This was much debated during the sixties and the seventies of the last century.

TWO PERSPECTIVES OF ECONOMIC SYSTEMS

The contrasting views of anthropologists and economists have created two broad divisions in economic anthropology—*formalists* and *substantivists*. These two designations appeared in the works of historian-economists Karl Polanyi (1957) and Dalton (1975).

The Formalist Approach

The subject of Economics may be viewed as either the allocation of the means or resources to alternative ends (or uses) or the patterning of choice. The former focuses on the resources available to people, how are they utilised, who gets what and how much under what circumstances. In the above definition, the second (patterning of choice) focuses on the actors, the members of society, and how do they choose among alternatives in producing and distributing goods. In both the views, individuals have skills and opportunities to maximise the total goods, and it becomes necessary for them to indulge in exchange of goods and services.

The existence of rationality and 'market mentality' is another problematic issue. It is not very easy to resolve this issue for want of sufficient data from non-industrial societies. To be sure, market rationality is the part of the motivational system but other considerations such as kinship and friendship do intervene. Some anthropologists have shown that rational attitudes may be dominant in some societies if not all of them. They probably play some critical role in most of the societies in determining individual action.

The Substantivist Approach

Substantivists look for substance hidden in the society. They maintain that the ways of allocating goods and services in small-scale societies differ fundamentally from those of formal economics. In other words, economic system of tribal societies cannot theoretically be compared with western or industrial societies. The chief proponent of this approach was Karl Polanyi who, following the ideas of Max Weber (the German sociologist), argued that pre-industrial economics can well be understood in social context and not in economic terms. To quote him, *"All societies exhibit substantive rationality, and some societies have techniques allowing them to speak of and define formal rationality, while fewer societies actually have institutional arrangements permitting them to behave in terms of formal rationality"* (Polanyi, 1957, p. 15).

Polanyi cites examples from some African state-like societies such as the Dahomey of west Africa to show that three kinds of relations (transactions) appropriately can be subscribed to economics—*reciprocity*, *redistribution* and *exchange*. Each of these transactive modes can be found in primitive, archaic and industrialised socio-economic systems. The primitive societies are more integrated by reciprocity, the archaic societies (The Dahomey) by redistribution and the western, i.e. industrial societies by the market exchange.

FORMALISTS AND SUBSTANTIVISTS VIEWS COMPARED

While Polanyi, George Dalton, Paul Bohannan and their followers continued emphasising 'substantivist' mode of analysis, some other anthropologists of relatively younger age generated the ideas of 'formalist' view in the analysis of cultural data. Prominent among them are Robins Burling, Le Clair, Scott Cook, Cancian and Lee. Manning Nash (1966) is of the opinion that the cultural anthropologists can be benefited by the works of formal economists in restricted sense; they can work on the ideas about the 'choice making' and 'allocation' processes and they can use the method of quantifications (input and output analysis), demand and supply interactions, etc. Likewise, Richard Salisbury, a foremost economic anthropologist, is of the opinion that exposure to economists and their methods could be invaluable and anthropologists should study Economics not to become economist, but to become a better anthropologist.

In order to compare and contrast these two approaches, we may consider examples of goods produced in pre-capitalist and capitalist societies. Some goods have 'use value' for they directly benefit the user. Substantivists maintain that the pre-capitalists produce usable goods, i.e. production for use. In contrast, capitalist economies are characterised by 'production-in-exchange' economic systems. A former of capitalists society produces goods largely for exchange. In other words, their motive is making profits. It is no denying fact that in these two types of societies both 'use-value' and 'exchange-value' coexist, but the patterns of production in these two societies are dominated by different mentalities. Sahlins (1972) has rightly noted that production for exchange in capitalist society is based on unlimited needs.

Anthropologists of late twentieth century believe that contribution of both the perspectives is rewarding; therefore, collection of qualitative and quantitative data are must for any economic anthropologist.

The difference confronted by substantivist and formalist anthropologists force us to recall the difference faced by Palaeo anthropologists. A given hominid fossil in relation to form and size may be assigned to 'genus' Australopithecus, but viewed in the perspective of evolution, it might be included under the genus *Homo*. One may also note that the Trobrianders are neither 'primitive' nor 'Archaic' or 'industrial'. The fact that they do have a system of exchange pattern (also described in this chapter), the distinction lies in the *degree* and not in *kind*.

THE CONTENT OF ECONOMIC ANTHROPOLOGY

The involvement of Economic anthropologists can briefly be described by looking at researches and publications since late sixties of the last century. Economic anthropology is one of the substantive fields of inquiry, on par with the family, the kinship, the political organisation or the religious system. Therefore, the foremost task of economic anthropology is to describe the range of economic system found across the societies. Obviously, it requires both fieldwork and comparative illustrations.

Economic anthropology classifies the diversity of economic systems into useful types such as societies at various technological levels have different systems. Content analysis of many modern text books in anthropology exhibit this trend, that is they present the materials in evolutionary categories—hunter-gatherer or band economies, pastoral economies, hoe and forest cultivators, sedentary cultivators and so on.

Economic anthropology examines the correlations or coexistence of various types of economic arrangements with other sets of socio-cultural arrangements. Following structural-functional analysis combined with statistics, economic anthropologists try to see 'what goes with what'. Economic anthropology sets out the conditions of continuity and change of economic systems in general terms.

Above topical areas are not exclusively for economic anthropologists. Anthropologists, working in pre-industrial or modernizing societies try to see how a specific area (here economy) is related to other areas irrespective of specialisations. In this sense, Economic anthropology is a general and desired sub-discipline of anthropology, but it should be noted that while doing fieldwork Economic anthropologists have been greatly inspired by the developments in related disciplines. In doing so, they have developed some useful insights. It is worth noting a passage from Manning Nash's work:

"Economic anthropology has the task of describing, ordering and explaining the range of human economic organisation in a manner contributing not only to factual enrichment of anthropology but also to its theoretical sophistication and penetration. It must develop a body of theory (to) explain... real, significant, and puzzling economic and cultural facts... the causes and directions of change in primitive and peasant economic systems" (Nash 1966 : 16–17).

A DESCRIPTIVE MODEL OF PRE-INDUSTRIAL ECONOMIC SOCIETY

In their attempts to describe and understand the economy and economic behaviour of the pre-literate societies anthropologists have worked out to elaborate frameworks. The ideas concerning characteristics of *primitive* and *peasant* economies are inherent in these societies. Here, primitive refers to the tribal societies. Peasants are defined as *part-culture* and *part society*. That is, they are part of a larger stratified society. On the other hand, tribal societies are autonomous, that is, they are not a part of the larger society. Usually, but not necessarily always, peasants are engaged in cultivation of crops and agricultural tasks (See Appendix I). The distinguishing features of tribal and peasant economies are noted below in brief.

Level of Technology and Division of Labour

Conventionally, anthropologists have viewed technology as an aspect of culture mainly related to production and utilisation of foodstuffs, shelter, clothing and implements desired to satisfy physical wants. Judging from any measure, simple societies display relatively simple technology.

A simple technology has some cultural correlates. One of the correlates is that the number of tasks involved in productive activity is a few. Very often, tasks are performed by a limited number of tools even for specialised operations. The division of labour in such societies tends to follow the natural line of sex and age. Both the simple division of labour and the simple technology set limits on the size of the task groups.

Structure and Membership of Productive Units

The second set of feature that distinguishes the peasant and primitive economy is the structure and membership of productive units. The prior existing social relations determine membership of economic units. In other words, various sorts of kinship groups described in the preceding chapter serve the structure of the economic units. Thus, nuclear or composite and extended domestic groups, lineage, clan, kindred, phartry and compromise kin groups are the basic units of production. In the world of pre-literates, labour market does not exist. Works are done on cooperative basis. Recruitment of persons for productive tasks depends on the prior relations between or among the persons of the domestic groups.

Media of Distribution and Exchange

The third distinguishing feature of primitive and peasant societies is the media of exchange on the basis of their comparative study of exchange systems, economic anthropologists have delineated four types of exchanges, viz. market, re-distributive, reciprocal and mobilisation exchanges. It is to be noted that any society may exhibit more than one of these types, but one of them is usually dominant.

Reciprocal Exchange

A common system of exchange is reciprocal exchange, which is based on the principle of reciprocity. It involves exchange of items between units of about same kind among the persons, domestic groups, kin-groups and communities. Reciprocity of exchange is exemplified by the practice of gift giving (Mauss, 1954) or 'kula exchange' of the Trobrianders of Melanesia). In gift exchange situation, the economic purpose is not crucial, rather the emphasis is on maintenance of social relations and social structure. Radcliffe-Brown in his famous monograph on the Andamanese wrote, the object of the exchange was to produce a friendly feeling between the two persons concerned (1922; 84).

It is worthwhile to note that items involved in the Kula are of no 'intrinsic' value or outside use. Their worth comes from their role in the cycle of exchange, and their value is increased during the process of exchange. This value is a reflection of social prestige and social position of the Kula partners. Under the shelter of this exchange, there is bartering (but not between Kula partners) of useful goods, which are usually unavailable on the islands.

Firth's account of Tikopian 'spheres of exchange' (*Primitive Polynesian Economy,* 1939) is the clearest analysis of exchange of goods between the persons in particular status relationships or in trade partnerships. He has also shown that particular types of goods tend to be associated with one another and with certain categories of social relationships. In brief, what is important in reciprocal exchange, according to Firth, is to realise the role status within the specific context. Social significance of exchange of goods in a tribal society is the manner in which they formed a nexus within concatenations of social relationships, where they come to symbolise the rights and duties obtaining between the parties.

In his work among the Trobrianders of the Pacific, Malinowski (1922) describes a complex set of reciprocal relationships among different groups with which the natives trade. The system is called Kula. In this system, a series of island-groups exchange shell ornaments and other items. The trading ring is organised in such a manner so that the various items travel in different directions. For example, the Trobriands trade armbands (MWALI) for necklaces (SOULAVA) with the people from Dabu. This exchange will never be reversed, i.e. the Dabun islanders will not give the armbands, to the Trobriands and this ritual exchange goes to other types of practical items for exchange. The Trobriands will never give necklaces for the armbands. "...On every island and in every village, a more or less limited number of men take part in the Kula—that is to say, receive the goods, hold them for a short time in his possession for a short time, and then pass them on...one transaction does not finish the Kula relationship, *once in Kula olways in the Kula*" (p. 82). (see Box).

The Kula Ring
A complex type of
reciprocal exchange

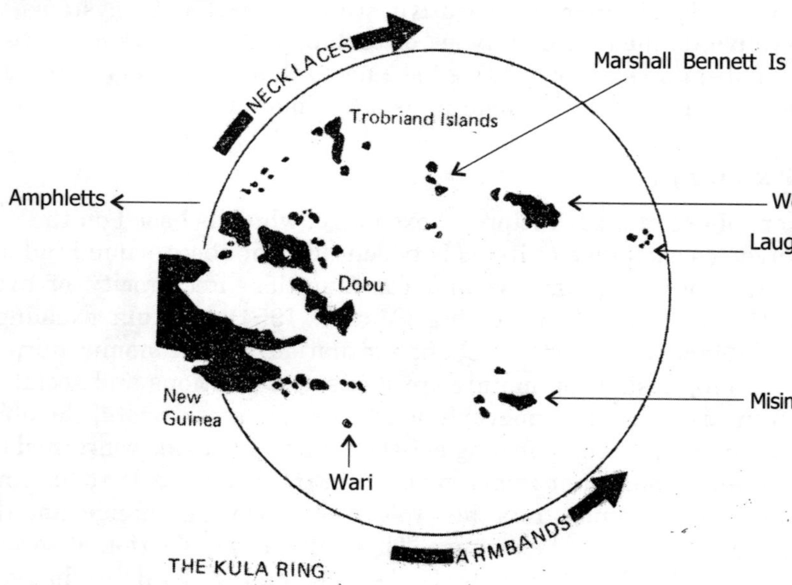

In his work among the Trobrianders of the Pacific, Malinowski describes a complex set of reciprocal relationships among different groups with which the natives trade. The system is called ***Kula.*** *In this a series of island-groups exchange shell ornaments and other items. The trading ring is organised so that various items travel in different directions. For example, the Trobriands trade arm bands for necklaces with the people from Dobu (see map). This exchange will never be reversed, i.e. the Dobuans will not give the Trobriands the arm-bands and the Trobrians will never give necklaces for the arm-bands. Alongwith this ritual exchange goes other type of practical items for exchange.* (Adopted from Malinowski, 1922, p. 81–83.)

'Face-to-face' barter is the frequent mode of economic exchange among the non-industrial societies. It may or may not involve bargaining and haggling and may occur at any place or at a special place, e.g. market. Some of the pre-industrial/pre-literate societies have also developed what is termed as 'silent trade' or 'dumb barter'. In this situation, one party leaves the items at a specified place; the other party comes to that place, takes those items and leaves its items without meeting or seeing the first party.

Redistributive Exchange

This exchange is the foundation of complex societies. It existed among the Sumerian, Mayan, Indus valley civilizations. Among the state like the tribal kingdoms of Africa (see Chapter 8), redistributive exchange also exists.

In the redistributive mode of exchange, the labour products of several different individuals (producers) are brought to a central place; and they are given away to producers and non-producers alike. The principal individual involved in this is known as re-distributor. Thus, a Trobriander chief acts as a distributor when his fellowmen bring gifts to him. In modern system, the principal distributor is an agency like the state. The *Jajmani* system in village India is another example of re-distributive exchange. It would be worthwhile to describe Jajmani system in rural India.

Jajmani System

In villages of India, landowning and occupational castes exchange goods and services in a traditional manner. Each caste is associated with a set of occupations—agriculturists, priests, potters, blacksmiths, washermen, carpenters, oilmen and so on. The households of the landowners (also called *jajmans*) are provided with services that they consider are the jobs of lower castes and with ritually pure services by the Brahmins. They pay the service to the castes in kind with grain or other products. The redistribution often takes place on threshing floor and shares may be defined as a part of the heap of the grain. In this system these relationships are hereditary, that is, patronage-client relationship.

W.H. Wiser (1958) has been credited to portray an account of jajmani system in northern India. However, local variations such as the *Bathula* system in western India have been well reported by Henry Orenstein (1966). Here, service castes and hereditary officials (headmen, washermen, accountants) serve a village as a whole. It has also been reported that in life cycle ritual, priests and artisans who largely live in ritual belt come to serve their jajman who reside in town. In recent years, the traditional system has undergone change due to market mentality on the part of clients.

How Does Redistribution System Develop?

The American anthropologists Elman Service suggested that agricultural societies distribute their products across different communities of the some of the neighbouring regions. We have noted above that in reciprocal exchange, two persons are involved; that is goods and services are exchanged between the two. In redistributive system, a person, usually a chief or a leader (Zamindars in feudal system), co-ordinates the tasks of exchange. Agricultural communities tend to orient toward redistribution. It must however, be noted that redistribution is not radically different form of economic relations, it involves reorganization of reciprocity.

Potlatch: An Example of Ceremonial Feasting Exchange System

Among the Indians of the northern shore of Vancouver Island, in British Columbia such as the Kwakiutl, a tribal feast ceremony called *Potlatch*, is accompanied by the gift-giving to the invited guests. (The word potlatch is from the Chinook language means "gift".) These local or distant kinsmen are their own people but of different rank and social status. They were divided into about 25 village groups, each of which was politically autonomous. In 1930, their population was less than 2000. In earlier days, it was celebrated with a great vigour. Some valuable material goods such as furs, clothes and utensils were destroyed in large quantity amidst the invitees by the host to humiliate the rivals of the equal rank. For a vivid description, Ruth Benedict's *Patterns of Culture*, Chapter 5 may be consulted.

Now-a-days this custom no longer exists due to destruction of property and life. But, the institution of Potlatch was very much established among the coast Indians. Thus, Potlatch was a feast given by an individual to another family and one clan to another clan. The more lavish the destruction of property, the greater the feast and the prestige accruing to the host. To regain prestige, the guests had to give present in return some other time on other occasions at a greater feast. On some occasions, during the Potlatch, the host boasted of his family prestige and its right over property. See Codere, 1950.

Both the cooperation and the competition are hidden in the Potlatch. Chiefs arranged elaborate feasts since they had to requisite power to make demands on other people for help. Thus, cooperation developed in order to accumulate property so as to give it away (destroyed). In some of the textbooks, the example of Potlatch is cited as a mechanism of redistributive exchange system (Piddocke, 1965: 258). But, in the eyes of present author this is incorrect.

Levelling Mechanism

Potlatch is a form of 'levelling mechanism'. It refers to a cultural device which reduces wealth differentials between individuals by organizing feast or distributing surpluses to visitors.

According to Manning Nash, "*levelling mechanisms* are ways of forcing the expenditure of accumulated resources into channel (social ends) that are not economic or productive. It may take various forms. Social loans to relatives, a large feast following economic success, etc." (Nash, 1966 : 35–36).

Trade and Market Exchange

In ethnogrophies terms like gift, trade, clumb borter occur. There is difference between trade and gift. The former emphasises economic redistribution, the latter involves social relationship. Silent or dumb barter occurs in some tribal communities. The semang of Malaya, for example, exchange forest items for goods offered by their enemies, the Sakai. During the transaction both are absent.

In modern (industrial) economy, the term 'market' has a special meaning. It refers to systems of exchange of goods and services using 'all purpose' or 'general-purpose' money (defined below) as a standard measure of relative value. In specialised market procedures, supply and demand adjust themselves to one another with respect to availability of goods. In this, the consumers directly influence production patterns. In tribal economies, this phenomenon is lacking, and particular items and quantities of these items tend to be stabilised in exchanges against one another. Among the tribals, in case of food crisis, i.e. famines, loss of crops, there can be no rise in the price of food since there is nothing against which food can be exchanged. Storage facilities do not exist. It must be noted that in non-western economy, particularly in subsistence-economy, market does not display the characteristics of market principles. As Bohannan has remarked, "A subsistence economy is one in which the factors of production are not transacted by the market mechanism. In subsistence economy, some produce may enter the market. Such a situation is called *peripheral market* (Bohannan 1975 : 241).

Anthropologists have noticed that in the subsistence economy, people work less than the commercial economies. In pre-agricultural stage, people collect food from forest and indulge in small game hunting and fishing in their off time.

Economic anthropologists, thus, make a distinction between market principle or market and market as an institution whose purpose is to bring a large number of people of varied social groups together in a non-controlled commercial situation. The most important function of pre-literate or tribal market is display of a network of communication (a non-economic function) among the people. In many parts of the world, 'market sites' provide a place to meet one's kinsmen and friends for exchange of their views. Tribal markets are used as the centre of political and religious activities. Simultaneously, people may also exchange their economic items and indulge in trade business. But, the notion that 'money' (see below) can buy almost everything has been alien to most of the human groups. Money (or price) market implies the existence of state form of control. The most developed market exchange is associated with the political economy of capitalism. Here, virtually everything can be bought and sold in organized manner.

Primitive and Modern Money

As empirical studies clearly reveal, some of the sections of tribal and peasant societies know the operations of modern money (*general purpose money*). Many of them have what Dalton has called *limited purpose money*. Money is *general purpose money* if it serves three functions, viz. as a medium of exchange for buying and selling, to discharge obligations such as taxes, fines, debts and to provide a standard of value for different kinds of goods and services. But, if money serves only one or two of the functions, then it is known as *limited purpose money*. It may also be noted that *limited purpose money* fails to manifest four physical characteristics (homogeneity, divisibility, durability and portability) of modern money. Some of the non-literate societies have indigenous money form (cowrie, sheep, teeth, rice, pigs), but, in essence, they lack physical characteristics of modern money and their commercialisation.

West African Cowrie-shell: One of the clearest examples of an approach of using money is to be found in the West African cowrie shells. It is a well-known fact that trade flourished between West African and European/the Mediterranean regions for centuries. With rise of western money in this part, cowries altered their value in relation to French currency. It has been reported that there were professional money-exchangers, like the Mahajan's of central India, who exchanged/sold/used cowries for currency-notes. Cowries now have been ousted by western money, but have survived in two spheres of activity—they are still used in small exchanges of produce and also on ritual occasions.

Property Rights in Economic Activity

Property is a social creation; hence, it is regarded as a 'cultural universal' (defined in Chapter 2). E.A. Hoebel defined property as "a web of social relations with respect to the utilisation of some non-material or material objects in which a person or group holds connections" (1972 : 270). To put this in simple terms, property is a defined status relation between person(s) and thing(s). Gluckman puts it as, "Property law in tribal societies defines not so much rights in respect of things, as obligations owned between persons in respect to things" (1963 : 75).

Non-professional anthropologists often hold the view that tribals were 'communistic' whereas modern societies are 'individualistic'. These terms are loose expressions of reality, In analysing property rights in relation to economic activity Gluckman remarks, "What is owned, in fact, is a claim to have power to do certain things with that land (property), to possess immunities against the encroachment of others on one's rights in them and to exercise certain privileges in respect of them...but *other persons may have certain rights, claims, powers and privileges of some property*" (1963: 77, emphasis added).

Land Rights

Land holding or land tenure varies in the line of technological skills of the people. Those who live by hunting and gathering have little significance of land than those who have elaborate systems of agriculture. Even in the former, each band had the right to hunt freely over a defined territory. Among the cattle keepers, there may be areas where right to graze stocks are restricted or open.

Tribal agriculturalists have more complicated system of land tenure. In most of the agricultural tribes of central India, such as the Munda and Oraon of Chotanagpur land belong to the original settlers of the area, the first lineage or clansmen are the owners of the land. They are known as the *Khunkattidar*. In primitive state type societies, the owner of the land is the king, but he, as in the Lozi of Upper Zambia, demands allegiance from anyone who wants to settle on the land; he has the power to distribute any land to people; he has the right to ask the subjects to give him a portion of land they are using, but he cannot dispossess them. Once the king has given land for cultivation, the subjects have rights in it that are protected against the outsiders including the king himself. Should he desire the land, either for his own use or to give it to another, he must ask for it. That is the reason, Lozi says, "the king is also a beggar" (Gluckman: 1955). Hoebel has presented a well-comparative account of the system of land tenure among technologically varied communities (1973 : 272–76).

In brief, in tribal and peasant societies the crucial point is 'who have rights, what rights over the property' and not who owns the property.

Common Criteria of Claims to Property

Philip Bock (1978) has noted the following criteria which people claim to tangible or intangible property.

1. Membership in corporate group and
2. Claim based on personal and/or social role of individual.

This includes the following:

(i) Individual inheritance,
(ii) Purchase of property,
(iii) Manufacture/original creation,
(iv) Discovery,
(v) Leasing,
(vi) Status rights, and
(vii) Custodianship (temporary control over the property).

Examples of above criteria are reported in rich ethnography.

To Sum Up

Economic anthropologists relate economic behaviour of people to their entire socio-cultural systems. This behaviour is tied to the society in more than one ways, viz. normative, integration, functional, interdependence and causal interaction. One should always remember that the differences in the operation of the two types of economies—tribal and western are not due to any difference in intelligence of the peoples concerned. "Difference is imposed by the types of productive tools the predominance of primary goods, and the restricted ...external connections. As a result, general social considerations are dominant over specific economic calculations, though these always enter" (Gluckman, 1964 : 98–99).

The most obvious application of the economic anthropologists is their studies of the changes occurring around the world as traditional including the tribals societies become part of larger national system. (see Belshaw, 1965).

SUGGESTED READING

- Barth, Fredrik, *Capital and Investment in a Pastoral Community*, Tavistock, London, 1963.
- 'Basseri of Southern Iran.' Included in edited volume *Capital, Saving and Credit in Peasant Societies*, Aldine, Chicago, 1963.
- Belshaw, Cyril S., *Traditional Exchange and Modern Markets*, Prentice-Hall, Englewood Cliffs, New Jersey, 1965.
  This is a short survey of different types of exchange system. For Belshaw's another provoking article on theoretical problems in Economic Anthropology, see *Social Organisation* edited by M. Freedman, 25–42, 1967.
- Bock, Philip, *Modern Cultural Anthropology*, Knof, Chicago, 1978.
- Bohannan, Paul and G. Dalton (Eds.), *Markets in Africa*, 1962. (Paperback edition in 1965 by the American Museum of Natural History.)
  The presence and absence of clearly defined trade, exchange, market, market principles in the focus to 8 essays by scholars such as Robert Gray, M.G. Smith, Mary Douglas and P.H. Gulliver. Introduction covers the conceptual framework.

- Codere, Helen, *Fighting with Property,* Monograph of the American Ethnological Society, No. 18, New York, 1950.
- Cohen, Y., The cultural present, *Man in Adaptation*, Aldine, Chicago, 1974. This is an excellent treatment on the relationship between culture and adaptation.
- Cook, Scott, "Economic Anthropology: Problems to Theory, Method and Analysis", Published in John J. Honigmann's edited volume *The Handbook of Social and Cultural Anthropology*, Rand MC Nally Publications, 795–860, New York, 1974. It presents a concise treatment on the subject with more than 550 bibliographic references.
- Dalton, George, *Economic Anthropology*, Basic Books, New York, 1975. Author's articles written during 1965–1975, including those published in *Current Anthropology* and *American Anthropologist.*
- Dalton, George, *Primitive, Archaic and Modern Economics*, 1971. This volume contains essays of Karl Polanyi.
- Firth, Raymond, *Primitive Polynesian Economy*, Tavistock, London, 1929. It presents a brilliant field study on primitive economic system. In 1967, Firth edited a volume on *Themes in Economic Anthropology* (ASA monograph, London) which is useful for more advanced students.
- Forde, Daryll, *Habitat, Economy and Society*, Dutton, New York 1963 (First published in 1934.)
  Beginners in anthropology would get a lot of information on way of life of pre-literate societies.
- Forde, Daryll and M. Douglas,: "Primitive economics", included in *Man, Culture and Society* H.L. Shapiro (Ed.) (Revised edition), 402–416, 1971.
- Gluckman, Max, *Custom and Conflict in Africa*, Oxford University Press, London 1955.
- Hoebel, E.A., *Anthropology, the study of man* McGraw Hill Book, N.Y. 1970.
- Harris, Marvin, *An Introduction to General Anthropology, Culture, People and Nature*, Alfred Knof, New York (Revised edition), 1980.
  Chapter 13 (Economy: Exchange and Control, 225–250) summarizes the findings of economic anthropologies both at descriptive and methodological level.
- Lee, R.B., *Kung Bushman subsistence*, 1969, An input-output analysis. See article in Vayda (1969). One of the specialists defines the meaning scope and method of economic anthropology. Nash has also contributed a short essay on "Organisation of Economic Life". See Tax (1964).
- Malinowski, B., *Argonauts of the Western Pacific: An Account of Native Enterprise and Adventure in the Arehipelagoes of Melanesian New Guinea,* London, 1922. (Paperback, Anchor, 1970). An epoch making ethnography in anthropological research.
- Mauss, Marcel, *The Gift, Forms and Functions of Exchange in Archaic Societies,* Cohen, London, 1925, 1954.

- Nash, Manning, *Tribal and Peasant Economics*, University of Chacago Press, Chicago, 1966.
- Piddocke, Stuart, The Potlatch system of the Southern Kwakiutl: a new perspective. *Southwestern Journal of Anthropology,* 21: 244–264.
According to the author Potlatch has several functions. It *redistributed* food and wealth. It validated changes in social status..." (p. 258).
- Polanyi, Karl, Conord M. Arensberg and Harry W. Pearson (Eds.), *Trade and Markets in the Early Empires*, Free Press, Glencoe, 1957.
- Pospisil, Leopold, *Kapaliku Papuan Economy*, Yale University Anthropology Paper No. **67**, 1963.
This is an excellent study of transaction of 'money' in a primitive society, New Guinea Islands (North of Australia). Pospisil relates his findings to the principle of formal economies.
- Radcliffe-Brown, A.R., *The Andaman Islanders,* Cambridge University Press, London (1922), Paperback in 1958, Harper.
- Tax, Sol, *Penny Capitalists: A Guatemalan Indian Economy*. Smithsonian Institute Publication, No. 16, Washington D.C., 1953.
- Tax, Sol, *Horizons of Anthropology*, Aldine, Chicago, 1964.
This volume is a collection of 21 articles on various facets of anthropology; for Economic Anthropology, see articles by Nash and Sahlins.
- Vayda, A. (Ed.), *Environment and Cultural Behaviour,* Natural History, Garden City, New York, 1969.
In this edited volume, articles by the renowned cultural anthropologists on economic systems published over the period of three decades.

Chapter 8

The Political Sphere of Culture

Anthropologists have devoted much time to the study of political system of the pre-literate societies since the beginning of the twentieth century. Various captions have been employed to describe these systems such as customs, laws, order and social control. In the present chapter crucial terms and their contextual meanings related to organised activities will be presented. Thereafter, analysis of data concerning political organisation and conclusion will be drawn.

POLITICAL ANTHROPOLOGY

Under the banner of Political anthropology, both social and cultural anthropologists analyse the aspect of social behaviour known as political organisation. The British social anthropologists view political organisation as the networks of social relationships that permit the regulation of the behaviour related to the maintenance of public order. On the other hand, the cultural anthropologists look for various cultural means by which political problems are solved. In doing so, anthropologists always remember that the political organisation of society cannot be approached apart from the rest of social organisations.

Recognising this view, the American anthropologist Morton Fried defined the field of political organisation as "those portions of social organisation that specifically relate to the individuals or groups that manage the affairs of *public policy* or *seek to control* the activities of those individuals or group" (1967 : 20–21).

Two terms (italicised above) require further clarification. Under "public policy" both modern state and local (Panchayat, municipal) are included. 'Seek to control' includes political parties, unions, corporations, activists and religious groups. Fried's definition can also be applied to pre-literate societies (the band, the tribe, chiefdom, etc.). In the latter public policy may not be easily detected but, altogether it cannot be ignored. This requires a good deal of academic exercises in treatment of individual-group relationships. The British social anthropologists have devoted much time and have focused on this exercise.

E.E. Evans-Pritchard has emphasised the study of primitive political system in terms of its relationship to the ecological, structural and ideological aspects of the society. Since the publication of *The Nuer* (1940) and *The African Political System* (1940), both British and American anthropologists began to study political behaviour in comparative perspectives. As a result, several approaches have emerged during the past five decades. Here, we are concerned more with the ways the anthropologists analyse and compare the organised activities known as politics or political organisation of simple pre-literate societies.

Bohannan is of the opinion that anthropologists must recognise at least three factors in the study of political organisation:

1. the territorial extent and organisation of the society,
2. the dimension of utilisation of resources by the people, and
3. institutional means of controlling force (i.e. law enforcement and warfare.) There is no such thing as politics without force organized in one way or another. "There is no such thing as politics divorced from territory. *Politics is the spatial aspect of social force*". (Bohannan 1975 : 266). A few crucial term inologies need to be considered here are *force, power* and *authority*.

Although social thinkers have used and developed above concepts in more than one ways, their operational meanings are well recognised. It was Max Weber, the noted German sociologist who introduced concepts of power and authority that have been accepted by cultural anthropologists. Paraphrasing Weber, power is the ability to do something or to act upon a person or thing. Social power is an aspect of human relationship. In all of the societies, some power relationships are institutionalised; as such, it becomes part of all of the social relationships. In many of the societies, a portion of this power relationship is legitimate. Legitimacy is always rooted in the values of the people who grant it. When power is combined with legitimacy, it becomes authority, that is legitimate power. Weber recognised this legitimate power as 'political power,' i.e. the ability to achieve personal ends despite opposition. In this sense, political power can be based on physical or psychological coercion. Therefore, the most of the members within a society recognise political power as legitimate.

The most effective form of political power is based on authority (defined above). Members recognise or perceive this power as legitimate rather than coercive. Political anthropologists look for the mechanisms developed by the societies with legitimate power (political power). They also look for how societies lacking legitimate power tackle their social behaviour.

Analyzing Political Systems: Comparative Perspectives

With the publication of *The African Political Systems* (Evans-Pritchard and Fortes, 1940) a tendency developed among the anthropologists to evaluate the political system of the traditional societies in terms of two categories, namely society with the organisation known as 'state' and 'society' without state. The former is termed as 'state society' while the latter is called 'stateless' or 'acephalous society'. Here, the crucial term is 'state' which is usually defined in western terms involving the notions of 'government', 'administration' and other formal categories (described at the end of this chapter).

The political specialists have suggested the following scheme of classification of political structures:

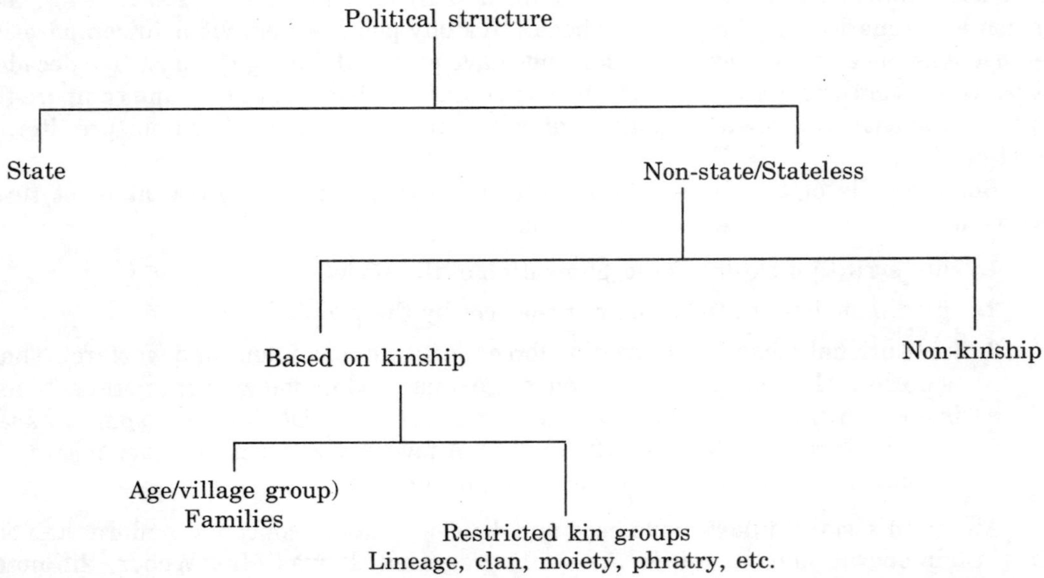

Two Approaches of Political Anthropology

Above classification has become a popular framework in the analysis of political behaviour of the traditional societies. With the emergence of Steward's *Theory of Cultural Change* (1955), some American anthropologists oriented their views in different directions. Their approach is known as neo-evolutionism and is well-documented in the works of Elman Service (1982) and Morton Fried (1967, see Chapter 3). Around the same decade, a few cultural anthropologists of North America and Great Britain presented a framework of analysis of political processes and decision-making popularly known as *processual approach* (Swartz 1966, 1968, also Gluckman, 1965, Bailey, 1968). This approach involves detailed ethnographic descriptions; in particular, functions, conflicts, manipulation, norms and values in relation to demography and economy to understand dynamics of political behaviour.

First development evolution of political organisation will be taken up.

Evolution of Political Organisation

As early as 1962, American cultural (neo) evolutionist Elman Service presented a four-fold scheme of development of human societies on the basis of socio-economic and political-religion. This scheme has been frequently noted in anthropological textbooks. They are—*the band, the tribe, the chiefdom* and *the state.* In modern time, Morton Fried made some changes with regard to terminologies, e.g. for primitive state-like societies, he preferred to label *the Archaic societies* (see box, Chapter 2 of the present book).

The above level of societies may also be considered as economic types based on adaptive strategy described in the preceding chapter. Major variations are found if we take up cross-cultural analysis of band, tribal, chiefdoms and state-level societies. These will be taken up under the processual analysis of political system. For immediate purposes, we may note briefly varied levels of political system in idealised manner.

Thus, a band is a small kin-territorial based group and is seen among the hunters and gatherers. A band is always a food-collector and not food-producing community. All decisions are taken up at the level of group itself.

A tribal-level society is associated with non-intensive food production (horticulture, pastoral and settled cultivators). Some of the tribal societies use their skills and goods to support large dependant populations. The political system is largely based on the bond of kinship. Chiefdom is intermediate between the tribe and the state. Though it is kin-based, it has differential access to resources. Some have more wealth, prestige and power than others. They display quasi-permanent political structure; social stratification begins to emerge at this level. According to Murdock's *Ethnographic Atlas* (1967), chiefdoms emerged in the lowland Amazon, the Circum-Caribbean, the southeastern United States and in Polynesia. American cultural anthropologists have largely worked among the Polynesian Islanders.

A state displays elaborate administrative and government structure along with the forms of social stratification based on wealth, political status, power and social status. Prestige enters into politico-economic life of state people. In some parts of the world, tribal-level societies grew into diversed states. Anthropologists including archaeologists and historians have reconstructed sequences of events leading to the formation of primitive states in the Old and the New world. The British social anthropologists have presented a vivid account of such states in their ethnographies.

Max Gluckman, a leading British social anthropologist is of the opinion that 'two types of societies can be contrasted without considering development perspectives, although it is certain that the type antedated the society in the whole march of human history. Gluckman, as the present writer, is a processual analyst of political system.

PROCESSUAL ANALYSIS OF STATELESS SYSTEM

The meaning of processual analysis has already been noted above (see also Chapter 5). Societies organised around the band, tribal and chiefdom are examples of stateless or acephalous systems. Each of these three types are discussed below.

Band Societies

Anthropologists have used the term 'band' to describe a small, loose-knit social group based on the nearness of its members. Many hunting-gathering societies display the characteristics of a simple kinship organisation. Patterns of formal leadership and formal exchange such as a market place and distinct institutions are lacking in band societies. The most common type of band organisation is formed around a core of related males, usually male siblings, who are married to females born and raised in other bands. In this sense, a band is exogamy. Radcliffe-Brown used the term 'horde' for the Australian bands.

In brief, a band is 'undifferentiated', that is kinship and political relations are one and the same entity. Examples of patrilineal bands are the Arunta and Aranda of Australia, the Ona (south America), the Shoshonean Indians (southern north America), the Semang (Malay), Kung Bushman (Africa), the Birhor and the Kadar of India.

Bands of composite type (lacking perfect residence or descent rule) are found among the Alongkians Indians of Eastern Canada and the Yaghan of Terra del Fuege (South America). Elman Service (1971) has added another type called '*anamalous*' band. It has an irregular composition; it is organised at 'family level' such as the Eskimo.

A band unusually has a leader or chief. Among some of the Northwest coast (American) Indian communities ranked leaders are called 'chiefs,' but this term is inapplicable elsewhere. In the context of Africa, Schapera (1930 : 130) writes that "the Bushman or Bergama chief... has no judicial functions or penal powers, his main duties are to direct the migrations and subsistence activities of his people; the 'chief' can discuss matters with all the men with whom he is involved as they sit round the fire. But, there is succession to office, a chief being succeeded by brother or son, with age or ability taken into account".

The political systems of the Comanche and the Cheyenne of North America have far more complicated system though both are at band level development. This is because of their territories distributed over several hundred kilometers but have sparsely distributed natural resources.

Tribal Level Political System

As compared to the band, a tribe is more complex for it accommodates much larger population. Tribes do not have centralised and formal institutions but they do have well-developed kinship-oriented units, viz. lineage, clan, moieties, kindred, etc. Tribes also have sodalities, i.e. special-purpose non-residential groups (see Chapter 2).

An example of sodality is the *Age-set group*. The British social anthropologists have presented vivid descriptions of 'age set/age class/age village' in their ethnographic accounts of Africa' though it is rarely seen elsewhere. An 'age-set' group is different from associational organisation like the fraternity-based group. It is often called the *Secret society*. Hoebel defined it 'as a fraternity whose membership and activities are shrouded in secrecy'. It is found infrequently in North America and Africa. During the puberty rite or initiation ceremonies, certain activities are only for the males and others are for females. Here, girls are initiated by the women, and men and boys are strictly excluded or the vice versa. In other words, sex linked roles are operative in secret groups. The idea being, no body knows what is going on either side. Matters are kept as secret as possible. The following example of secret society comes from the Mendi and Temrie tribes of Sierra Leone, Northwest Africa.

Upon the completion of their puberty rites, all of the boys belong to the *porro* fraternity and girls to the *bondu* sorority. The *porro* is an integrating feature of tribal life—family, religious and political. The chief officer yields effective political power and social prestige.

In southwest North America, the Hopi (one of the Pueblo tribes) perform a dramatic rain-making ceremony. Secret ceremonial rituals are also prevalent among some of the Indians of the northwest coast of America. As compared to the 'age-set group' (described below), secret groups are oriented more towards rituals than the polity.

In the age-set group, political matters are largely in the hands of 'age-set members and their seniors. The following description is based on Monica Wilson's *Good Company* (1951).

The Nyakyusa are people practising mixed husbandry in the Living Stone Mountains of southwest Tanganyika. Organised in small chiefdoms; they are marked by agnatic lineage organisation and age—villages (composed of mixed lineages) of a neighbourhood. The effects of this situation enter into every aspect of their life.

Nyakyusa remain getting together to herd their father's cattle, and for several years, they are busy in these grand activities. When they reach around twelve, they leave off herding to take up the hoe in the gardens of their fathers; then they move into a village of older boys, away from their parents except for meals. All of the members must be together even when one visits his parents. When they approach adulthood they get marry one by one; each brings his wife into the 'age-village' of his peers. In this way, the village of the boys is developed into a family village of husbands, wives and their children. Each youth owns his own fields from his father and ceases to return to his parents' house.

In the next decade, when all the villages of a given age level have matured, the formal government of the territory is ritually handed over to them, and they rule the land, i.e. the Nyasaland. Their sons follow the same sequence.

The age-set groups are also prevalent in highly developed political system of the Nandi (Kenya) and Zulus (Swaziland), which are often cited as examples of primitive state-societies. Writing about the Nuer age-set, Evans-Pritchard remarks, "The Nuers age-sets have no corporate activities and cannot be said to have specific political functions ... There is no leadership in the sets".

What then the Nuer do? At this stage, we now move on to illustrate stateless societies. The Nuer, the Tiv and many others all over the world are organised at a tribal level in terms of kinship groups. Each group (segment or descent group) is complete in itself because of descent ties. One segment (lineage) enters into another segment for marriage alliances. Often conflicts occur between the groups over many grievances, viz. cattle theft, damage to property, adultery, rights over resources, etc. The Nuer resolve the issues in the following way:

How does segmentary lineage system work?

Let us consider the following diagram:

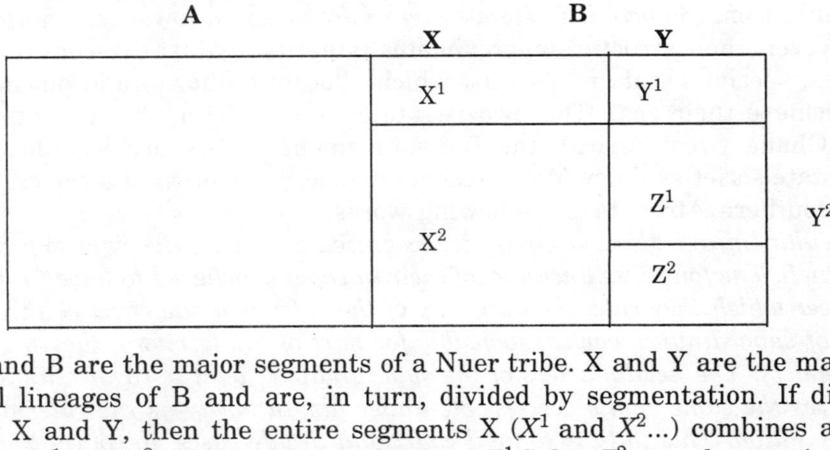

A and B are the major segments of a Nuer tribe. X and Y are the major branches maximal lineages of B and are, in turn, divided by segmentation. If dispute arises between X and Y, then the entire segments X (X^1 and X^2...) combines and stand by against Y (Y^1 and Y^2). When segment (lineage) Z^1 fights Z^2, no other section is involved.

It is called *principle of segmentary opposition*. This is noticed in such societies where the feuds can be resolved by anyone who stands outside the lineage. This person is often called the leader his strength lies in this influence over the people.

Management of Conflicts by the Village Elders and Council of Villages

Under this, there is no tribal government or corporate lineages as described above, but the authority is vested in village council. Here, each village consists of single clan households and has a headman (chief of the clan). If two or more clans are present, then the *headman* of the original settler represents the village. They are also called *the elders.* Among the natives of Melanesia, headman is referred to 'big man'. The kinship is not an important factor in the political decision. Territorial identity and personal qualities of leadership on the part of headmen are the determining factors. It is in this sense the headman is the local political leader.

Typically, lineage heads exercise authority over their descent groups. However, if conflicts arise among two or more villages, then the matter is resolved in a meeting of all the village headmen. Among the Munda and the Oraon, two linguistically contrasting agricultural tribes of Jharkhand state (central India), the institution of *Parha panchayat* (council of villages) works well in major disputes. The head of the Parha is called *Parha raja*. The original settler in the area is the head. His post runs in patri-lineage lines, the people of his clan enjoy much respect. "The primitive tribal societies", remarks Hoebel, "are always democracies, rarely are they subject to dictorial leadership. . . . The council is a democratic gathering of the adult men." (1972 : 430). This institution is adept in resolving conflicts of high intensity at a large level.

Decision making processes may involve 'trail' ('oath' and 'ordeal'). The oath is a declaration in the name of supernatural while the ordeal is a means of determining guilt or innocence by same tests.

State-level Political System

The anthropological category of 'state society' is derived from the western meaning of state. Unlike modern national states, which display the characteristics of a complex network organisation, the *primitive state-societies* are oriented towards definite goal or purpose. However, their structure approximates integrity against external threats. In these societies, special social groups exist which allocate authority and physical force in order to achieve their goal. The Swazi state of south Africa, the Ashanti state of present-day Ghana (west Africa), the Bunyaro among others are well-decumented examples of state societies. Lucy Mair presents a vivid description of a typical state in eastern and southern Africa in the following words:

"A particular lineage (descent group) is recognised as having the right to provide the ruler (king, chief). The founding ancestor (of their lineage) is believed to have first entered the country over which they rule; the authority of the ruler is made effective through the appointment of subordinates, each responsible for part of his territory; they may be his kins or commoners. The headquarters of the subordinate official is royal establishment, and he exercises the same rights over people under his authority as the ruler does over the whole population. This duty is to hold court and decide cases, to collect the tribute, and to organize manpower required at the capital (*Mair,* 1975 : 113–114).

Thus, a primitive state system is not based on 'kinship', but kinship implicitly plays some crucial rules. A primitive state differs from the modern state system in respect of formation of state bureaucracy that governs society (nation) on behalf of ruling authorities through extensive procedures and mechanisms that direct plan and coordinate complex political processes.

STRUCTURE AND ORGANISATION OF PRIMITIVE STATES

Societies organised along the lines of band and tribe implicitly make a distinction between leaders (headmen) and followers, but those leaders are never set so above explicitly as they are in state-level societies. Unlike primitive (tribal) societies, the state-societies are composed of two classes of people—commoners and elites. The latter are kings, priests and aristocrats. 'Ties of authority and worship' rather than ties of kinship bind these two classes. This would become clear considering the following description of the *Swazi, a South African Kingdom* (Hilda Kuper, 1963).

The Swazi are a Bantu-speaking people living in Swaziland—a country surrounded on three sides by the Union of South Africa and on the fourth by Portuguese Angola. Before 1968, it was a British colony now ruled by King Sobhuza II in the capital town of Lobamba.

Swazi commoners live in homestead (a cluster of 7–20 households). The eldest man acts as the head (patriach). The Swazi king lives in a homestead much larger than that of the commoners for non-kinsmen are included in his group. King's compound is a sacred area (Great Abode). As Swazi practise polygamy, the senior most wife occupies a central place called Queen mother. As a child, the king lives in his mothers village, but on adulthood, he moves away from his mother's village and establishes his own village (nation capital). The king's village serves as the administrative and military headquarters, while the Queen mother's village serves as the ceremonial or ritual centre. In brief, the villages of the king, his mother and wives are major sites of activities.

The territory of Swaziland is divided into districts, each is ruled by the relatives of the king, royal governors and hereditary chiefs. The king is the owner of all the lands; he allots plots of land to his people. If a commoner feels that he has been treated unfairly by a local leader, then he may appeal to the King or the Queen.

As a local settlement or district is likely to include several clans, therefore at the time of household disputes the clan-authority related to them must be consulted rather than the people. What we get here is 'clan authority gives way to government authority'. Swazi society has been a hierarchical structure of clans and lineages, with the Dlamini clan at the apex. Many clans no longer maintain their own territorial clans, but they contribute directly to royal clan. Thus, the Swazi has become increasingly centralized, and the local territorial loyalties has become arms of the King-central government. Swazi's age-grade/age-class structure has now transformed into 'age-graded warrior-regiments'. Each Swazi male owes military service directly to the head—the king. Every 5 to 7 years, the king forms a new regiment. All men of age-range leave their homestead, and take up group residence. Each group is organised into squads (8–20 men) who dance and drill together ceremonially. Several squads make up a platoon under the command of a Prince (one of the sons of the king). Platoons are combined into local regiments which, in turn, culminates into 'age-class regiment'. Living, eating and smoking together by the age mates develop a strong group feeling. It is to be noted that a member is away from his father, brothers and sisters. Loyalty to the age-group reflects loyalty to the Supreme Commander—the King.

Kinship and Ritual (Ritual of Rebellion)

As the king is the focal point of the Swaziland all the ritual and the Divine power protect him. In order to strengthen his health and wealth, several types of rituals are performed. One of them is ritual of *Incawala*. It is not possible here to describe this complex ritual, but it allows Swazi citizens to display openly their ambivalent and hostile feelings towards the King's authority. This ultimately strengthens the kinship. That is why Gluckman called this ritual a 'ritual of rebellion' (see Gluckman, 1963).

The Swazi case study clearly demonstrates how a primitive state-level is structured. It is to be noted that this structure was not present at a particular period of time, rather it evolved over a period of hundred years. Africa and Asia seem to be abode of primitive states. (See box below)

The Barotse: A large kingdom on the upper Zambezi (northern Rhodesia) is dominated by the Lozi tribe. Gluckman (1955) has described and analysed the intricate administrative system of the Lozi.

The Bemba: Established east of Lake of Bangweolu (the Cango) with a ritual and secular paramountacy. British anthropologist Richards has given fine accounts of how the Bemba make their living.

The Dahomey: The most bureaucratic state in South of the Sahara. Under the king, it has developed an elaborate administration controlling economic and political life. Professor Herskovits has described the Dahomey in details.

The Bunyaro: An African kingdom studied by John Beattie in a simple text (1960).

The Nupe: One of the Emirates created by the Muslim Fulani conquest of an indigenous state. This is a non-tribal state studied by Nadel.

The Ruanda: In the west of Lake Victoria, Cattle-keepers Tutsi established dominance over Hutu peasants. In this area, number of kingdom developed.

The Xhosa: This is a small chiefdoms lying to the south of Zulu. This is quite different from the Swazi.

The Zulu: A Kingdom of southeast Africa, of the people similar to the Swazi. Shaka created it during 1816–22. Its polity was marked by civil war. Though they are patriarchal, the position of Zulu women is high.

Note: Lucy Mair in her *Primitive Government* (1970) has described some of the above state-level societies suited to the students. A brief note on the origin and development of state system has been provided at the end of this chapter.

SOCIAL CONTROL AND LAW

The term social control broadly indicates those aspects which are concerned with the maintenance of social order and stability. There are two mechanisms of maintenance of social control, viz. internal and external. The internal mechanism is built into the process of *enculturation*. Enculturation (Chapter 2) means the elders teach the youngers about the cultural norms. People internalise the specific norms regarding society's expectation. A 'norm' is the average (standard) behaviour of a social group. A societal norm is manifested in custom. However, despite this, people violate the norms since enculturation alone is not a perfect social control within a society. Hence, external mechanisms are required to enforce norms. This mechanism is known as *sanction*. Rewards are positive sanctions for appropriate behaviour and punishments (negative sanctions) for inappropriate behaviour.

There is a good deal of variation among the societies with respect to external sanctions. In pre-literate societies, sanctions tend to be informal. Smiles, pats on the back, hugs, and compliments are examples of positive sanctions. Examples of negative sanctions are gossip, ostracism, raising eyebrows, and restricted access to some goods and services. In complex societies, sanctions are highly formalised. Thus, while public awards, educational degrees, banquets are example of reward; negative sanctions include fines, imprisonment, expulsion and sometimes death.

What emerges from the above brief discussion is relationship between *social norms* and *legal norms*. Customs are social 'norms', while law is a 'legal' norm.

As compared to the American cultural anthropologists, British social anthropologists are more oriented towards studying customs of the non-western (tribal) societies. Their focus is on the role of persistent customs in maintaining a social system in equilibrium. "The social-anthropological study", writes Gluckman, "seems to go further in stressing that customs themselves have an interdependence, which controls the behaviour of those who practise such customs... Cultural anthropologists look for relations between customs themselves without as much reference to social relationships. They have tended... to see customs as forming patterns with dominant themes" (1963: 336).

What is Law? The Terminological Problem

Although anthropologists have written much on primitive law, there is no agreement in defining the term. Not even this word is defined in 'one sense' in Jurisprudence. It is, therefore, natural that students of tribal societies face problem as soon as they try to apply this word to the activities in other cultures.

Radcliffe-Brown and other have defined 'law' by the sanctions behind it. Others stress on social control through the systematic application of the force of politically organised society. If we mean 'politically organised society' as having existence of courts, then there are societies without the law. At one place, Evans-Pritchard stated that "in the strict sense of the word, the Nuer have no law' yet at another place he spoke of Nuer law and of legal relations (See *The African Political Systems*).

Malinowski, in his *Crime and Custom in Savage Society* (1926) wrote that "law is a body of binding obligations, regarded as a right by one party and acknowledge as a duty by the other". The difference between Radcliffe-Brown and Malinowski in their treatment of law is that while the first applied the word to one set of facts, the latter to another. Gluckman has suggested that although there is no harm if the word 'law' is used loosely as long as ethnographic details make it clear that there exists a body of obligatory rules in the society under study.

One of the authorities on primitive law is E.A. Hoebel. In his widely circulated text book on Anthropology Hoebel wrote, "Law consists of social norms, *plus*".

Under 'plus' he noted three features of law, viz. (1) The legitimate use of physical coercion or economic deprivation, (2) the allocation of official authority and (3) the element of regularity (consistency). It is these qualities through which a law is distinguished from custom in any culture. Custom is a traditional way of behaving or doing something that is specific to a society, place or time (see also, *The Macmillon Dictionary of Anthropology*, p. 164)

Under the above framework, Hoebel classified law in various cultures into three—

(1) Civilized law,
(2) Archaic law and
(3) Primitive law. Under the primitive law, he noted "law of pre-literate societies such as the Eskimo, the Comanche, the Ifugao, the Nuer, the Ashanti among others (For details see Hoebel, 1972 : 504–516).

Socio-cultural anthropologists study primitive law by analysing empirical cases of disputes and conflict in tribal societies.

Functions of Political Institutions

In the preceding sections, we have discussed the nature of political system from the points of view of neo-evolutionists and processualists. The common element of these two groups is inherent in the rule of institutions in decision-making process. We may now ask, regardless the complexity of the society, what are the functions of political system (organisation) under society. Here, we may refer to a good framework provided by David Easton in his cross-cultural analysis of legal system (1959). According to Easton, the major functions of political institutions are:

(1) To formulate process,
(2) the legislative process,
(3) the administration (implementation and enforcement of rules/decisions),
(4) the adjudication (settling disputes) and
(5) the supporting functions.

The supportive functions answer some of the critical problems—Why a few give a good deal of support while others give only a little? Is the support directed at a person/agency/system? Are there elements of the population whose support is more crucial than that of others? (For detail see Easton, 1959).

THE ORIGIN OF THE STATE

The Background

According to Fried (1967 : 230), holding a 'monopoly of force' is crucial to the nature of the state, other characteristics of state-level polity are that the state emerges under conditions in which the significance of kinship ties is reduced and the kinship ties serve to mitigate the development of coercive power.

A state has elaborate legitimising idealogies. Legitimising idealogies have taken a variety of forms, but a very common tactic has been for the rulers of the state to justify their rule in religious terms. Finally, states, unlike chiefdoms, have generally not been redistributing centres. The flow of the surplus to the state has been a one-way flow, and such surplus expropriation has resulted in substantial enrichment of the ruling powers.

As a stage in political evolution, the state typically emerges within agrarian societies, and most of the states throughout history have, therefore, been *agrarian states*. While these states have shared certain basic characteristics, there have been several different forms of the agrarian state. There have been a few instances of *primitive states,* those formed within essentially primitive, intensive horticultural societies. The most significant are some of the intensive horticultural states that flourished in the nineteenth century in western and southern Africa. George Peter Murdock (1959) has called such states *African despotisms.* Despotism refers to a system of government in which the ruler has unlimited power. He lists as among their prominent features such attributes as monarchical absolutism, conceptions of divine kingship, ritual isolation of kings, insignia of office royal courts, territorial bureaucracy and ministers of state.

In order to analyse the rise of the state in human society, it is useful to follow Morton Fried's (1967) distinction between *pristine* and *secondary* states. According to Fried, secondary states are those states that have arisen as the result of the presence of one or more pre-existing states. Many, if not most, of the primitive states in Polynesia and Africa arose in this manner. Secondary states, however, need not be formed through inter-societal contact. The overwhelming majority of the states in human history have been secondary in nature.

On the other hand, the very first states arose under conditions in which there was no pre-existing state. These are the states that Fried has termed pristine. As he says, "When a pristine state emerges, it does so in a political vacuum" (Fried, 1967 : 231–232).

Pristine states arose in four regions of the Old World and two regions of the New World. The earliest of the Old World states evolved in Mesopotamia (what is now mainly Iraq) and Egypt approximately 6000-5000 B.P. (before present). The first state arose in China with the creation of the Shang dynasty in approximately 3750 B.P. In India, state-level society was evolving around 4500 B.P. All of these Old World states emerged in geographical regions dominated by major rivers.

In the New World, pristine states evolved somewhat later. The two regions of New World state formation were Mesoamerica, what is now mostly Guatemala and Mexico and Peru.

Theories of Origin of the State

The Functionalist Theory

A well-known functionalist theory of the state is found in the work of Elman Service (1975, 1978). Service thinks of it as a form of centralised leadership that organises and coordinates society for the mutual benefit of its various individuals and groups. When the state arises, the principal distinction within society is not between wealthy and poor or oppressors and oppressed, but between governing and governed groups. The state originates in order to serve the needs of the governed more effectively,

Service sees three principal types of benefits arising from the creation of the state. The first concerns with economic redistribution. The state is an organ that mobilises natural resources and persons for important production and consumption functions. A second major benefit which Service views is that provided by new forms of war organisation. Intensified warfare is said to be an integrative feature of society in that it brings in increasing wealth in the form of booty, captives and tribute and thus, enhances the 'national pride'. A third major benefit allegedly produced by the state is that of public works. The state oversees the construction of temples, tombs, pyramids, walls, roads, irrigation systems and many other public projects.

The Marxian theory

The alternative to a functionalist interpretation of the origin of the state is a conflict theory, one version of which is the Marxian theory. The classical Marxian view of the state holds that the state, in Marx's own words is "the executive committee of the ruling class." That is, the state is a political body that exists primarily as a mean of protecting the economic interests of the dominant social class within a stratified society. With the division of society into classes, the state becomes a virtual necessity from the standpoint of the dominant class.

Morton Fried (1967, 1978) is a defender of this view of origin of the state. For him, once a society has adapted to a system of social stratification, the emergence of the state is all but assured. The appearance of differential access to resources means the emergence of privileged and disprivileged groups, and those holding a privileged position must secure and protect it against the threats of the disprivileged to take it away. Indeed, Fried's conception of 'state' and of 'stratified society' are fundamentally the same (1967 : 225–226).

The demographic theory

Many scholars have called attention to the role of demographic and ecological factors in the rise of the state. Population growth, density of population, changes in environment, resource decline, etc. are some of the crucial variables. The best-known theory of this type is Robert Carneiro's (1970, 1981, 1987).

Circumscription theory is, in fact, more than just a theory of the origin of the state. It is a theory of the entire course of political evolution.

Carneiro notes that a factor common to all the major areas of the world where pristine states arose was what he has called *environmental circumscription.* This exists when areas of rich agricultural land are surrounded either by areas of very poor or unusable land or by natural barriers such as major mountain ranges. The potential operation of this factor can be seen in the areas of pristine state formation like the Middle East.

SUGGESTED READING

- Balandier, George, *Political Anthropology*, Random House, New York, 1970. Originally published in French in 1967, it presents a short account of contribution of political organisation to social sciences. Chapter 1 is recommended for the beginners.

- Banton, Michael (Ed.), *Political Systems and Distribution of Power*, Tavistock Publications, London, 1965.
  Some noted social anthropologists have dwelt on the subject. 'Introduction' to this edited volume written by Max Gluckman and Fred Eggan is worth reading.
- Bohannan, P., *Justice and Judgement among the Tiv,* International African Institute, Oxford University Press, London, 1957.
  The volume presents a detailed account of a stateless society of West Africa. Its materials are also incorporated in Bohannan's *Social Anthropology* (Chapters 16 and 17).
- Bohannan, Paul (Ed.), *Law and Warfare: Studies in Anthropology of Conflict*, Natural History Press, Garden City, New York, 1967.
  This edited volume contains a collection of articles on law and warfare in non-western societies.
- Cohen, Ronald and Middleton, John (Eds.), *Comparative Political Systems*, Natural History Press, Garden City, New York, 1967.
  Twenty articles are on the studies in the politics of pre-industrial societies.
- Davenport, W., The Hawaiian Cultural Revolution, *American Anthropologist*, **71** 1–20, 1969
- Easton, David, "Political Anthropology", *Biennial Review of Anthropology,* (Editor, Benard J. Siegel), Standford University Press, California, 1959.
- Evans-Pritchard, E.E., *The Nue*r: "A Description of the Modes of Livelihood and Political Institutions of a Nilotic People", Oxford University Press, London, 1940 (paperback 1969).
  This is one of the classics in cultural anthropology. Segmentary principle of lineage is described in the context of blood-feuds.
- Evans-Pritchard, E.E. and M. Fortes (Eds.), *The African Political Systems,* Oxford University Press, 1940. London (Paperback edition, 1970).
  This is path–breaking volume displaying formal and informal means of social control among African societies.
- Fogeoson, Raymond D., R.N. Adams (Eds.), "Ethnographic studies from Asia, Oceania and the New World," *The Anthropology of Powers,* Academic Press, New York, 1977.
  The volume contains specialised works.
- Fried Morton H,: *The Evolution of Political Society: An Essay in Political Anthropology*, Random House, New York, 1967.
  An introduction to the anthropological study of political organisation in non-western societies, presents an evolutionary approach to the rise of the state. Fried's anthropological essay on *State: the institutions* can be consulted. See *International Encyclopedia of the Social Sciences*, **15,** 43–150.
- Gluckman, M., *Politics, Law and Ritual in Tribal Societies*, Oxford University Press, London, 1965.
  Chapters 3 and 4 are worth reading; they deal with stateless societies. Gluckman is the leading specialist on the judicial processes in Africa, especially of Lozi courts.

- Hoebel, E. Adamson

  1. *The Law of Primitive Man: a study in comparative legal dynamics*, Harvard University Press, Mass, Cambridge, 1954.
  This is one of the earliest studies of legal anthropology, a survey of different forms of legal institutions around the world, emphasizing on non-western societies.
  2. *Anthropology: The Study of Man*, Macmillan, New York, 1972.
  This is a popular textbook. Chapter 26 provides a discussion on law among the Eskimo, Comanche, Ifugao, Nuer and Ashanti.

- Krodor, Lawrence, *Formation of State*, Prentice-Hall, New Jersey, 1968.

- Lewis, I.M., *A Pastoral Democracy* "A Study of Pastoralism and Politics among the Northern Somali of Africa". *A Pastoral Democracy*, Oxford University Press, London, 1961.

- Lienhardt, R.G., *Social Anthropology*, Oxford University Press, London, 1964. Chapter on politics presents an account of social anthropological writings on this subject, also how balance of power is maintained in stateless societies.

- Mair, Lucy
  1. *Primitive Government,* Harmondsworth, Pelican Books, 1962.
  The authoress presents a description of the major types of government in African tribal societies and also their role in modern times.
  2. *An Introduction to Social Anthropology*, Oxford University Press, London, 1975.
  Chapters 7 to 9 are on political and legal systems of pre-industrial societies. At the end of each chapter reference of ethnographies on African tribes is presented.

- Midleton, J.F. and D. Talt (Eds.), *Tribes Without Rulers*, London, 1958. Short description of stateless societies by field Political anthropologists.

- Nader, Laura, *Law in Culture and Society*, Aldine, Chicago, 1969.

- Pospisil, Leepold: *Anthropology of Law: A Comparative Theory*, Harper and Row, New York, 1971.
  This volume is on the theoretical and empirical treatment of law and society from an anthropological point of view. Pospisil also had worked on the Kapauku Papuans of New Guinea in 1958.

- Roberts, Simon, *Order and Dispute: An Introduction to Legal Anthropology*, Hermonds-worth, Penguin, 1979.
  This is a concise treatment on the subject.

- Schapera, I.
  1. *A Handbook of Taswana Law and Custom*, Tavistock, London, 1955.
  This is a classical treatment of the social system and formal law of an African Tribe.
  2. *Government and Politics in Tribal Societies*, Tavistock, London 1958.
  It surveys the views of writers on political system.

- Seaton, S. Lee and H.M. Classen (Eds.), *Political Anthropology*, Mouton, The Hague: 1979.
  This edited volume contains a collection of works on the subject during 1960–70 including the changes in the traditional political structures.

- Southal, A, "Stateless Society", *International Encyclopedia of the Social Sciences*, **15,** 157–168, 1968.
  Structure and function of stateless societies are discussed.
- Swartz, Marc J., Victor Turner and A. Turden (Eds.), *Political Anthropology*. Aldine, Chicago, 1966.
  This edited volume presents a collection of articles on political organisation from a cross-cultural perspective. The editors discuss the growing concern of anthropologists on the study of political powers and processes rather than on political institutions. This edited volume represents processual analysis of political system of traditional societies.
- Swartz, Marc J. (Ed.), *Local-Level Politics: Social and Cultural Perspectives.*, Aldine, Chicago, 1968.
  A collection of essays on decision making processed in simple and peasant society.
- Wilson, Monica, *Good Company: A Story of Nyakyusa Age Villages*, Beacan Press, Bostan, 1951.
  This is an excellent ethnography on the primitive state.

Chapter 9

The Religious Sphere of Culture

"There is probably no single subject with which anthropology concerns itself today, one that the literature is larger than that on tribal religion. It is also the only anthropological subject on which there have been more than two or three original minds at work—Tylor, Frazer, Durkheim, (Malinowski), and so on". (Bohannan, 1963 : 310).

ANTHROPOLOGICAL APPROACH TO RELIGION

In 'Anthropology of religion', there is an implicit assumption that human beings are biologically similar, and the variation in beliefs and practices called religion, has little to do with physical variations. Another crucial fact is that religion is the man-made part of culture and, therefore, a creation of man. Cultural anthropologists are not interested merely in describing a particular ritualistic belief or practice. Rather, they focus on the supernatural beliefs (symbolised in gods, witches, ghosts, evils, etc.) and relate them to other aspects of society. Therefore, their primary concern is to examine the relationships between religion and socio-cultural aspects of a given society.

Raymond Firth, in his textbook *Elements of Social Organisation* (1951), views religious systems in terms of means for handling the fundamental problems of social organisation, "for reducing uncertainty and anxiety, for increasing coherence in human relationships, for assigning meaning to human endeavour, for providing justification for moral obligation" (1951 : 250).

Malinowski, another British functionalist, emphasised the manner in which religion enters the cultures; among simple societies like the Trobrianders, this is more prominent. This point will be taken up in this chapter under magic and science.

Anthropological method of studying religion is simple: "Anthropologists concentrate on the deed (ritual) in order to understand the explanation of the deed in the practitioner (creed); one must set ritual and creed into their larger context. Finally, one must compare rituals and creeds among societies both in their substantive statements and in their symbolic reflection of the rest of culture" (Bohannan, 1963 : 326).

In the above passage, the term 'ritual' is crucial, and it must be handled carefully. Sometimes, ritual and religion are used as synonyms. The members of any society have culturally defined feelings of all sorts of things; people symbolise these feelings in some standard ways. The means of expressing these feelings and sentiments is called 'ritual behaviour'. Honingman has defined ritual as "the symbolic expression of the sentiments which are attached to a given situation" (1959 : 509). A *ceremony* is a complex of rituals associated with a specific occasion or a kind of occasion, e.g. the ceremony associated with the Kula ring (see Chapter 7).

The techniques and objects used in rituals are highly diverse. Manipulating body, folding hands to pray God, weeping and crying to express solidarity, clapping the hands to show approval, dancing, etc. are some of the ways used in ritual behaviour. Similarly, objects in ritual action include animals, tobacco, drink, etc.

Rituals are of many categories. One such category 'rites of passage' has been described under 'communistic cult' in this chapter. In brief, the effect of ritual behaviour is unification of the group.

Max Gluckman, with reference to his studies of the Lozi and Zulu of South Africa, has suggested that sometimes, people are encouraged to do the opposite of what is culturally prescribed, and in doing so, the prescriptions actually are strengthened. He calls this 'rites of reversal' (Gluckman, 1955 : 109).

Socio-cultural anthropologists investigate ritual not only in religious sphere, but also in economic, political and other aspects of the society. This topic will be taken up at the end of this chapter.

THEORETICAL PERSPECTIVES ON RELIGION: SOME CLASSICAL APPROACHES

Anthropologists of late nineteenth century such as Tylor, Marett and Frazer were interested in propounding theories of origin of religion. They were intellectualists (see Chapter 3) and believed that beliefs in supernatural beings were products of reason (rationality).

One of the earliest and the best-known intellectualist was Sir Edward B. Tylor. His well-documented classic is *Primitive Culture* (1871) in which he looked for, among other aspects of culture, origins of religion. Tylor defined religion as *'a belief in supernatural beings'*. From this 'minimal definition of religion' he developed the main theory known as the *theory of animism*. According to Tylor, primitive human-beings must have tried to explain the differences between human beings before and after death. What happened to them during their sleep or when they were unconscious or in trance; they saw other persons in their dreams, they themselves appeared in dreams of other. He then concluded that it is obvious that man must have seen a person as possessing a life and a phantom, in addition to a body. Tylor went on, "These terms are evidently in close connection with body, the life as enabling it to feel and think and act, the phantom as being its image or second self; both, also, are perceived to be things separable from the body, the life as able to go away and leave it insensible or dead, the phantom as appearing to people at a distance from it" (Tylor, 1871 : 138).

Briefly stated, Tylor sets forth his views in this way, "man had a *phantom, a life, and a material body*. Life enabled the body to be a sentient being, and the phantom was the body's image (second self). Combination of life and phantom formed the concept of soul that could detach itself from the body and wander about appearing in dreams. Since the dead and the living beings appear in the dreams, it is believed that the soul continues to live after death".

In Great Britain, Tylor's successor Robert Marett (1866–1943) found elements of his predecessor's animistic theory well reasoned, but not necessarily reflecting the thought that early humans would have employed in trying to make sense of the most puzzling aspects of human experience. Searching for more generalised 'pre-animistic' notion, Marett (1909) came upon the *concept of mana*, widely found in cultures of the Pacific Islanders. Mana refers to an impersonal supernatural force that may be concentrated in persons or inanimate objects. It creates religious feelings of fear, wonder, respect, etc. in human beings and fertile domestic animals due to *mana*. It was Robert Henry Codrington (1830–1922) who, during 30 years of missionary service in Melanesia, wrote extensively on the Islanders beliefs system, locally called Mana. Later on, it was used by the Polynesians in its referenced form Codrington defined *mana* as a force, altogether distinct from physical power, which acts in all kinds of ways for good and evil and which is of the greatest advantage to posess and control..." (quoted by Piddington, *An Introduction to Social Anthropology*, Vol. 1, 1958). In Polynesia, where social standing determines the degree of *mana*, some persons, it is believed, are so highly charged as to be dangerous to the people of lower ranks, who, therefore, must be protected from overexposure by a variety of taboos. Marett claimed that the concept of *mana* is universal and thus, basic to his *theory of animatism*. It appears that primitive, in Marett sense, did not differentiate between 'natural' and 'supernatural'.

Another Englishman, Sir James George Frazer (1854–1914), endeavoured to show that any discussion of religious behaviour must include the consideration of magical activities and religion evolved from magic.

Frazer's *The Golden Bough* (1911–1915) is a masterpiece account of primitive people. Here, some passages will be noted from an abridged edition of this book (1922). He drew a distinction between different kinds of magic with respect to the principles on which magic is thought to operate. He concluded:

"Magic will probably be found to resolve themselves into two: first, that like produces like, or that an effect resembles its cause; and, second, that things which have once been in contact with each other continue to act on each other at a distance after the physical contact has been severed. The former principle may be called the *law of similarity,* the latter the *law of contact* or *contagious*" (Frazer 1922 : 11).

Law of similarity works in a type of magic what Frazer termed *imitative magic*. In this, attempts are "made by many peoples in many ages to injure or destroy an enemy by injuring or destroying an image of him, in the belief that just as the image suffers, so does the man, and that when it perishes, he must die," (Frazer 1922 : 12–13).

In another type of magic *contagious magic*, "the most familiar example is the magical sympathy which is supposed to exist between a man and any served portion of his person, as his hair or nails; so that whoever gets possession of human hair or nails may work his will, at any distances, upon the person from whom they were cut" (Frazer 1922 : 38). In the following chart the classification of magic has been shown:

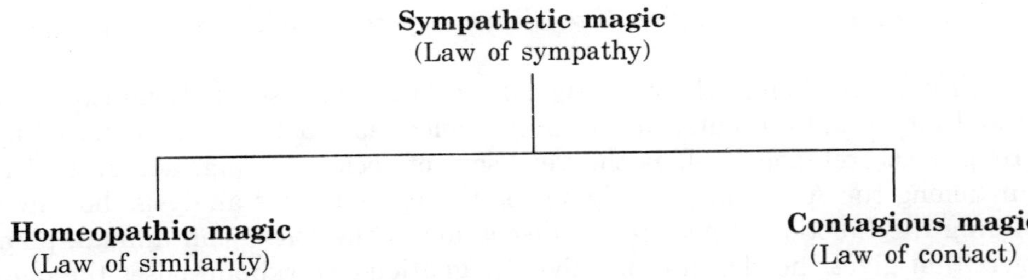

In brief, magic, in Frazer's views, refers to the techniques manipulated to achieve desired goals. It is this characteristic that magic differs from religion; magic is not a force as in *mana*. Frazer contrasted between magic and religion and viewed that magic preceded religion (to be described shortly). Anthropological studies have confirmed that both magic and religion occur side by side in many societies and complement each other; both magical and religious attitudes and practices share a common basis in dealing with the supernatural. In other words, they frequently overlap to a considerable extent.

Emile Durkheim (1858–1917) argued that magic is an individual offer, while religion is a collective enterprise involving collective feelings. Similarly, Malinowski claimed that magic is a mean to an end, while religion is an end in itself. Before we examine their views in some details, it seems worthwhile to see how Durkheim attempted to find the common dominator for all the religions. To quote a passage, "A religion is a unified system of beliefs and practices relative to sacred things, that is to say, things set apart and forbidden-beliefs and practices which unite into one single moral community called a Church, all those who adhere to them" (Durkheim, 1965 : 62; orig. 1912).

The first definition given above is very famous and has been cited repeatedly by a host of sociologists. For Durkheim, the crucial characteristic of the religion was that it was oriented towards a realm defined by human beings *as sacred*, that is, the object of special reverence, respect and even, awe. This realm stood in sharp contrast to the realm of the *profane* or the world of ordinary everyday existence.

Malinowski offered illuminating ideas on nature of magic and religion. For him, magic arises to fill a gap in empirical knowledge. It develops at the point where primitive technology no longer produces results and do specialists for very specific ends engaged in a practical art. Religion, on the other hand, has roots and purpose that are much more complex.

Malinowski denied that magic and religion grew out of speculation. He held that both arise from emotional needs and they are the ways of coping with situations that cannot be controlled.

Social Nature of Religious Behaviour

Common to all of the above-mentioned approaches has been their primary concern with the individual's relationship to the realm of the supernatural. There is, however, another important aspect to religion that must not be neglected—its social nature. The most influential proponent of this approach was Emile Durkheim, who argued that the root of religious behaviour lies in social experience. The main source for this idea is his classic study of primitive religion, *The Elementary Forms of the Religious Life* (1912, 1965).

According to Durkheim, whereas magical activities are essentially an expression of personal and individual pursuits, the tribal mythology is a belief system shared by the entire group. Also, religion itself is the very soul of society. Using, accounts of ritual behaviour among the Australian aborigines as the basis for his analysis, he saw their clan as filling the function of god. In his discussion of the *totem*—an animal, plant, or other object that gives the clan its collective designation—Durkheim poses the question of what the totem is a symbol or material expression of "in the first place, it is the outward and visible form of... the totemic principle or god. But, it is also the symbol of the... society called the clan. It is its flag... so if it is at once the symbol of the god and of the society, is that not because the god and the society are only one?" (Durkheim 1965 : 206).

The Australian natives, e.g. the Arunta and Aranda, move around their environment in small bands and join together periodically in large ceremonial gatherings. It is on such occasions that primitive men came to realise unconsciously that society is the sole of strength and survival; so they made its 'totem', the objects of their sacred symbols.

(Totemism will be discussed separately under 'religion and social organisation'). At this stage it would be worthwhile to recall Durkheim's notion of 'social fact' and method to understand social fact, that is the beliefs and corresponding rites (see Chapter 3).

While Durkheim's theory of social origin of religion has been subjected to have its criticism, his view of religion as a powerful symbolic system has been accepted by almost all of the anthropologists.

MAGIC, RELIGION AND SCIENCE

Earlier thinkers on primitive religion made distinction between magic and religion. Both Tylor and Frazer viewed that there is a difference between religion and magic; and that there is a significant relationship between magic and science. Malinowski too subscribed to this view in functional terms.

Evans-Pritchard explained Tylor's views in this way: "everywhere, there is magic and science and religion.... but in the latter stage of development or in the more advanced societies, magical and animistic ideas play a lesser part in the thought and behaviour of men than in the earlier stages of development or in the more primitive societies." (1933)

Paraphrasing Evans-Pritchard, the following chart makes the point clear:

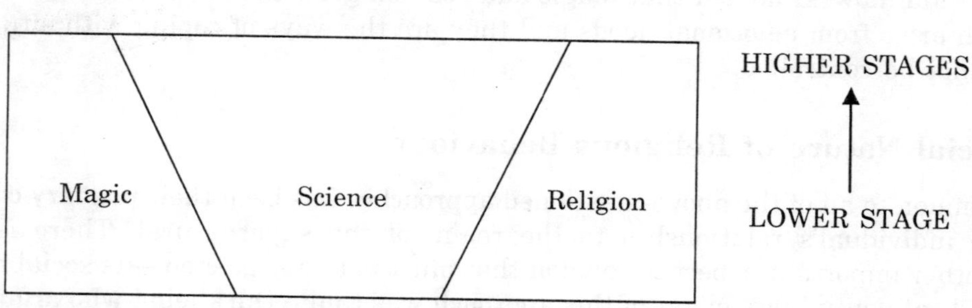

Tylor's conceptualisation of magic, science and religion.

According to Tylor, magic is associated with commonsense behaviour that magic itself does not achieve. Bohannan has interpreted Tylor's ideas to the theory of magic on two points—First of all, the ideology and logical quality of magic, though it may be on false premises; and second an analysis of the causes that prevented magic's exposure are fraud. These two ideas of Tylor are still current, precisely because they are capable of being significantly tested. Through the fieldwork, the logical processes involved in magical ideas and the ways in that the magicians defend their failures.

Frazer's views on magic have already been presented above. He asserts that magic is primitive man's attempt at science, but it is only a pseudoscience. He maintained that the logic of the magician was an erroneous application of the two laws of similarity and control. He argued that the primitive magician knows magic only in terms of its practical side; he never analyses the mental process on which his practice is based. To Frazer, magic is an art, never a science; the very idea of science is lacking in primitive mind. Frazer's ethnocentric ideas are quite apparent here—primitive people have underdeveloped minds because they use magic. As they begin to employ science there, magic and science are the polar opposites in the developmental scheme. Let us consider the following chart:

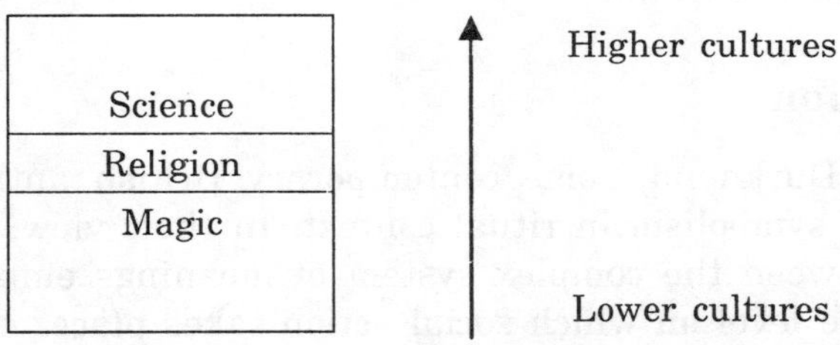

Frazer's view of magic, science, and religion

According to Bohannan, Frazer was wrong in comparing the science of one society with the magic of another; better to compare the empirical behaviour with the magical behaviour within a single society, or the magical behaviour in two (1963 : 320). Malinowski does so.

Malinowski's View

Frazer has been criticised for his unsupported arguments. When the tradition of fieldwork began with Malinowski, a new orientation followed. Malinowski felt that magic had been misunderstood. He demonstrated how Trobrianders use both magic and science, and therefore, we need to understand relationship between magic and science. His first hand experience with the Trobrianders shows that they possess a rich store of empirical and rational knowledge about the environment and how to adapt to it. They are fully skilled to ensure life from their environment. Yet, despite all these efforts, sometimes there is failure. Crops do fail, Kula exchanges become blocked, canoes are destroyed, etc. To control these mishappenings, they employ magic. Thus, to Malinowki, magic is purely a practical act, performed as a means to an end. Magic is regarded as indispensable to the success of garden economy and Kula. At every stage, the magicians must perform magic rites—use of words that invoke or command the desired end.

Malinowski tells us that the Trobrianders keep magic conceptually apart from empirical knowledge.

Levi-Strauss, in his *Savage Mind* (1966), revives the issue of 'primitive thought' and 'civilised' thought. He argues that for the both, the universe is an object of thought. Instead of contrasting magic and science, it is better, he held, to compare them as two parallel modes of acquiring knowledge. He rejected Frazer's notion of pseudoscience and Malinowski's spurious science. He said, "Our view is that the kind of logic in mythical thought is as rigorous as that of modern science, and that the difference lies, not in the quality of the intellectual process, but in the nature of the things to which it is applied." He uses examples from the field of technology.

Malinowski offered illuminating ideas on nature of magic and religion. For him, magic arises to fill a gap in empirical knowledge. It develops at the point where primitive technology no longer produces results, and is a practical art engaged by specialists for very specific ends. Religion, on the other hand, has roots and purpose that are much more complex. He denied that magic and religion grew out of speculation. He held that both arise from emotional needs, and they are the ways of coping with situations that cannot be controlled. He cites the Kula expedition of the Trobrianders to illustrate his views.

Symbolism in Religion

Directly influenced by Durkheim, some contemporary British anthropologists have focused on the study of symbolism in ritual context. In their view, ritual provides a symbolic connection between the complex system of meanings embedded in a given cultural thought and the level on which social action takes place. A good example of this approach is Victor Turner's account of curing among the Ndembu of northwestern Zambia. Disease among these people is seen as not merely afflicting the sick individual but as having a profound effect on the structural framework of their society. Nur Yalman (1967) and Geertz (1966) have also subscribed to this view. To quote a passage from latter's writings:

"For an anthropologist, the importance of religion lies in its capacity to serve, for an individual or for a group, as a source of general, yet distinctive conceptions of the world, the self, and the relations between them, on the one hand... and of rooted, no less distinctive "mental" dispositions... on the other. From these cultural functions flow, in turn, its social and psychological ones," (Geertz 1966 : 40).

Another American anthropologist Gregory Bateson (1904–1980) in his ethnographic account of a New Guinea tribe (*The Naven*, 1958), suggested two principles, viz. the principle of coherence to beliefs system, and the other, the principle of value system. Bateson termed them as 'Ethos' and 'Eidos', respectively (see Glossary, Appendix I).

OCCULT POWERS: WITCHCRAFT AND SORCERY

Many tribal societies of Africa, Melanesia, Asia, South and North America follow various magical practices under the category 'shamanic and communal cults' known as *witchcraft* and *sorcery*. Though their explanation varies remarkably, in common they are used to influence social relationship. A distinction is made between witchcraft and sorcery. The former refers to innate, psychic ability of some people to harm others; in the later, the performer manipulates objects to bring about harmful or beneficial effects. The classic examples of these practices on grand scale are furnished by Evans-Pritchard (1937), and Kluckhohn (1944).

Example of Azande

When Evans-Pritchard was conducting fieldwork during 1930's in Zire (southern Sudan, central Africa) Zande people numbered about half a million. They were shifting cultivators growing maize, sweet potatoes, and groundnuts. Fishing, small game hunting also contributed to their subsistence economy. Their social organisation was based on partilineal extended household consisting typically of a man, and occasionally a few close patrilineal relatives.

Zande, unlike many tribal communities of Africa and elsewhere, make a clear-cut distinction between two occult powers, that is witchcraft and sorcery. Sorcerors are the people who indulge magical spells, rites and medicines to achieve their felt ends. Their operands are tangible and are external to themselves. On the other hand, witches do not need these external aids; occult power is inherent in them. In other words, witches have innate psychic capacity to cause harm. Their tool is malicious thought itself. Among the Zande, this innate capacity has its seats in a distinct physical organ within the witch's stomach. (*mangu*, in essence intestine). 'Red eyes' individuals are witches, declare the Azande. The art of witchcraft passes from father to son/mother to daughter. Sorcery is considered as an upper class phenomenon, i.e. man of his social status. It is not employed between commoners. Witchcraft in contrast is thoroughly plebeian. Chiefs are neither accused of it nor attacked by it; witchcraft is never suspected between close kins. Here, we get an idea of mystical relationship between social organisation and rituals. Further, gender issues are unattached with witchcraft.

What we get from Evand-Pritchard's masterpiece account of Zande mystical action is not just about what people do, but why people are indulge in witchcraft and sorcery. "They explain different things; or different parts of the same thing... without creating deep conflicts in those who employ them with discrimination and precision. Witchcraft and sorcery is generally invoked to explain why misfortunes befall pontrader victims, where how they occur is explained in the matter-of-fact fashion we thing of as being empirically true. Zande are fully aware of the fact that certain things can never be blamed on or explained in terms of witchcraft. Lying is never due to witchcraft, nor can it excuse adultery. Witchcraft cannot be easily applied to violet or circumvent social norms. It works within the framework of Zande legal system." (1948, 101).

Why do many societies believe that there are 'ways' to invoke the spirits to work harm against the people is a problem still not fully explained. Cross-cultural analysis of this sort of beliefs and practices suggested that societies lacking formal mechanisms such as judiciary system to deal with enemies and other offences employ witchcraft and sorcery as a mean of social control (for details, see Whiting, 1950 and Chapter 8 of present book).

RELIGION IN COMPARATIVE PERSPECTIVE

How to compare religious practices across the societies has been a major concern of sociocultural anthropologists. Classical scholars presented varied categories of religion under the labels 'animistic', 'animatism', 'ancestor-worship', 'totemism,' and so on. Modern anthropologists have concluded on the basis of ethnographies that any category is overlapping with elements of other categories. Hence, neat categorisation cannot be made in explicit terms.

Types of Cult Institutions

The American anthropologist Anthony F.C. Wallace considers the religion of any society to be a conglomeration of *cult institutions*. A cult institution is 'a set of rituals all having the same general goal, all explicitly rationalized by a set of similar or related beliefs and all supported by the same social group' (1966 : 75). The four main types of cult institutions identified by Wallace are the following:

1. ***Individualistic cult institutions:*** These exist when there are no shamans, priests or other religious specialists available to perform rituals. Rather, each person acts as his or her own specialist, performing specific rituals as the need arises.

2. ***Shamanic cult institutions:*** In these institutions, there exists a part-time religious specialist are supposed to a shaman-deemed to have special religious qualifications and powers. Shamans are supposed to intervene with the supernatural powers on behalf of their clients. In contrast to individualistic cult institutions, shamanic cult institutions maintain a religious division of labour, in which there is a distinction between the religious specialists possessing special skills and the powers and laymen who lack such special attributes.

3. ***Communal cult institutions:*** These institutions are characterised by groups of laymen who "are responsible for calendrical or occasional performance of rituals of importance to various social groups ranging in scope from the members of special categories such as age grades, the sexes, members or secret societies, particular kinship groups, and sufferers from particular diseases to the whole community" (1966 : 86–87). Communal cult institutions include the agricultural rituals of the Iroquois, the ancestor ceremonies of the Chinese and some African tribes, and totemic and puberty rituals among the Australian aborigines. A specific type of religious specialisation characterises communal cult institutions, there is no full-time priesthood or extensive religious hierarchy.

4. ***Ecclesiastical cult institutions:*** These institutions are based upon the existence of professional priesthoods organised in bureaucratic fashion. Members of the priesthood are full-time religious specialists elected or appointed to permanent religious offices. A sharp demarcation exists between priests and religious laymen; the former monopolise religious knowledge and the direction of religious rituals, while latter are typically passive recipients of knowledge and ritual.

Types of Religions

Wallace identifies four evolutionary types of religion based on the combinations of cult institutions:

1. ***Shamanic religions***, which contain only individualistic and shamanic cult institutions;
2. ***Communal religions***, which contain communal, shamanic, and individualistic cult institutions;
3. ***Olympian religions***, which contain individualistic, shamanic, and communal cult institutions; as well as ecclesiastical cult institutions organized around polytheistic pantheons of high gods and;
4. ***Monotheistic religions***, which contain individualistic shamanic and communal cult institution along with ecclesiastical cult institutions organised around the concept of a single high god.

Wallace believes that shamanic religions prevail primarily among the hunting and gathering societies. The Eskimos have a shamanic religion. They populate the world with a variety of greater and lesser spirits, the most important of which is Sedana and Keeper of the Sea Animals. The most important activity performed by the shaman is his annual trip to the bottom of the sea, a trip in which he attempts to persuade the Sedna and Keeper of the Sea Animals to release the game they control in order that the Eskimos can live through another year. Eskimo shamans are also frequently called upon for the diagnosis of illness. The Eskimos also maintain two individualistic cults—the Spirit Helper Cult and the Game Animal Cult. Religious activity in these cults involves the individual enactment of certain ritual performance as well as the individual avoidance of certain taboos.

Communal religions are the most important characteristic of horticultural societies. Wallace indicates that such religions have been found among many of the North American Indian societies, among African societies (except Muslim North Africa and the centralised African kingdoms) and among a number of Melanesian and Polynesian people. The Trobriand Islanders of Melanesia are organised along the lines of a communal religion. The major cult institution is what Wallace terms the 'Technological Magic Cult'. In this cult, public magicians preside over communal rituals involving garden magic, canoe magic and fishing magic. These rituals are calendrical in nature, being tied to the cycle of the seasons. In addition to this communal cult, the Trobriand Islanders have another communal cult, shamanic services and engaged in a variety of individualistic religious practices.

In Wallace's views, the individualistic category refers to the rituals performed by the persons who are not religious specialists. Societies having simple habitat and economy usually reside in nuclear domestic group and display individualistic cult. An experienced elder member officiates ritual-performance. Band–level societies represent this category. Some of them like the Eskimo, however, have part-time religious specialists known as *shamans*. He is a religious specialist who has individual ability to communicate and deal with supernatural. Other terms used for this type of person are medicine-man/witch-doctor, healer, diviner, curer and so on.

The shaman or medicine–man may be viewed human being's first specialist, although not on a full-time basis. In a hunting band, he is a hunter like anyone else. In most of the hunting-gathering societies and among many simple agriculturists, there are religious practitioners of this sort. They are also found among the pastoral and horticulturalists. In stratified societies, they coexist with another type of religious specialist—the priest. The shaman is an intermediary between the members of his society and the supernatural world with which he supposedly communicates either by talking to the spirits and listen to their replies or through spirit possession. They are some times believed to learn about hidden matters and believed to influence the weather or to cause or stop the rainfall. By employing various techniques of *divination* (singing, dancing, eating, drum-beating etc.), shaman or medicine men cure diseases. Objects used in magic are called medicines; pre-literate societies often do not distinguish medicine from actual or modern medicinal value.

Role of Priest in Communal Religion

A *priest* is the full-time religious practitioner. Societies having stable subsistence system organised around corporate descent principle, develop leadership and decision- making patterns characterise what Wallace termed communal cult institution. Such cults are largely integrated with calendrical *(rites of intensification)* or life-cycle ritual *(rites of passage)*, lineage and clan on ancestor worship. The worship of lineage and clan ancestor is also known as totemism. Usually, the rituals of various sorts are performed at the level of entire tribe or its segments under a shaman. Depending on the nature of the rituals, the social position of shaman varies. While a detailed account of totemism will be taken up under relationship between religion and social organisation, here a brief note on 'rites of intensification' and rites of passage will be presented.

Rites of intensification

Intensification rituals are also known as calendrical or time-bound rites; they are associated with events that occur repeatedly (weekly, monthly, annually, etc.) in societies under study. Rites of intensification may occur at irregular intervals, i.e. they are performed whenever needed.

Rites of passage

These rites occur when an individual or a group of individuals move(s) from one social status to another. Naming ceremonies, baptism, initiation rites, birth, marriage and funeral are examples of such type of rites.

Olympian Religions

Olympian religions are most commonly found among intensive horticultural and early agrarian societies. Olympian religions have been found among the early civilisations of the New World such as the Mayas, Aztecs, and Incas; among many of the centralised chiefdoms or kingdoms of Africa; among East Asian societies on the edges of China and India such as the kingdoms of Burma, Indonesia and Korea and among the ancient Greeks and Romans. The African kingdom of Dahomey possesses an Olympian religion. In addition to individualistic, shamanic and communal cults, the Dahomeans have a Great Gods Cult. This cult has many of the features of an established church, as it actively supports and legitimises the Dahomean ruling class. This cult possesses a priesthood and many temples. The pantheon of gods is divided into four subpantheons, and each of them is associated with a separate religious order. Each religious order contains its own priesthood, temples and rituals. As typically the case in Olympian religions, each deity is associated with a particular aspect of nature over which it exercises control.

The great world religions such as Judaism, Christianity, Islam, and Hinduism are, of course, monotheistic religions. Such religions arose in the context of complex agrarian societies and have continued right into the modern industrial era. Although there are a number of fundamental differences among these great monotheistic religions, all of them share in common the conception of a single high god to whom great reverence and obedience is due.

Ecclesiastical Religion

Among the highly ranked societies, the ritual practices are more elaborate than those among the tribal groups; some are prescribed for the commoners, others are for the nobles or chiefs. In these societies, religious specialists enjoy a special status. In Wallace's scheme, this category is ecclesiastical religion.

Agricultural-state-literate civilisations developed in Asia, ancient Mesopotamia, Greece, Rome, Maya, Inca, Aztec in Meso America and South America are excellent examples of ecclesiastical religion. Usually in this type of religion, there is no separation between state and religious authority. In other words, social system, authority pattern and religion are closely interlinked. In such traditions a special person, i.e. a full-time religious specialist—the priest—supervises rituals of all sorts. They are either elected or appointed to the post by the chief. The post may or may not be hereditary. Written ritual texts are interpreted by them. In state-organised rituals, the duty of the priest was chanting hymns and prayers, addressing to gods and rulers, this authority is derived from the organisation of which he is a part. Among the Hindu society, the specialised persons of the Brahman *varna* perform these tasks.

Ecclesiastical and Universal Religion

Sometimes, a distinction is made between ecclesiastical and universalistic religions. As discussed earlier, the former is oriented towards the region (area) based politico-cultural heritage, while the latter is applicable to all the mankind.

"A universal religion", says Bohannan, "is one primarily independent of any specific social group. It is independent of specific mores... Universalistic religions have emerged only in a few places in the world; the rest are national or *tribal religion*" (1963 : 328). In tribal religion, participation in rites is limited to a specific social group.

RELIGION AND ECONOMY

Drawing insights from the Wallace's evolutionary scheme, the relationship between the religion and economy has been summarised in Table 9.1.

In a nut shell, there is an implicit evolutionary progression in Wallace's above scheme. In societies containing an ecclesiastical cult institution, there will also be communal, shamanic and individualistic institutions. Where there is no ecclesiastical institution but a communal one, there will be also shamanic and individualistic

Table 9.1 Religion and Economy

Type of religion (Wallace's scheme)	*Technological level of society*	*Examples*
Shamanic: only individualistic and shamanic cult institutions present.	Hunting and gathering	Eskimos, Kung, Mbuti of central Africa.
Communal: individualistic, shamanic, and communal cult institutions present.	Simple horticultural	Trobriand Islanders, many North American Indian Tribes.
Olympian: individualistic, shamanic, communal and polytheistic ecclesiatical cult institutions present.	Intensive Horticultural and early agrarian.	Mayas, Aztecs, Incas, acie-ent Greeks and Romans, A-frican kingdoms.
Monotheistic: individualistic, shamanic, Communal and monotheistic ecclesias-tical cult institutions present.	Complex agrarian and contemporary industrial.	Ancient China and India, medieval Europe, contemp-orary Japan.

varieties. Also where there is neither ecclesiastical nor communal institution, there will be shamanic and individualistic cults.

FUNCTIONS OF RELIGION

Following Durkheim, the functional anthropologist Bronislaw Malinowski and his students have concluded that religion is not what *religions are but what they do in society*. Raymond Firth had written religious system "as means for handling the fundamental problems of social organisation... for reducing uncertainty and anxiety, for increasing coherence in human relationships, for assigning meaning to human endeavour, for providing justification for moral obligations" (Firth, 1967 : 250).

Paraphrasing Firth, religions offer four functions—*explanatory, validating, reinforcing and integrative.*

Religion explains

Religion has explanatory functions. American anthropologist Spiro (1968) said that it can be shown that humans everywhere have a desire to know, to understand and to find meanings of any entity. Belief systems provide the members of society with meanings and explanations for otherwise meaningless and inexplicable phenomena. For example, the Azande described earlier have a satisfying explanation of why unfortunate and unusual events take place.

Religion plays a significant role in every activity of Azande life in agricultural, fishing and hunting pursuits; in domestic life of homesteads as well as in communal life of district and court. It is an important theme of mental life in which it forms the background of a vast panorama of oracles and magic. Its influence is plainly stamped on law and morals, etiquette and religion. It is prominent in technology and language and there is no niche of Azande culture into which it does not twist itself.

Religion validates

Religion has validating functions. Malinowski has shown how a myth functions to legitimise the social order of the Trobriand Islanders. With reference to the Trobriand origin, he wrote. "Members of a Trobriand subclan know, mark and recount the history of the 'hole' through which their ancestress (matrilineal descent) and her brother emerged from the underworld. In that underworld, in the days before life on the earth, men lived as they do now. The ancestral brother and sister brought up with them the sacred objects and knowledge, the skills and crafts, and the magic that distinguish the group from others" (Malinowski, 1948 : 132).

It is brother and sister who emerge, because they represent the two essential elements of the sub clan; a husband does not emerge because he is, in terms of the sub clan, an irrelevant outsider. The ancestral pair lives in separate domestic groups because the relationship of brother to sister is marked by sharp taboos. Thus, we can see how this myth validates, justifies and reinforces Trobriand social relations.

Religion is psychologically reinforcing

Kluckhohn (1944) was emphasising this very aspect of religion when he told us that its basic function is to provide people with a sense of security which derives from belonging to a group and sharing its beliefs, attitudes, values and sacred symbols.

Religion integrates

Both Durkheim and Radcliffe-Brown viewed religion and ritual as reinforcing collective sentiment and social integration. Rituals and beliefs are often elaborated around the focal points of individual and group experience such as birth, puberty, marriage, death succession to leadership, warfare, harvest, etc. Some of these are irregular as with death; other is cyclical and involves systematic preparations. System of beliefs and rituals not only integrates in a social sense but also functions to weave together, as Keesing (1970) has pointed out that many segments of the customs and beliefs of a people into an overall conceptual design. That is, religions can function to integrate in a social sense and also in a conceptual sense. Clifford Geertz (1968) formulates a definition of religion that integrates its functions in a broad framework. Religion bridges the gap between reality and the people's ideal view of what reality should be, so that both the nature of the universe and the emotions and motives of the people are confirmed and reinforced.

A cautionary note must be made regarding the above functions of religious beliefs and practices (see also, Fadwa Guindi: *Religion in Culture,* 1977). Any claim that religion has a function presupposes a number of assumptions. If we take a closer look at the Trobrianders' claim, we find that it presupposes that the natives' activities, behaviour and beliefs are dictated by decisions taken within a purely rational framework. It also assumes that the natives are mystified by certain phenomena that seem unexplainable and that they formulated theories (the theory of the soul) in order to explain such mysterious phenomena. Clearly, these are assumptions, and hence do not represent an objectively verified set of facts.

RELIGION AS ADAPTATION TO CULTURE AND ECOLOGY

In their tenth updated edition of *Anthropology* (2002), Ember and others have cited the example of Harris' study on India's sacred cows (already discussed in Chapter 3 under materialist approach to cultural evolution) as adaptation to ecosystem. What authors want to convey is that certain beliefs and practices are directly adaptive practices. The Hindu belief in the sacred cow has seemed to many to be very opposite of a useful (adaptive) custom. Their religion does not permit to slaughter cows. Why? Harris has suggested that it is because of "the cows do not themselves consume resources needed by the people and it would be impossible to provide traction, fuel, fertiliser as cheaply by other words, the taboo against not is very adaptive."

RELIGION AND POLITICAL ORGANISATION

The specific ways in which religion and politics are associated in various societies have been subject to commentary by social scientists. Many scholars have taken the view that religion has primarily served as a mean of legitimising and protecting the interests of the ruling class. It was James Frazer, who held that "religion and magic bolster the political organisation of a society". It may be recalled the way he equated a king with priest and sometimes, with deity so that political control was made easier. Both the king and the priest became the centre of rituals. Durkheim too believed that the social, political and kinship organisations of a society are reflected in its religion. In other words, in Durkheimian sense, all the institutions of a society are related to one another. In the preceding chapter, we have defined politics as a behavioural process of resolution of conflicts between the common goals and interests of the groups by use of power. Ritualistic activities in such societies become a source of maintenance of social order, values and normalcy. Social anthropologists such as Gluckman and Turner, in the context of African societies, have analysed these phenomena in depth. Kings, chiefs and village headmen, are the specific persons to handle matters related to decision-making. They perform ritualistic functions as well.

To understand the relations between rituals and the political system or authority pattern, the following passage of Fortes and Evans Pritchard's *The African Political System* (1940, Introduction) may be helpful:

"African rulers have mythical and rituals-warranty for their authority. In a stateless society, this warranty attaches to the inter-relations between the various segments of the society. As we have seen, these societies are not 'models' of continuous harmony. Acts of violence, oppression, revolt, civil war, etc. forth chequer the history of every African state'. The stateless societies are also full of strife. But once the society has achieved a degree of stability, these internal struggles do not necessarily wreck the social system. In practice, they themselves are protective devices against abuse, or they set processes in motion which deploy representatives or symbols of the widest common values of the society since people have to think and feel about it. The symbols, being themselves 'sacred', endow the social system with mystical values, which evoke acceptance of the social order on a plane that secular force and sanctions cannot attain. The social system is, 'as it were, removed to a mystical plane, where it figures as a system of sacred values beyond criticism or revision'. The bad kind or usurper is overthrown without the kingship being questioned. All of the individuals and sections accept these symbols as common values."

Many ritualistic observances such as rain making, sowing-harvesting crops are performed in the presence of these persons. In addition, there are a few religious specialists whose duty is associated with the office of the kings.

Richards (1940) has written about the Bemba of Zambia in details. How the *Bakabilo* (ritual functionaries) become important at the sacred shrines when the chief dies. He has privilege to light the sacred fire. Thus, among the Bemba, the hereditary Bakabilo form a council that exerts a check on the paramount chief's power. With some variations, the processes of checks and balances between ritual and political affairs are found in many parts of the tribal world. Reference to the Nuer 'Leopard-skin chief' (Elder) or 'priest of the earth' as reported by Evans-Pritchard has already been made earlier (see Chapter 8). In this stateless society, the ritualistic person becomes the intermediary between two fighting lineages. At least, he plays significant role in reducing the conflict if not reasoning forever.

In the tribal belts of Jharkhand (south Bihar) the coexistence of secular head (*Mahto*) and the ritualistic head (*Pahan*) among the Munda and the Oraons fits well supporting the intricate relationship between the religion and politics. (For detail, see Sachchidananda, 1968). It may also be noted that both the secular and sacred tasks may be assigned to the same individual; but by and large, they are assigned to different individuals.

RELATIONSHIP BETWEEN RELIGION AND SOCIAL ORGANISATION

Durkheim has a well-perceived link between society and ritual behaviour. In the primitive world, the institution of totemism may illustrate this link. *Totem* is a belief in a spiritual association between a clan/lineage/moiety and a bird, animal or a natural phenomenon. Twentieth Century ethnographers working in Australia and North America had explored the relationship between social organisation and religion. Goldenweiser (1910) among others was interested more in totemism. The anthropologists of modern time, both Radcliffe-Brown (1952) and Levi-Strauss, (1963) look at totemism as a recurring way of conceptualising relationships between kinship groups and of the natural world. For example, among the Crow Indian of North America, Crow and Eaglehawk moieties are conceived totemically not because members of the Crow moiety are like birds in any way but because the relationship between two moieties is conceived as like the relationship between two species of bird. A totemic system makes use of the natural differences among selected species (plant, animals) to reveal the relationship. A number of tribal groups of middle and south India believe that they are related to some plants and animals that are sacred to them. The Ho of Jharkhand Pradesh have clans (*killis*) and each killi bears a totemic object that is sacred to them. The Gond, the Munda and the Oraon also have totemic clans.

THE WORLD RELIGION

In the academic context, the expression 'world religion' differs from 'religions in the world'. The former expression includes world's major religions, viz. Christianity,

Hinduism, Islam, Buddhism, Confucianism, Taoism, Zoroastrianism and Judaism. A large number of world populations can be identified with these religions.

On the other hand, 'religions in the world' connotes 'ethnography of religions'. These can be grouped conveniently under typological headings arranged in a culture area framework. The types of religions considered here are *shamanic, communal* (totemic), *olympian* or *polytheistic–fetishistic* and *monotheistic*. We have already described some of these types in the previous section.

It would be interesting to pinpoint some of the remarkable elements of world religions. These points would help separate world religions from the *tribal (primitive) religion*.

All of the world religions have one or more sacred texts. Preaching and teaching of their founders/prophets/followers are reflected in these writings. All of the religions are complex.

All the major religions have become institutionalised. They have churches, temples or mosques. Here, devotees gather for worship or teaching. Most of the religions claim a real or stipulated founder a charismatic teacher, prophet or a teacher who is revered and sometimes, worshipped. In most of the world religions, these special persons such as priests, monks or ministers carry out prescribed functions and rituals. Some of them have developed elaborate institutionalised structures with hierarchies of functionaries.

The world religions differ from the tribal religions in the fact that there is, if not usually, the possibility that one may accept or reject membership in the group, though this may not be so in practice. Of all the world religions, many have crossed their original borders to become competing religions in other areas. Some of them make converts, and some of them are actively missionary. In British India, for example, Christianity was introduced in early 18th century, and thereafter, it flourished in south and northern regions.

All of the world religions had their origins in Asia. Southwest Asia was the birthplace of Zoroastrianism, Judaism, Christianity and Islam. India gave rise to Hinduism and Buddhism, while Confucianism and Taoism had their origins in China.

The world religions differ in the degree to which they demand the complete and exclusive loyalty of their adherents. Judaism, Christianity and Islam are exclusive in the sense that each requires for its followers absolute allegiance to the one God though differently interpreted in each case.

As compared to the above-mentioned religions, the religions having their origin in India or China are highly permissive. Hinduism has absorbed and incorporated many gods. Some of the Hindus see the millions of gods as separate deities; others look upon them as aspects of Brahmanism.

It is important to realise that none of these religions is a single entity. Several divisions exist in a particular religion. Christianity has its major divisions into Roman Catholicism, the Eastern orthodoxies, Anglicanism and Protestantism; Buddhism had its Hinayana and Mahayana divisions as well as Tibetan Lamaism, Muslims may be Shias or Sunnis, and Judaism has its orthodox, conservative and reform groups. Hinduism has many sects.

World religions did not originate as a completely new system. All of them developed out of some earlier form of beliefs and practices. Almost all of the magical practices found today among the tribal religions can be found, to some degree, among the less sophisticated peoples in the world religions.

World religions have taken different forms and have had varied emphasis in different periods of history. There is also difference in the ideal and the actual practices. The exalted teachings of the founder or prophets may be given lip service while practice fails far behind. The world religions are sometimes called the living religions. Perhaps, one of the reasons for their enduring quality is the fact that their teachings have lent themselves to adapt a man's changing life through the ages.

REVITALISATION MOVEMENTS: CHANGES IN INDIGENOUS RELIGIONS

We have already dwelt on the terminology 'revitalisation' (see Chapter 3). Some anthropologists have been concerned more with the phenomenon of vital changes in the native religions. This change usually, not necessarily always, occurs when natives come into contact with dominant cultures. Several terms are used by the ethnographers to denote this type of situation, viz. *nativistic movement*, *messianic movement*, *cargo cult*, *revivalism*, *millenarian cult*, etc. Anthony F.C. Wallance has proposed a term *revitalisation* to accommodate all these expressions. He defines it as a deliberate and organised movement by some of the members of a society to create a more satisfying culture. These movements give rise to extreme stress, social disruption and cultural disintegration. Such conditions may be caused by forced acculturation, natural disasters, or some other factors that create rapid change. It would be worthwhile to note here a couple of cases reported from the tribal world.

Cargo Cults and the Ghost Dance

Beginning around the end of the nineteenth century, many areas of Melanesia fell under European colonial domination, resulting in severe dislocations in the lives of native inhabitants of the region. Under these conditions, revitalisation movements known as *cargo cults* developed. The most persistent ideological element in these cults is the belief that shiploads of modern Western industrial goods (cargo) will be arriving at any moment for the complete use and enjoyment of the natives. These goods are being sent and accompanied by the natives' dead ancestors, who have come back to life. When the goods arrive, a new age of joy and prosperity will commence. In earlier times, the cargo was believed to be arriving by ship, and the natives occupied themselves building ports where the ships could dock. But with the arrival of the airplane, the cargo was said to be coming by plane, which prompted many cult members to build runways on which the planes could land. The cults have also perpetuated dectrines regarding the reorganisation of native society. Above all, the Europeans would be thrown out and native society returned to the control of the natives themselves.

Peter Worsley (1968) has described the nature of many of these cults. One such cult is the Vailala Madness, a movement that first developed in Papua New Guinea in 1919. This movement was led by a prophet named Evara, a man filled with divine revelations. He prophesied the arrival of a steamer that would be bringing cargo and the spirits of the dead ancestors. This cargo—flour, rice, tobacco, rifles and other items—was claimed rightfully to belong to the Papuans, not to the whites. In order to obtain the cargo for themselves, the Papuans had to drive the whites out. Many of the adherents to this cult referred to themselves as 'Jesus Christ men', and some claimed to have visions of God or Christ and to have received messages from them. The movement also embodied a belief in the ascent of the dead to Heaven as a central theme.

Revitalisation movement arose among a number of North American Indian tribes in the nineteenth century as a response to the encroachment of the whites and the destruction of traditional cultures. The most famous of them was the Ghost Dance, which appeared in two waves—the first in 1870 and the second in 1890 (Lanternari, 1983; cf. Thornton, 1981). The first wave of the Ghost Dance occurred among the Paviotsos—the Indians living between Nevada and California. A prophet named Wodziwob, who founded the movement after receiving a vision in 1869, led the Paviotsos. In his vision, Wodziwob saw a railroad train carrying the native Indians' ancestors. He held that these travellers were going to announce their return to Earth with a great explosion: "Wodziwob's revelation occurred at the top of a mountain: the Great Spirit announced that a major cataclysm would soon shake the entire world, in the course of which the white man would vanish from the Indian land. The earth would open up to swallow the whites, while all their buildings, goods and tools would remain for the use of the Indians" (Lanternari, 1963 : 132).

Wodziwob's revelations began to spread in two different directions, and soon they had reached to the tribes all over the western part of the United States. A Paiute Indian named Wovoka started the Ghost Dance in 1890. Wovoka preached a strict moral code to his people: They were not to fight, lie, steal or drink whisky, and they were to work hard and love one another. He prophesied that the whites would be blown away by high winds, but that all their possessions would be left to the Indians (Malefijt, 1968). Like the earlier version of the Ghost Dance, this one spread widely and rapidly to other tribes such as the Shoshoni, Arapaho, Cheyenne, Kiowa and Sioux.

Marvin Harris (1974) has provided a provocative analysis of Jewish military messianic as it existed around the time of Christ. In addition, he has attempted to demonstrate the way in which it gave birth to Christianity.

The ancient nation of Palestine had long been subject to colonial rule by a host of powerful empires. Under the Roman rule, which prevailed for many years both before and after the life of Jesus, most of the Jews who inhabited Palestine were subject to enormous oppression and exploitation. As Harris has pointed out, Palestine was a victim of extreme colonial misrule. The vast majority of the population consisted of landless peasants, poorly paid artisans, servants, and slaves. Apart from them, there were tiny elites of priests, landowners and merchants who lived in magnificent luxury. Peasants were subjected to especially heavy taxes and various forms of labour conscription by absentee landlords. Administrative corruption and inflation in the economy were rampant. The result of all this oppression and exploitation was an intense hatred on the part of the Galilean peasants for the Jerusalem aristocrats.

Jesus was one of many Jewish messiahs who arose in Palestine to fight against Roman oppression and exploitation. It is widely believed—indeed, it is a cardinal principle of Christianity—that Jesus's teachings were strictly of a peaceful nature, and he was opposed to violence and vengeance. Harris sharply disputes this image of Jesus as the

'Prince of Peace' and claims that Jesus' activities were actually highly consistent with the whole tradition of Jewish military messianism (Harris, 1974 : 187–188).

As indicated above, a revitalisation movement may be of a special category such as 'millenarian' or 'messainic' concerning around a cult of a saviour (*messiah*) who is believed to be presented or about to appear. Such movements have been common in the Judaic Christian tradition, but have also occurred in other parts of the tribal world. In this situation, messiah is not a God but as a reincarnation of tribal cults. Kopytoff (1964) has suggested that each revitalisation movement must be analysed in local situation, and no attempt should be made to generalise it. In this sense, it yields little theoretical understanding. Several examples from the tribal communities of India can be furnished here (Srivastava, 2010, see also Appendix-VI).

SUGGESTED READING

- Banton, Michael (Ed.), *Anthropological Approaches to the Study of Religion*, ASA monograph, Tavistock, London, 1966.
  This volume contains specialised essays by the noted anthropologists.
- Bateson, Gregory, *The Naven,* The Oxford University Press, London, 1958.
  A survey of the problems suggested by a composite picture of the culture of a New Guinea tribe drawn from their points of view.
- Durkheim, E., *Les Formes Elementaries la vie Religieuse*, Paris, Alean, 1912.
  Translated by J.W. Swain as the *Elementary Forms of the Religious Life,* Allen and Unwin, London, 1912.
- Evans-Pritchard, E.E.
  1. The Intellectualist Interpretation of Magic Cairo, Bulletin-1, Part 2.
  2. *Witchcraft, Oracles and Magic among the Azande*, Oxford University Press, Oxford, 1937.
  This is a classic account of magio-religious beliefs of an African society.
  3. *Theories of Primitive Religion*, Oxford University Press, London, 1965.
- Firth, R., *Elements of Social Organisation*, Oxford University Press, London, 1975 (First published in 1951).
  Chapter on 'Religion' for social functions of religion is worth reading.
- Frazer, James G., *The Golden Bough: A study of Magic and Religion*, Macmillan, London, 1922.
  Originally published in 12 volumes, now available in abridged form. One of the best known works in anthropology, full of examples and sources.
- Geertz, C., 'Religion: Anthropological Study', *International Encyclopedia of Social Sciences*, **13**, 398–406, 1968.
  A specialist on culture and religion presents a brief summary of anthropological interpretation of religion beliefs.
- Guindi, Fadwa El, *Religion in Culture*, Elements of Anthropology Series, W.C. Brown Company Publishers, Dubuque, Iowa, 1977.
- Harris, Marvin, *Cows, Pigs, Wars, and Witches: The Riddles of Culture*, Random House, New York, 1974.

Provocative discussions of Jewish military messianism, early Christianity and the great witch craze of early modern Europe.

- Kluckhohn Clyde, *Navajo Witchcraft*, Peabody Museum of American Archaelogy and Ethnology No. 22, 1944.
- Keesing, Roger M., *Cultural Anthropology*, New York, 1970.
- Lawson, E. Thomas and Robert N. McCauley, *Rethinking Religion*, Cambridge University Press, London, 1993.
  A very important book that marks a turning point in the way anthropologists thinks about religious ideas and practices.
  This is a comprehensive survey of all the major religions of the world.
- Lessa, William A. and Vogt, Evon Z. (Eds.), *Reader in Comparative Religion*. Harper and Row, New York, 1972.
  An excellent collection of articles on the anthropology of religion. Several experts in the area are represented in this volume. Pages 253–559 contain original articles on the subjects.
- Levi-Strauss, C., *Totemism*. Trans. R. Needham, Beacon Press, Boston.
- Lewis, I.M., *Ecstatic Religion*, An Anthropological Study of Spirit Possession and Shamanism, Penguin, Harmondswarth, 1971.
- Lowie, Robert H., *Primitive Religion*, Liveright, New York, 1942.
  Overview of several primitive religions followed by a critical appraisal.
- Malefijt, Anne Marie De Wall, *Religion and Culture: An Introduction to Anthropology of Religion*, New York, 1968.
- Malinowski, Bronislaw, *Magic, Science and Religion and Other Essays*, Free Press, Glencoe, 1948. First published in J. Needham (Ed.), *Science, Religion and Reality*, Macmillan, London.
  A collection of Malinowki's papers, including the famous article distinguishing magic, science and religion, myth in primitive society.
- Marett, R.R., *The Threshold of Religion*, London, 1909. In the Preface of the book, the author has dwelt on the terms 'pre-animism' and 'animatism'.
- Middelton, John (Ed.), *Gods and Rituals: Reading in Religious Beliefs and Practices*, National History Press, Garden City, New York, 1967.
- Nielson, N.C. and Others, *Religions of the World*, St. Martin Press, New York, 1983.
  This is almost like encyclopedia on religion. It introduces readers to the major living religions as well as to a number of significant faiths of the past. Chapter 1, *What is religion*? poses problems of cross-cultural definition of religion.
- Radcliffe-Brown, A.R., *Structure and Function in Primitive Society*, Oxford University Press, London (One of the articles is on relationship between Social organization and religion.)
- Radin, Paul, *Primitive Religion: Its Nature and Origin*, Doven Publications Inc., New York, 1957 (first published in 1937).

A classic treatment by a noted anthropologist. Several primitive societies such as Arunta, Bushman, Crow, Dakota and Aztec are dealt with. Radin discusses Winnebago Shaman in depth.

- Sachchidanand, *The Changing Munda,* Concept Publishers, New Delhi, 1968.
- Spiro, M., *Burmese Supernaturalism,* The Prentice-Hall Inc., New Jersey, 1968.
- Smart, Ninian, *The World Religion*, Cambridge University Press, London, 1992.
  This is a comprehensive survey of all the major religions of the world.
- Srivastava, A.R.N. *Tribal Freedom Fighters of India,* Publication Division, New Delhi, 2010.
- Turner, Victor
  1. *The Forest Symbols*: Studies in Ndembu Rituals, Ithaca, New York, 1967.
  2. *Drama, Fields, and Metaphors*, Symbolic Action in Human Society, Ithaca, New York, 1974.
- Tylor, Edward B., *Primitive Culture*, Researches into the Development of Mythology, Philosophy, Religion, Language, Art and Customs, Murray, London, 1871.
  Includes an early anthropological view of religion and Tylor's analysis of animism as the most basic form of religious belief.
- Wallace, Anthony, F.C., *Religion: An Anthropological View*, Random House, New York, 1966.
  One of many modern-day texts dealing with the anthropological approaches to the study of religion.
- Whiting, B., *Paiute Sorcery,* Viking Fund Publications in Anthropology, New York, 1968.
- Worsley, Peter, *The Trumpet Shall Sound: A Study of Cargo Cults in Melanesia,* 2nd ed., Schochen Books, New York, 1968.

Chapter 10

Language and Culture

"Brain size and prewiring for language were coterminous with the humanity of man. Language led to the formation of human group. Language is not only a component of culture, but also is the vehicle of culture." Therefore, the study of language in cultural anthropology and linguistics goes hand in hand. It has now become an established core branch of anthropology (Pattanayak, 1994).

ANTHROPOLOGICAL LINGUISTICS

Anthropological Linguistics or Linguistic anthropology is one of the four core branches of anthropology. As anthropology is the study of man and his biological and cultural achievements, and language is considered as the functioning aspect of culture; its importance was realised from the very beginning by the first generation of professional anthropologists. Anthropological linguistics is divided into two subdivisions *Descriptive Linguistics* and *Historical Linguistics*. The former, also called *Structural Linguistics*, focuses on recording, transcribing and analysing the structure of languages distributed across the world. Historical or comparative phylology deals with comparison of texts and determination of dates. Comparative reconstruction recreates an earlier stage of the language on the basis of cognates. Researches have shown that reconstruction of modern spoken European language does not lead to Latin. Researches have also indicated that reconstruction on the basis of modern spoken Indo-Aryan languages does not lead to Sanskrit. At the first instance, it leads to a spoken sister language of Latin, while in the other to a spoken sister language of Sanskrit.

Historical linguistics is concerned with evolution of language and language groups through time and space. Its field is wide, for it reconstructs extinct proto–languages from which historically known languages differentiated.

Anthropological Linguists during the past several decades have been researching on native languages in their efforts to relate them with ethnographies. During this process, they have developed rigorous techniques and theoretical insights. Some of them are discussed under *metalinguistics.* These insights may be viewed as *linguistic models* for understanding culture in more than one ways.

What is Language?

Of all the animal species, humankind has developed the most precious communication system—language. Anthropologists think of language in terms of thirteen design features proposed by a British linguist, Charles Hockett (1958). In Hockett's terms, language is characterised as follows:

1. ***Vocal-auditory channel:*** Language is produced through the nose and mouth and is received through ears.
2. ***Broadcast transmission and directional fading:*** A speaker can be heard in all the directions. A listener can hear a speaker no matter which direction the signal is coming from.
3. ***Rapid fading:*** As soon as they are spoken, words dissipate and subsequently cannot be retrieved.
4. ***Interchangeability:*** All the speakers of a language can both utter and understand the same words.
5. ***Total feedback:*** A speaker hears everything she or he says, can monitor it and can correct or account for mistakes.
6. ***Specialisation:*** Speech serves no other purpose than to communicate; as a specialised system, it can be used even when the speaker and the listener are engaged in other activities.
7. ***Semanticity:*** There are systematic connections between the spoken words and their standard accepted meanings.
8. ***Arbitrariness:*** The connections between the words and their meanings are a matter of convention; hence it is possible both to create new words and to change the meaning of the old words.
9. ***Discreteness:*** Human beings can produce enormous range of sounds, but each language makes use of a very small subset of these sounds.
10. ***Displacement:*** Human beings can use language to communicate about the things and events that are far removed from the immediate context in which they are interacting. Time, distance or both may separate these distant events.
11. ***Productivity:*** People regularly utter sentences that have never been said before in exactly the same manner, and they can talk about the things that have never been observed.
12. ***Traditional transmission:*** It appears that human beings are genetically predisposed to learn a language (or even more than one). However, the specific language that an individual eventually speaks is acquired solely through learning in a social context and it is not inherited genetically.
13. ***Duality of patterning:*** Language is patterned on at least two separate levels—phonemes, the sounds a language recognises as significant but which by themselves have no meanings; and morphemes, the invisible unit of meaning of a language. The word dog, for instance, consists of three phonemes (/d/ /o/ /g) and one morpheme (/dog/).

DESCRIPTIVE LINGUISTICS

Descriptive linguistics is synchronic comparison of languages/statements in a time-scale that yields diachronic linguistics. Descriptive studies primarily started with recording non-literate languages.

Invariably, people studied by anthropologists lack writing. That is, they are *pre-literate*, but this does not mean that their languages cannot be grasped. Anthropologists by means of scientific study of language learn others' languages. They do it by analysing three basic elements of a language, viz. *sound, meaning* and *structure*. Analysis of these elements is the purview of descriptive linguistics.

Phonology, Phonemes, Phonemics, Phonetics, Morphemes

The study of the sound used in speech is called *phonology*. In a situation in which one is unable to understand what was being said, the first thing the person does is try to recognise the sound of the speakers.

Phonetics is the study of sound in general—what people actually say in various languages. *Phoneme* is significant sound contrasts in a given language. *Phonemes* lack meaning themselves, but they are the smallest sound contrasts that distinguish meaning, for example *pit/bit*. These two English words are distinguished by a single sound contrast between / p / and (b). Thus, by comparing words that resemble each other in all but one sound is called *minimal pair*. Take another example of different vowel sound of *bit* and *beat.* Although it is difficult to get contrast, but two phonemes / i / and / t / in English are uttered differently. Tongue high (spread) leads to / i / as in / beat /, lower high front tongue is used for / t / as in bit. (Practice it, you will feel!).

Thus, important or critical sounds of a language are called phonemes. The study of phonemes also includes elements such as stress of accent. For example, the difference between *present* (a verb) and *present* (a noun or adjective) is of *pitch* and *tone*.

In brief, every language has its own characteristics sounds, and these sounds as distinguished from one another is known as phoneme. For example, in English *a, t* and *s* are phonemes.

After identifying phonemes, the next step is to put these sounds together into a meaningful unit. A unit of meaning is called *morpheme* that includes one or more phonemes. In English, there are 30 to 45 phonemes depending on scholars. *Morpheme* is a meaningful unit of sounds in a particular language. They may be words, or parts of a word, e.g. *and, it, ed, es*. Morphemes should not be thought of in terms of what written words represent. There are morphemes in languages for which there is no writing. Some morphemes have several forms both written and spoken.

Grammar and Syntax

How morphemes are put together to form words and meaningful sentences? The term grammar simply refers to the rules relating to speech with meanings. In other words, grammar is rules governing construction of morphemes. It consists of unconscious rules for speaking and writing a given language. Every language has syntactic rules that govern how words are put together. Thus, the linguists insist that the phonemics and morphological arrangements of a language can be understood adequately only within the context of syntax interpreting the meaning of words. Rules for speaking in ways that are appropriate in a particular context is also a part of grammar. Similar unconscious rules govern the combination of morphemes into sentences. This branch of grammar is called *syntax.*

TRANSFORMATIONAL GRAMMAR

The above fact led the American linguist, Noam Chomsky to develop a new explanation called *Generative of transformational grammar* (1968). In Chomsky's views, a language is more than just sounds, words and word order. These are the surface features discovered through analysis of a language; there are deep features as well. He views language as a uniquely human possession. A normal child growing up in a society develops language easily and automatically. It occurs because the human brain contains a genetically transmitted blue print (a basic plan) for building languages. He calls this plan *universal grammar*. Chomsky reasoned that the arrangement of the components of sentences is governed by basic rules intuitively known to the speakers of a language in early stages of life. He held that there must be a set of underlying linguistic rules that permit a person to generate his language. Chomsky recognised difference between two levels of language and called them as *surface* and *deep* structures. The former is the overt aspect of linguistic behaviour. Deep structure represents the psychological level underlying this linguistic behaviour. It contains the basic units that the speaker of a language unconsciously selects to convey his message before he encodes them into physical noises of speech. The process of moving from those underlying rules (which Chomsky called deep structure) is termed a *transformation*.

Some anthropologists have begun to think that the capacity to generate linguistic utterances according to a set of rules is an inborn trait of all the human beings. Researches on higher non-human primates indicate that these characteristics are *species* specific. Building larger units using smaller units, known as duality of patterning, separates human communication from animal communication.

Transformational Grammar

Difference between phonetic (d) and (th)	
Spanish	English
(d) as in dia (day)	(d) as in dia
(th) as in nada (nothing)	(th) as in they

Both differentiate between two sounds.

English and Spanish languages are similar in surface structure. But, an examination at deep structure reveals that the two languages are not at all similar.

The difference between (d) and (th) are phonemic in English but nonphonemic in Spanish. The difference between (d) and (th) is relevant not only at surface level but also in the deep structure.

The conclusion we draw from the above discussion is: surface structures are often misleading, for they may show very similar patterns in cases where the deep structures are radically different.

This means, in Chomski sense, that children start learning their native language not from the scratch but because they have already an outline in-built in their brain. Children experiment with different parts of the blue print. In doing so, they discover that their language uses some of the sections but not the others. They reject principles used in other languages and accept only the ones in their own language.

Briefly stated Chowsky's major innovation was to conceive language akin to a mental organ.

Comparative or Historical Linguistics

Another important branch of linguistic anthropology is comparative linguistics. It is the comparison of languages with one another in terms of their phonetic, phonemic, morphological and syntactical characteristics. This enables linguists to classify languages into families according to their varying degrees of similarity. It is assumed that those languages, which are similar enough to one another to be put in the same family, have a common origin. About nine language families are spoken by close to ninety percent of the world population. One of these is Dravidian and includes Tamil, Malayalam, Telugu and Kannada—all languages of India. Another is Indo-European, which includes Hindi, Sanskrit, Greek and Slavic including Russian, French, German, English and a number of others. One sub-branch of Indo–European language is Indo-Aryan. Some of the areas of these places are linguistically more variable than others. (see chart : Indo-European language stock on the next page).

Method of Comparison and Reconstruction

Some of the scholars have tried to determine whether or not vocabulary and grammatical changes occur at constant rates, hoping that they will be able to determine how long ago similar languages splitted off from one another. *Lexico-statistics* (also known as glotto-chronology) is such a method derived from the pioneering works of Morris Swadesh. This is the study of history of written languages and their comparisons based on the number of similar keywords. Not all the scholars accept glottochronology as a valid technique, but it continues to be used. Using this method, some of the American scholors, e.g. Beals and Hoijer have found that the Navaho Indian language of the southwestern U.S. got separated from the Kutchin language of Alaska about 850 years ago.

Another development in historical linguistics is comparative reconstruction. Comparative study of Indian languages dates back to Sir George Grierson who conducted language survey of India in the late 19th century. Suniti Kumar Chatterjee's *Origin and Development of Bengali Language* (ODBL) is held as a watermark in comparative linguistics. However, these persons compared languages but did not attempt to reconstruct them. In India, the first theoretical methodological breakthrough is represented by a controlled historical reconstruction of Oriya, Assamese, Bengali and Hindi by Debi Prasanna Pattanayak. Comparative reconstruction of Roman languages

Indo-European Language Stock

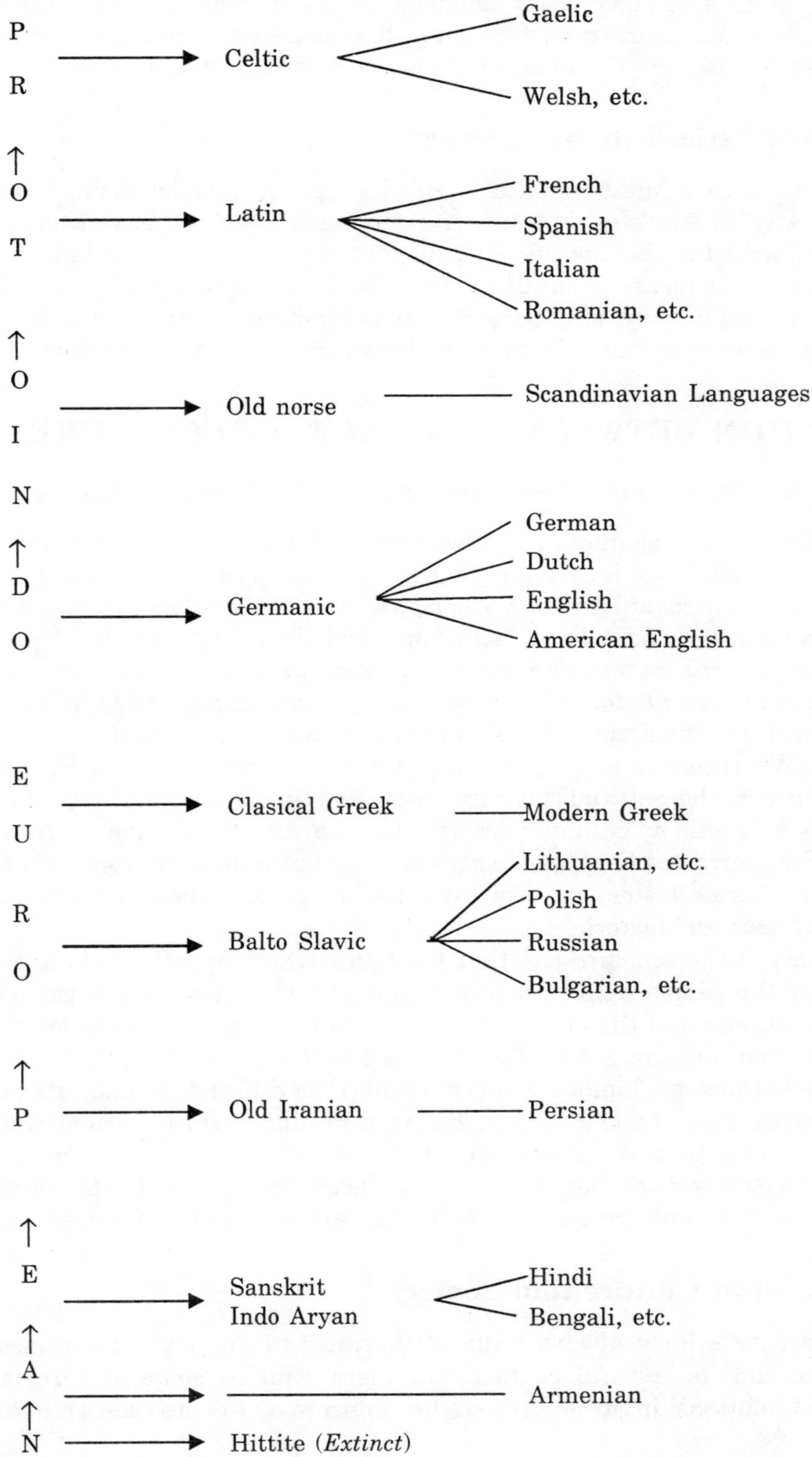

established that the modern European languages, when reconstructed, do not go back to Latin, but to a speaker sister language of Latin. Similarly the modern Indo–Aryan languages, when reconstructed, do not go back to Sanskrit, but to a speaker sister variety of Sanskrit. (*Source :* Personal communication with Prof. D.P. Pattanayak, 2003).

Metalinguistics/Ethnolinguistics

This sub-branch of Anthropological linguistics explores the relationship between a language and the way the speakers view their total environments. Another version of metalinguistics is Ethnolinguistics that specifically explores the linkages between linguistic customs and nonlinguistic elements of culture. Some of the anthropologists have preferred to call it 'Language and Culture' or a 'Language and Cognition.' Briefly stated, both language and cognition is an aspect of culture. Some knowledge on this branch is required here.

RELATION BETWEEN LANGUAGE AND CULTURE

Sapir-Whorf Hypothesis: Language and Thought Habits

Edward Sapir (a student of Franz Boas) developed the idea that in real serise "language and our thoughts are inextricably interwoven, are ore and the same" (1921: 232) He, along with his student Benjamin Whorf, were the first scholars to focus on the relationship between language and culture. Both Sapir and Whorf together developed the idea that *language structures our perceptions of environment, and the speakers of different languages will react to the same environmental stimulus differently*. Whorf cites examples from ore of the American Indians' language–Shawnce in support of views. Based on this method, Whorf compared the Hopi language with 'standard average European' languages with respect to their attitudes towards space and time. He claimed that the Hopi language contains no words or grammar forms that refer directly to time, or to past, present or future. He contrasted European usages and suggested that they concern with time, clocks, calendars, diaries, history, etc. Chinese verbs lack distinctions of tense, but they were great record keepers and historians.

Some of the scholars feel that the Sapir-Whorf hypothesis is untenable because there are the people with unrelated languages who share otherwise similar cultures, (e.g. the Munda and the Oraon of Chotanagpur, India. Also there are the people such as the Oraon and the Sauria Pahariya of the Rajmahal Hills, south Bihar, who have essentially the same language, but are otherwise different in habitats and cultures. In record years time, scholars of the Behavioural and cognitive sciences have taken the issues related to S.W. hypothesis, for a detail investigation. However, cognitive anthopologists for more than three decades have been interested in the problem of the way in which a given culture percives its world. (see Appendix-I, Ethnoscience).

Language in Culture and Society

Anthropologists have always realised the importance of the relationship between a language and its cultural context, but there remains some disagreement as to the degree of relationship. Recent researches indicate a growing concern in anthropological linguistics to relate the phenomena of elements of language to specific aspects of a culture. Dell Hymes (1962) calls for *Ethnography of Speaking.* Similarly, Ward Goodenough (1970) and others are for *Componential analysis* while Marvin Harris (1968) has developed *Etic Emic approach* in analysis of cultural data.

Within the field of linguistic anthropology, the above approaches are basically methods of investigation of how people categorise their experience through the language they speak and also how should anthropologists explain the cultural phenomena in order to arrive at some generalisation. In recent decades, *Cognitive anthropology* has emerged as a sub-branch accommodating these developments (see Chapter 3).

Relationship between Linguistic Anthropology and Cultural Anthropology

1. Language is a powerful mechanism of communication. In any society, members react constantly with set of vocabularies, and all of the vocabularies are expressed through their customs and institutions. Therefore, understanding of institutions require perfect knowledge of language.
2. People learn most of the elements of culture primarily through their native languages. To a large extent, language determines how people will think and act. Arbitrary classification inherent in each language may influence habits of perception and of reasoning. (This is also known as Whorf-hypothesis).
3. Linguists have been able to analyse the basic units/elements of a spoken language. They have been able to generate objectively verifiable elements within particular societies. Cultural anthropologists have realised that comparable units might be identified for other aspects of culture. In other words, following analogy of structural linguistics, cultural anthropologists can prepare 'grammar' of religion, kinship, politics, music, etc.
4. Both language and culture do change. Historical linguistic helps cultural anthropologists to extrapolate the past and reconstruct the stages of development of culture.

Primitive societies lack written evidence of history. Linguistic evidences alone can add a great deal of information through the study of comparative linguistics.

To conclude, the aim of Anthropological linguistics (or Linguistic anthropology) is to account for what people know about their language-usage. From the viewpoint of formal structure, emphasis is on the native speaker's knowledge of what constitutes a grammatical sentence. From the viewpoint of semantics, emphasis is on his knowledge of what makes senses, and finally, from the viewpoint of sociolinguistics, the emphasis is on the speaker's knowledge as to the appropriateness of a given dialect, style, etc. under social conditions.

SUGGESTED READING

- Bloomfield, L. and H. Hoijer (Eds.), *Language History,* Macmillan, London, 1965. It covers the basic principles by which historical derivation of languages is worked out.

- Burling, R., *Man's Many Voices: Language in its Cultural Context*, Harper, New York, 1970.
  This book deals with effects of the cultural setting on the whole process of communication. The emphasis is the nonlinguistic factors which affect the use of language; linguistics with a strong cultural anthropological slant.
- Chatterjee, S.K., *Origin and Development of Bengali Language*, Calcutta, new edition, 1980.
- Chomsky, N., *Language and Mind*, Mass., Harvard University Press, New York, 1968.
  The book is written by the formulator of modern transformational methods.
- Fried, Morton H. (Ed.), *Explorations in Anthropology*, Alfred Knof, New York, 1973.
  'Part 5' has three articles on aspects of Linguistics by Chomsky, Labov and Gumperz dealing with property of language, and language and communication.
- Goodenough, Ward H., 'Componential Analysis", *Description and Comparison in Cultural Anthropology*, Aldine, Chicago, 1968.
- Greenberg, J.H., *Anthropological Linguistics: An Introduction,* Cambridge, London, 1968.
  This is a basic book for Linguistic Anthropology.
- Gleason, H.A., *An Introduction to Descriptive Linguistics,* Cambridge, London, 1961.
  A well-balanced and not-too-difficult textbook.
- Hammel, E.A., *Formal Sematic Analysis*, American Anthropological Association Papers, Washington, D.C., 1965.
- Harris, Marvin, *An Introduction to General Anthropology*, (*Culture, People and Nature*, 3rd ed.,) Harper and Row, New York, 1980.
  Chapter 23(437–454) introduces the subject matter related to culture and language systematically.
- Hickerson, Nancy P., *Linguistic Anthropology*, Holt, Rinehart and Winston, New York, 1980.
  This is a brief introductory survey of the subject.
- Hockett, C.F., *A Course in Modern Linguistics*, London, 1958.
  This is a clear introduction to the subject.
- Hymes, Dell H. (Ed.), *Language in Culture and Society*: A Reader in Linguistics and Anthropology, Harper and Row, New York, 1964.
  A thorough collection of articles on many different areas of anthropological linguistics, designed for the advanced students.
- Hymes, Dell H., *Foundation is Sociolinguistics*: *An Ethnographic Approach*, University Press, Pennsylvania, 1974.
- Lehmann, W.P., *Historical Linguistics: An Introduction*, Holt, Rinehart and Winston, New York, 1962.

- Pattanayak, D.P., *A Controlled Historical Reconstruction of Oriya, Assamase, Bangali and Hindi*, Mouton The Hague., 1980; Communication with the author in 1994.
  The book covers the techniques of reconstruction of the genetic relationship of languages. See especially, 83–114.
- Philip, Lieberman, *On the Origins of Language*: An Introduction to the Evolution of Language, Harper, New York, 1975.
  The author discusses various theories of the evolution of language, including the question of when speech became possible.
- Romney, A.K. and R.G. Andrade (Eds.), *Transcultural Studies in Cognition*, American Anthropological Association Publications, 1964. Among the papers particularly important are W.C. Sturvent's 'Ethnoscience' and Dell Hymes "Ethnolinguistics".
- Sapir, E., *Language*, Harcourt, New York, 1921. see also *Sound Patterns in Language,* In D.G. Mondelbaum (Ed.), Selected writings of Edward Sapir, University of California Press, pp. 33–45.
- Tyler, S.A. (Ed.), *Cognitive Anthropology,* Harper and Row, New York, 1969.

  Essays on method and results in the study of how different people define and classify the world, experience and ideas. See Introduction, 1–21.
- Whorf, B.L., Linguistics as an Exact Science, 220–32. See also Whorf's another volume, *The Relation of Habitual Thought and Behaviour to Language*, University Press of California, Berkeley, 134–159, 1956.

Chapter 11

Anthropological Perspective on Art

"In one-way or another esthetic pleasure is felt by all members of mankind." (Franz Boas, 1929 : 9).

The Anthropological study of art, sometimes called 'primitive art,' focuses on the contextual setting in which art is produced and used. Anthropologists study art not as a critic, but as an ethnographer and try to find out the meaning behind it.

Franz Boas' *Primitive Art* (1927) was the first comprehensive work in the field of the art of pre-literate societies. The persons who systematised study of primitive art are Herskovits, Dundes, Lomax, Otten, and Anderson.

WHAT IS PRIMITIVE ART?

Primitive art refers to the art of the people of pre-literate societies. They are also referred to tribal, exotic, traditional, simple and small-scale societies. "In the widest sense... art is to be thought of *as any embellishment of ordinary living that is achieved with competence and has described form . . .*" (Herskovits, 1955 : 235, emphasis added).

"Regardless of differences in wording, certain basic elements are stated or implied in most of the definitions of art—there is a creator(s), a process, a medium, a product presented for public (sometimes limited) view, a content and meaning, and a response on the part of the beholder (s)" (Hoebel, 1970 : 32).

In this, at several places, we have emphasised on the fact that the subjects of the socio-cultural anthropology are 'non-western' tribal societies. Whenever the tribal-art is present, it is an integral part of their social, economic, political and religious life. However, most of the societies may not have a proper word for it.

Raymond Firth, in his introductory text book on social anthropology writes: "... the primitive artist is first and foremost a craftsmen, from whom arts flows as an extension of his craft ability. By this is meant that he is essentially a constructor of things for use, which are also regarded as giving enjoyment. He does not make things simply for the aesthetic satisfaction to be got out of looking at them. Even songs are not composed simply to be listened to for pleasure, they have work to do..." (1956 : 171).

The message Professor Firth wants to convey is that primitive art is not for art's sake alone but it has *utilitarian value*. Earlier anthropologists described the various forms of art in descriptive and narrative styles; contemporary anthropologists try to identify the historical relationships between and among the societies, and try to understand development of their taxonomies.

THE FIELD OF PRIMITIVE ART

Nelson Graburn (1975) an American anthropologist has summarised the scope or field of primitive art as follow:

Primitive art covers the range of activities found in western art; it includes sculpture, painting, basketry, weaving, clothing, masks, body decoration, architecture song, dance, instrumental music and poetry. Inspite of these parallels, primitive arts are characterised by some unique factors, though it is difficult to generalize them. In most of the cases, non-specialists and part-time artists produce arts for their friends and neighbours. Primitive arts follow local traditions and are not set apart from life. In this sense, they are static or even consciously changing. They are embedded more in the fabric of society than the 'art for art's sake' characteristic of the highly specialised civilisations of the eastern and western worlds.

In the absence of literacy, these arts bear religious and spiritual messages and are major forms of communication promoting conformity, identity and solidarity. Often, the arts themselves are thought to have magical and protective powers. In tribal societies, the artist is an ordinary or respected person, rather than a marginal person. Whether a specialist or a part-time artist, he or she is a key person in the non-formal education and religious and social life of the people.

Under conditions of acculturation and change, primitive art may still be produced for sale to outsiders for whom it is fashionable or decorative to collect. It may, thus, become simplified and repetitive, as with the souvenir arts or individualised and fast changing.

Ethnomusicology: Music, Dance and Drama

Herskovits has put music, dance and drama as the least tangible aspect of primitive art under *folklore,* which will be discussed shortly. Despite the universal importance of music as an aspect of culture, a channel for aesthetic creativity, a mean of communication, a mechanism for the achievement of emotional release and a source of pleasure for both the performer and the listener, its study has recently been neglected badly by most of the anthropologists. In recent decades, a new subfield within cultural anthropology, appropriately called *Ethnomusicology* has come up. The unit of analysis of music begins with the instruments through which it (music) is produced in scaling, rhythm, melody, vocal technique, song-style, harmony and polyphony.

Music functions in many ways—social, economic, political and religious. The ceremonial aspects of culture are intimately related to music. Anthropologists as participant observers of a culture understand the importance of music well (see Herskovits, 1955 : 282–286).

Dance

Dance is associated with other aspects of culture as closely as music. Often, it plays important roles at every stage of rite-de-passage. Peter Hammond writes: "For children, dance may be an important part of play. At adolescence, it provides a means of sexual display, stimulation or sublimation. Marriage ceremonies often involve dancing. Many people dance to celebrate events like a successful harvest, a victory in battle, the initiation of boys and girls at puberty or the accession to power of a new political or religious leader. Men also dance during periods of crisis and anxiety, to cue sickness, to drive out evil spirits and to placate angry gods. Frequently, dancing is a part of the death ritual" (1973 : 326). Lomax in his survey study found that song styles tend to vary with the socioeconomic variables of the societies, especially level of subsistance activity (1968; iv).

Drama

Among the art forms, drama is neglected the most by the anthropologists. The reason behind this, perhaps, is that in so many societies, it is not separated from ritual observances. Herskovits' dramatic experience among the primitive people is an example of this sort. He writes:

"The drama in non-literate societies affirms some of the deepest sanctions of living. The myths declaimed and acted, the choreography of the dances, the rhythm of drums, the verses sung call forth responses from participants and onlookers that bear profoundly on the value system of the individuals who compose the group and on their adjustment within this system. They give assurance that rains will come, that crops will be abundant, that calamity will not befall, that the group will continue. Participation in dramatic presentations may range from complete participation to performances by trained specialists.

"There is one features that forms of dramatic expression have in common whether simple or complex, performed by specialists or the group as a whole, manifested in the open-air performances of non-literate folk or in the modern theatre. All performances have structure; all manifest the unities that distinguish any artistic production. There is a beginning and an end; there is sequence in time and in incident. There is a sense of progression of climax—whether the tradition of the group orders heightening or diminishing of effect, or conceives it in a more flexible mold." (Herskovits, 1955 : 276–276).

Music

The comparative study of the music of the tribal people leads us to some of the most fundamental truths about the nature and functioning of culture. The great number of musical instruments that have been devised by non-literate people can be classified into the categories with which we are familiar—string, wing and percussion—of which the first two have the most restricted distribution and the fewest types, while the last has the greatest number of different forms and the widest spread. Music, like language, has basic structural forms that are revealed only after their manifestations in the everyday life of the people. These forms are objectively investigated. On analysis, however, they go far in disclosing the cultural factors, in both pattern and process, from which they take on their ascribed form and meaning (Herskovits, 1955).

Hammond wrote: "The role of music as an integral aspect of nearly all other cultural institutions, from work and play to politics and warfare, religion and death rituals, is clearly evident. How to go beyond assertions that its presence indicates its importance? Our data is still crude. For instance, it is still not certain how far our understanding of the emotional functions of music can be extended beyond trite allusions to the varieties of 'pleasure' it provides."

We need to know more about who the musicians in a society are, and about the relationship of music to the social structure. For example, is musicianship reserved for the elite? Or is it a role set aside only for low-status persons or even more specifically, for people with certain kinds of infirmities? In parts of West Africa, for example, blind children are frequently taught to sing and to accompany themselves on the gourd fiddle in order to earn their living as entertainers. How are the musicians trained and treated in other societies? Where do they 'fit' in their culture? Further in what way can study of the people's music assist in understanding other aspects of their ways of life, their perception of reality and of the problems of human existence (1971 : 325)?

Alan Lomax, in his famous project wanted to establish that to what extent "song style symbolizes and reinforces certain important aspects of social structure in all cultures" (1968, Preface).

Folklore

It is worth noting that the word 'folklore' was first employed in a letter signed by Ambrose Merton, published in *The Athenaeum* of London, August 22, 1846. Its writer, who used this pseudonym for his real name, William J. Thom, urged that accounts of the "the manners, customs, observances, superstitions, ballads, proverbs, etc. of the olden time" be recorded so that later students could turn for information to these dying remnants of the unrecorded past that were termed 'popular antiquities, or popular literature' (Quoted in Herskovits, 1955 : 275).

One of the authorities on folklore oral literature is Alan Dundes (1989). To him, folklore is a broad category comprising all the myths, legends, folktales, riddles, proverbs and superstitions of a cultural group. In general, folklore is transmitted across generation orally through the process of enculturation.

In Dunde's view, oral literature is closely related to 'folklore'. Folklore includes both verbal and non-verbal forms. Oral literature, however, usually includes verbal folklore only and does not include games and dances. Different cultures have different categories of folk literature.

Folklore including oral literature is universal (written literature is not a universal). Dundes is of the opinion that contemporary study of oral literature tends to see folklore as a reflection of present culture rather than the past. His original motivation for collecting oral literature was partly a desire to return to the past (cf. Boas' view on reconstructing past).

Among the earliest anthropologists, it was Herskovits who systematised folklore studies in anthropology. He suggested five themes occurring in the myths and folktales of all the societies—catastrophe, slaying of monsters, incest, sibling rivalry and castration (for details, see Herskovits: 1955),

Primitive Art in Cross Cultural Studies

Some of the anthropologists have used data related to art to address questions of cross-cultural variation or universal. Thus, artistic style, which is the recurrence of clusters of formal features in art, was used along with other cultural traits as evidence of general hypotheses concerning evolution and diffusion in the 19th and 20th century anthropological theory. Boas introduced an early concern with the psychic and symbolic aspects or art styles, while Kroeber attempted to relate the historical development of artistic style to the development of civilisations. The cross-cultural approach to art attempts to establish broad correlations between art styles or forms and social or socio-psychological factors. Thus, Fischer argues, using statistical evidence, that egalitarian societies are characterised by graphic designs that repeat simple elements, while hierarchical societies produce designs integrating a number of dissimilar elements. Such analysis rests on the notion of a modal personality shared by all of the members of society and assumes the artist's conformity to social norms (cf. Culture and personality studies, Chapter 3). It has been criticised on the grounds that both values and artistic styles vary within a single socio-cultural context.

The views of Levi-Strauss have been influential in the anthropology of art. Following him, some structuralists like Leach have analysed mythologies and have shown how the underlying principles of artistic production reflect the structural patterns underlying the functioning of society. It has been suggested that in Walbiri (an American-Indian group) graphic art, the design patterning parallel the ordering principles, which govern the totemic system and other cosmological theories. Graphic designs, thus, become visual models for abstract principles of social and cosmological ordering. How styles of folk song and dance are related to social structure is well documented by Lomax (1968).

Primitive Art in Modern World

Art is always changing; however, in some parts of Africa, Polynesia and Southeastern islanders, the traditional elements are being preserved. Under the pressure of acculturation and globalisation, primitive art may still be produced, but largely for commercial purposes. Some countries including the United States and India, have opened a national forum to popularise tribal arts and crafts; the principal motive may appear to earn foreign currencies. In India, TRIFED (Tribal Cooperative Marketing Development Federation of India) is in operation since 1987. At many tourist centres, shops like 'TRIBE WINDOW ' have come up. India's cultural traditions are radiating through this forum.

SUGGESTED READING

- Anderson, R.L., *Calliope's Sisters: A Comparative Study of Art*, Prentice-Hall, New Jersey, 1990.
  This is a comparative study of ten diverse societies in order to discover similarties and differences in their arts.

- Boas, Franz (1955): *Primitive Art*, Dover, New York, 1927.
  One of the early anthropologists initiated studies of primitive art in modern American anthropology.
- Dundes, Alan, *The Study of Folklore,* Oxford University Press, Oxford, 1965.
- Hammond, Peter, *Social Cultural Anthropology*, Macmillan, New York, 1971.
- Herskovits, M.J., *Cultural Anthropology*, New York, 1955.
- Firth, Raymond, *Elements of Social Organisation*, Oxford University Press, London, 1956.
- Graburn, Nelson, Primitive Art, *Encyclopaedia of Anthropology*, Mouthon, 23–24, 45–46. 1975
- Hoebel, E.A., *Anthropology: The Study of Man*, McGraw-Hill Books, New York, 1970.
- Lomax, A. and others, *Folksong style and Culture*, American Association for the Advancement of Science, Washington, D.C., 1968.
  This is an excellent volume containing views of authors cross-culturally.
- Otten, C.M., *Anthropology and Art*, Reading in Cross-cultural Aesthetics, Harper, New York, 1971. It contains 24 articles on theory and method in studying primitive art.

Chapter 12

New Subfields of Anthropology

Anthropologists' efforts towards combining anthropology with other disciplines, viz. sociology, economics, psychology, geography, law, medicine etc. have stimulated the rise of some new subfields within cultural anthropology. We have already seen such development in subfields of Economic and Political anthropology (see Chapters 7 and 8). In this chapter, we will focus on the researches in some specified areas, viz. ecology, urban, and audio-visual and medicine.

The Panel on Anthropology, constituted by the University Grants Commission, New Delhi (*Anthropology Curriculum*), remarked:

"... Anthropology is being rediscovered in the area of health, rural and tribal development and voluntary activities. Medical anthropology is one of the fastest growing branch of anthropology, over being ecological, educational, communication, forensic, nutrition and visual anthropology..." (UGC, 2001 : 7). Keeping in view the spirits of the expert-members, we propose here to present the ideal structures of the course on a few selected areas within sociocultural anthropology, viz. **urban anthropology, ecological anthropology, visual anthropology** and **medical anthropology.**

URBAN ANTHROPOLOGY

Urban anthropology is relatively a new field within the general field of cultural anthropology, which developed as a consequence of the rapid worldwide transformation of rural population including so called tribal and peasants into urban, town or city dwellers. This sub-discipline involves the interaction between anthropology and other disciplines, more importantly sociology and geography. Of course, the urban anthropologists have retained their own discipline's flavour holistic as well as field-based comparative approaches.

Although all researches done in city are not urban anthropology, certainly the emphasis of the urban anthropologists is to view the 'city' as one of the focal points. In this sense, a city may be accepted as an 'institution' like any other institution, i.e. kinship, economic, political and religion.

It was Robert Redfield of Chicago University whose efforts (under the influence of Ecological approach led by Robert Park, Earnest Burgess and Roderick McKenzie), can be regarded as that of the first socio-cultural anthropologist to delve into urban anthropology. During the period 1920–1940, Redfield thought of a new perspective to the study of urbanism. In *Folk-Culture of Yucatan* (1941), he offered a comparative analysis of four communities of central Mexico, in which he introduced the notion that has come to be known as the *folk-urban continuum*. This was designed not only as a descriptive concept contrasting cities with rural communities, but also as an indicator of cultural changes as rural communities came into contact with urban influence at varying degrees.

The descriptive and analytic literature in this field remains sparse. Gans' work on the Italian enclave and Elliott Liebow's study of single Black males in a Washington neighbourhood in 1967 are, perhaps, the best descriptive works in recent years of aspects of urban life drawn in anthropological perspective. Through his studies in Black family life, Liebow became acquainted with a group of men who 'hung out' on a street corner, and this acquaintance led to friendship and intimate knowledge of their lives. *Tally's Corner* is an attempt to present the view from the street corner to illuminate the forces that defeat men in an urban *ghetto*.

One of the most popular concepts (still being popularised by contemporary urban researchers) to emerge from the work in urban anthropology has been that of the *culture of poverty*, which was introduced by Oscar Lewis in course of his field investigation among Latin Americans. The culture of poverty is thought of a 'sub-culture' located in urban slums; yet all slum dwellers are not part of the sub-culture. Today, many large metropolitan cities of this sub-culture can be traced out. There are numerous studies relating this sub-culture to the large national culture (see Chapter 2).

Among the contemporary British social anthropologists, J. Clyde Mitchell (1960) appears to be the first who had investigated the process of urbanisation in Africa. The works of A.L. Epstein (1958), Barnes (1954), Bott (1971) and Whyte (1955) are landmarks in urban anthropology.

While our aim is not to review the works of urban anthropologists completed so far, we may note the trends enumerating the following topics of interest in the field:

1. Social groups/communities of recently immigrated country folk,
2. The on-going rural-urban links or networks of interaction,
3. Voluntary associations and other institutions with a recent immigrants into cities developed to help them cope with the problems of city life in general, problems of slum culture, in particular.
4. Cultural change and survival of traditional themes in urban contexts and
5. Cross-cultural studies of cities in order to develop an applicable theory of urban life and development.

Note: See also entries in Appendix I and II (Folk-urban continuum, Culture of poverty, Redfield).

Industrial Anthropology

The classic studies made at the Hawthorne Plant of Western Electric under the aegis of Elton Mayo are the early examples of research done in industrial institutions. The essence of this work was to demonstrate that the status system and the structuring of social relationships were essential ingredients in work satisfactions and factory output. This initial source was the starting point for a body of literature analysing various work situations and institutions, including the motion picture industry and the restaurant industry. Charles Harding (1961) has summarised the anthropological study of industrial enterprises, pointing out that the factory or an entire industry is a social system, that it operates on the assumption of communication among its component elements, that it involves not only the formal system but also the informal, and that the latter is a major consideration in the daily operations of the work routine. Marvin Harris (1987), using Emic-etic approach has studied social stratification in modern American society.

ECOLOGICAL ANTHROPOLOGY

The Background

Descriptive ethnographic data under the caption of 'cultural anthropology, ecology and environment' do not necessarily mean that the respective ethnographers have followed the theoretical notions of ecology rigidly. Scholarly writings on the themes of ecology and anthropology make it clear that the interests of cultural anthropologists are extremely varied.

Cultural Environment Frame of Reference

The terms 'environment' and 'ecology' are widely prevalent in anthropology. Many anthropologists have used them interchangeably. These two terms do not always carry the same meaning though some common elements are present in both. The term 'environment' refers to something that surrounds—it is the complex of climatic, edaphic and biotic factors that act upon an organism. The term 'ecology' in broader sense refers to 'the totality of relations' between environment and organism. The line of demarcation may be hard to lay down between the two, but it is apparent that behavioural aspect may be absent with the use of environment while ecology does include behavioural pattern of the organism. The former is more popular among the behavioural scientists while the latter is among the biologists. With this general background, we may now note the two current frames of reference, viz. 'cultural environment' and 'ecological' as prevalent in cultural anthropology today.

Determinism and Possibilism

Two main views of relating cultural behaviour to environmental phenomena are *determinism* and *possibilism*. The former, also called *environmentalism*, states that environmental forms dictate cultural ones; therefore, cultural phenomena can very adequately be explained with reference to their environment. In other words, cultural practices are made intelligible only by environment. Those who held that environment has a limiting rather than determining effect on cultural behaviour have denied this. Its adherents are also known as 'possibilists', because in their views, environment permits alternatives; and there is no guarantee that any particular possibility will be the one to materialise. Marvin Harris has nicely presented these two views in his book *The Rise of Anthropological Theory* (Harris, 1968).

Culture Area Approach: A Compromise Way

To demonstrate the interplay of specific cultural variables and environmental factors, the 'culture-area' approach, conceived fully first by Clark Wissler (1917–1926) and in modified form by Kroeber (1923–1939) and other, may be accepted as a compromise between determinism and possibilism. But, one has to be careful in evaluating this approach as its methodological schemes differ markedly. Thus, early works of Mason (1896), Huntington (1915) lacked methodological rigour; while the schemes of Wissler and Kroeber entailed scientific insights. In a map of North America prepared by the Ecological Society of America, Wissler had presented distribution of cultural traits parallel to the distributions of floral and climatic factors and had tried to establish correlations between them. His observation was: "We find such a consistent relation between generalised culture areas on the one hand, environmental areas on the other, it may be that the form of the distribution (of cultural trait) is, in some way, based upon ecological relations" (Wissler, 1926 : 214).

This does not, however, mean that Wissler blindly supported the correspondence between the distributions of human traits and environmental traits, rather it was a limited accomplishment. He declared that it might be an 'essential step' towards the discovery of the mechanism whereby one class of traits affected the other (1926 : 212).

As was indicated earlier, Kroeber rejected environment determinism. He emphasized on the 'historical or cultural influence' as determinants of cultural phenomena (Kroeber, 1923 : 185). Later on, he presented detailed treatment of both natural and cultural areas of North America. His assessment was: "the immediate causes of cultural phenomena are other cultural phenomena" (Kroeber, 1939 : 1).

Contributions of Daryll Forde

We will now briefly discuss the contributions of Forde, a British anthropologist whose widely read book (1934) included descriptions on economics and habitats of several known societies across the world. He found no simple correlations or generalisations existing between environment and society. He criticised the doctrines of both geographical and economic determinism, and added "Indeed, the economy may owe as much to the social and ritual pattern as does the character of society to the economy" (Forde, 1934:465). He also emphasised the role of diffusion operating in the areas of cultural and social forms.

Emergence of Cultural Ecology

Interests in environment and culture continued and remained a major trend in American cultural anthropology during 1940–1960. Julian Steward rigorously developed the concept of cultural ecology in several of his articles beginning 1938, till the publication of *Theory of Culture Change* in 1955. This book remained as a prescribed major textbook in anthropology for several years. It would not be out of place to highlight major points of cultural ecology.

Julian Steward was interested not only in establishing 'environmental-cultural relationships', but also in developing a theoretical-methodological scheme for understanding development of human societies. According to him, cultural ecology differs from neo-evolutionist conception of cultural history in the sense that "it introduced the local environment as the *extra* cultural factor in the fruitless assumption that culture comes from culture" (Steward 1955; 36, see Kroeber's above–quoted passage). He is mainly concerned with the ways in which particular environmental features interact with specific features of culture (society), and in the patterns of activity adopted by social groups to exploit a particular ecological niche. Here the crucial term is 'ecological niche', which (borrowed from biological sciences) is taken to mean that the total environment can be divided into a number of areas within which different groups live. One may study the inter-relationship between a social group occupying one niche (habitat) and those occupying other niches.

Thus, although several social groups may live and subsist in the same geographical area, in fact, they occupy quite different niches and have very different subsistence patterns. Two groups may depend on each other for exchange of subsistence goods. In other words, they may develop a symbiosis relation. Steward, in his analysis of cultural ecology, has carefully demonstrated why a specific group adopts to a specific ecological niche.

The following are the three basic procedures of analysis of culture ecology:

1. Analysis of the interaction between the environment and technology that a group uses. Same environmental features may be more crucial than other in influencing technology (culture). To Steward, the simpler societies are more directly affected by the environment than the complex ones.
2. Analysis of the patterns of activity required by the exploitative technology used in a given area. Does the technology require cooperation? Therefore, to Steward, the important point is 'adaptive strategy of the group in a given environment' (1955 : 41).
3. Other aspects of the culture affect description of how the behaviour involved in exploiting the environment. The organisation, density, material cultures are some of the areas of social (cultural) life that may be involved.

In brief, cultural ecology, based on the principle of ecological properties (which will be described shortly) is how a wide variety of factors work in their specific culture without regard to their origins.

With the publication of the *Theory of Culture Change*, cultural anthropology and archaeology received a new dimension of study known as 'culture ecology'. Soon, culture ecology became an important frame reference for ethnographic studies, and for the archaeologistic fieldwork base. Replications and verifications of Steward's culture ecology and its refinement began to appear in many professional Journals, and books, viz. Eggan (1954), Sahlins (1964), Damas (1963), Nicholas (1962), Netting (1965), Rappaport (1967) and Geertz (1963).

Emergence of Ecological Anthropology

The expression 'Ecological anthropology' was used for the first time in definitive terms by Rappaport in 1963 when he presented a paper on the concept and methods in ecological anthropology in a symposium organised by David Damas. Further, Rappaport used it freely in a textbook on General anthropology (see Harry Shapiro 1971). Beneath the term Ecological anthropology, runs an idea that anthropological data can be subjected to methods and theory generated by the science of ecology. There are vast potentialities of certain concepts prevalent in science of Ecology for understanding human societies in a better way. Crucial concepts are ecosystem and ecological population.

Ecosystem is used for both biome and habitat. Biome refers to the whole complex of organism—animals and plants naturally living together as a coherent unit. The interacting factors in an ecosystem are organic, inorganic, biome and habitats. To describe an ecosystem, one has to consider spatial relations, inventories of its physical features, its habitats and ecological niches, its organisms, inputs and patterns of matter and energy. The principal characteristics of an ecosystem are the following (i) The following environment, man and the plant and animal worlds within a single framework, within which the interaction between the components can be analysed. (ii) Ecosystems are structured in a more or less orderly, rational and comprehensible way. (iii) Ecosystem functions. (iv) They involve continuous through-input of matter and energy. (v) Ecosystems are a type of general system.

In general terms, the ecosystem is an open system tending towards a steady state and obeying the open-system thermodynamics (for detail see Stoddart, 1973).

Ecological Population

In biological sense, a population implies a taxonomic position but in ecological sense, a population—human or otherwise—refers to an aggregate of organisms sharing distinctive means for maintaining common trophic (material) relations in the ecosystem in which they participate together. In case of human beings, ecological population consists of all the representative human groups to be found in a particular ecosystem.

Thus, pastoral and hunters may be in a similar geographical area; ecologically, they have two distinct populations. Below is depicted ecosystem of the Oceanic gardeners and fishing communities.

Empirical Test of Ecosystem

Above-mentioned properties of an ecosystem are well understood in simpler system, i.e. in plant island world. When situation comes to the world of human beings, its application becomes more complex. During the past three decades, numerous American cultural anthropologists paid more attention to understand primitive (small scale, simple) societies drawing principles of ecosystem as discussed above. To serious ecological anthropologists, it is possible to delineate ecosystem with as much precision as in the non-human population.

One of the earliest studies following ecosystem approach was that of Geertz (1963). He discusses how in rural Indonesia, the system of shifting cultivation and wet rice cultivation is operated. He viewed the characteristics inherent in shifting cultivation, in relation to the tropical forest it replaces. In this system of cultivation, burning is seen as a mean of channelling the nutrients locked up in the vegetation into certain selected crop plants; the general efficiency of the land is lowered, but the yield to man is increased. By contrast, the ecosystem structure is different in wet rice cultivation. The yield is high, and the system equilibrium is more stable. Although Geertz's analysis is in qualitative terms, it opens avenues to search for quantitative analysis. It must, however, be noted that both Geertz and Steward were greatly influenced by the notions of ecology discussed earlier.

Rappaport's (1971 : 251–261) analysis of role of the pigs in New Guinea subsistence in an example of ecosystem studies in explicit terms. With ecological perspective, socio-cultural anthropological researches, to an extent, have taken a new dimension.

Ecological analysis is not as just simple as the analysis of functional treatment of data by cultural anthropologists. For example, socio-cultural anthropologists try to understand the economic organisation in terms of environment, material culture, food producing techniques, kin groups, settlement patterns, land-tenure and so on. The focus of ecological anthropologists is rather narrowly confined. They require types of evidence different from those required by cultural anthropologists. Thus, to understand effective factors in the physical environment, an accurate knowledge of rainfall, types of soil temperatures, plant varieties, types of animal may be necessary. Some data must be long-term in order to be meaningful. Both longer period of participant observation and detailed notes on the topic under investigation are necessary for ecological interpretation of cultural data. Some of the convincing studies done in this direction are by Lee (1969), Netting (1969) Pospisil (1963) and Rappaport (1967–1971) among others.

VISUAL ANTHROPOLOGY

Visual anthropology is a newly developed sub-branch in cultural anthropology. It deals with the study of human behaviour through visual means incorporating the theories and technologies as developed in the anthropological traditions. It analyses the behaviour of the people, natives and their different modes of communication.

An International Journal *Visual Anthropology* defines the field of visual anthropology as "the analysis of the structuring of reality as evidenced by visual productions and artefacts; the cross-cultural study of art and artefacts from a social, cultural, historical and aesthetic points of view; the relationship of cultural and visual perceptions and the study of the forms of social organisation surrounding the planning, production and use of visual symbolic forms" (*Visual Anthropology*: Harwood Academic Publishers, New York, 1989). In addition, Visual Anthropology has the functions of 'preservation' and 'communication', which it fulfills through the use of films, videotapes and televisions.

Scientific research needs unbiased and reliable data. Film, sound and videotape records are today an indispensable scientific resources since they provide reliable data on human behaviour that may later be analysed by independent investigators in the light of new theories. They may also be found to contain data that may then give rise to new theories, or they may be used to corroborate already established theories. The advantage that films and videotape records enjoy over other tools of data collection is that they are independent of language, i.e. their communicative ability is independent of language and any one can understand them, at least to some extent. Films also help us in preserving the changing ways of life in action.

In an edited volume on Visual anthropology, Margaret Mead, says in her introductory notes, "anthropology as a conglomerate of disciplines has both implicitly and explicitly accepted the responsibility of making and preserving records of the vanishing customs and human beings of this earth". "Coupled with their ethnographies, the two can be incorporated under the wider scope of urgent anthropology." (1975 : 2).

Aims and Scope of Visual Anthropology

The aims of visual anthropology can be briefly enumerated as follows:

(i) to record data for future analysis,

(ii) to improve our descriptive ethnography increasing the quality of basisc observation,

(iii) to provide information for related cultural studies and to verify theories,

(iv) to provide an account ethnographer,

(v) and to put together a film that will convey to the audience a 'feel' of the people.

One of the major thrust areas of Visual anthropology is Ethnographic film, which may be defined as 'a film that reveals cultural patterning'. Walter Goldschmidt defines an ethnographic film as "a film that endeavours to interpret the behaviour of the people of one culture to the persons of another culture by using shots of people doing precisely what they have been doing if the camera were not there".

Visual anthropology classifies films into documentary, ethnographic and educational. Marcel Griaule is of the opinion that documentaries are intended for a relatively large and uninformed public, and ethnographic films are intended for educational use particularly in cultural anthropology. The latter must present cultural phenomena and human behaviour as accurately as possible and is less conditioned by aesthetic formal concerns.

Anthropologists always emphasise on the fieldwork through the use of 'participant-observation' while studying other cultures. This participation between the researcher and the subjects being studied should be reciprocal. According to Rouch, the way to achieve this reciprocity is through the use of ethnographic film, since it represents the easiest route to establish a dialogue between the anthropologists and his subjects. The dialogue's most decisive moment comes with the presentation of the complete film to the subjects filmed, that is with what Rouch defines as an audiovisual counter gift.

With the entry of Mead and Bateson in 1936–1938, the field of Visual anthropology, ethnographic filming underwent a profound change. There was a shift towards conceptual originality. Anthropological teaching has started taking greater support from films. The museums and universities are now supporting it. With the introduction of culture and personality studies in socio-cultural anthropology, Mead and Bateson made the most effective use of films for analysis of cultural behaviour. Collier is of the opinion that the works of Mead and Bateson depended not only on the viewing of the film footage, but also on detailed examination and comparison of enlarged prints of single frames. It is to be noted that Collier wrote the first Standard text book (Visual Anthropology) in 1967.

Visual anthropology makes an explicit distinction between the difference in approach regarding the preparation of ethnographic film and a documentary film.

How ethnographic films can contribute in understanding a culture or cultures of a region can best be understood by distinguishing between the various uses to which films can be put in the field of social research, education and visual anthropology.

Brigrad (1975) notes, "unlike the specialised uses of film in research where conclusions are expressed verbally, and unlike the use of film in education where effectiveness is dependent upon context, the use of ethnographic film as public information depends upon the presence, in self-contained form, of visual attractiveness and intellectual substance".

Film has played only a minor part in anthropological research. This is, in part, due to the fact that film is harder to harness as data than still pictures. But, it is also due to the temptation, or even the pressure, to make films in the field of anthropology for reasons other than research. Great 'documentary' films have been made in the field of anthropology by art filmmakers, and by expert anthropologists. These films have generally been produced for an audience, for aesthetic experience and for education. Anthropological films are used as an illustration of culture in teaching anthropology.

Ethnographic filming has its critics too. Maurice Block (1988), while relating ethnographic films to anthropology says that filmmakers should make films on a predetermined script, with a thesis and preferably without anthropologists since the presence of an anthropologist in the team is an excuse for an illusion of pseudo-objectivity. "Ethnographic films can be very useful if they can be used as data which is incorporated in teaching. Ethnographic films as form of public entertainment often make people very uncomfortable. What ethnographic films are trying to do is to give the idea that if you just stare at people, if you just hear their words out of context, you have learnt something about them. This idea that ethnographic film speaks for itself is wrong. The kind of thing one tries to teach in anthropology is, if you just stare at exotic scenes and listen to the things people are saying without knowing anything about these people, you understand less about them than if you have never seen them or heard them". *Anthropology Today,* U.K. 1988.

The other important tool of data collection for visual anthropology, the videotape, permits coverage of the stream of activity in the natural setting in much of its complexity over relatively extended time periods. Videotape records provide necessary detail on the activity of individuals in specific contexts.

Videotape coverage can be advantageous to visual anthropology in many different ways. It supplements the ethnographic accounts of the record of any particular culture. It permits review by scientists and informant-participants in the field to stimulate response and increase the scope of interrelation of both general and specific socio-cultural phenomena. Lastly, videotape records are employed to establish connections between abstraction and inferences and the observed phenomena upon which they are based.

Visual anthropology can play a very important role in developing an awareness of those aspects of culture that condition the formation of the value judgements. The development of such awareness is possible because visual communication can engrave itself directly upon the emotional element of one's psychic structure. Visual anthropology can also affect the rational level by virtue of its specific language—the language of images.

The IXth International Congress of Anthropological and Ethnological Sciences, held at Chicago in 1973, passed a resolution on Visual anthropology. The minutes of this resolutions as reported by Hockings (1975 : 483) are, "Film, sound and videotape records are today an indispensable scientific resource. They provide reliable data on human behaviour that independent investigators may analyse in the light of new theories. They may contain information for which neither theory nor analytical schemes yet exist. They convey information independently of language, and they preserve unique features of our changing ways of life for posterity. Today is time not merely of change but of spreading uniformity and wholesale cultural loss. To help arrest this process and to correct the myopic view of human potential to which it leads, it is essential that the heritage of mankind be recorded in all its remaining diversity and richness".

Development in India

Two cultural anthropologists—K.N. Sahay and B.C. Agarwala, were among the others to generate the scope of Visual anthropology in India. They were also the nominated Chairmen of the Commission on Visual Anthropology under the auspices of the International Congress of Anthropological and Ethnological Sciences for the years 1979 and 1982 respectively. Sahay took special interest in preparing the groundwork for introducing a full-fledged course on Visual anthropology for Ranchi University. He has also written series of research articles incorporating the aims, methods and contents of ethnographic and fictitious motion films in India. One of his research students has prepared a volume depicting the role of feature films in India in understanding society and culture. Since 1984, Anthropological Survey of India has been actively engaged in the production of ethnographic films on primitive communities in India. It is only during the last decade that the U.G.C. Committee on Curriculum development in Anthropology has approved an ideal course structure on Visual anthropology in India at Post-graduate level in Indian universities. As far the information goes, only University of Allahabad and Punjab University, Chandigarh have one-year course in Visual anthropology as part of post-graduate programme. It is heartening that both the ministeries of culture and Tribal affairs have started funding to the interested visual anthropologist. The most recent publication is of Lucknow University anthropologist, Anjali Chauhan's *Kumbh Mela,* The Macmillan India, 2011. It is worthwhile to present an extract of the course material on Visual anthropology, for it gives an idea what Visual anthropologists actually try to do:

(i) Definition, scope and uses of Visual anthropology, Views of prominent anthropologists regarding the discipline.

(ii) History and development of Visual anthropology. The different approaches to anthropological films. History and development of Visual anthropology. The different approaches to anthropological films. Types of films, movie films, feature films, ethnographic films, documentary. Visual Anthropology and analysis of cultural style.

(iii) Visual Anthropology as one of the Documentation methods in anthropology. Visual communication and its advantages; limitations of visual communication over other systems. Photography as medium of communication. Still and movie photography. Naandi, Hyderabad based N.G.O. has been publishing 'Photographic Album' on the tribes of India since 2001.

(iv) Television and Visual anthropology. New techniques of observation and analysis in anthropology. The videotape—advantages and limitations over other systems.

(v) Evaluation to some ethnographic films made in India by Anthropological Survey of India, Calcutta; Films Division of Government of India, New Delhi and Audiovisual Research Centre of Osmania, and other universities and Indira Gandhi National Open University, New Delhi.

MEDICAL ANTHROPOLOGY

(This section has been adopted from P.C. Joshi's article on Medical Anthropology published in 'Medical Anthropology' in India, 1990, Reliance, Delhi)

Medical Anthropology, as a sub-field of enquiry deals with the study of people's point of view in medicine. In its goals, it is not merely limited to the extent of assisting medical sciences in health care delivery but it also covers much broader spectra of enquiries. Its multifaceted objectives include study of culture-specific trends in the domain of illness; inter-relationship between medical arena with other spheres the society have; and finally identification, evaluation and utilisation of resource-potentials in a particular culture in terms of therapeutic cure, health care and adherence.

Although medical anthropology, as an independent sub-field of anthropology, is of recent origin, yet the roots of medical anthropology are as old as anthropology itself. The development of ideas and theoretical orientations in anthropology has a direct bearing on the style of enquiry in medical anthropology. It is not surprising, therefore, that we have different schools of thoughts in medical anthropology as well. For instance, the culture-trait approaches of anthropology (Clement, 1932; Murdock, 1978), the functional (Ackerknecht, 1958; Mead, 1953; Foster, 1979; Paul, 1955), the symbolic (Turner, 1964), the semantic (Fabrega, 1978; Kleinman and Dung, 1979; Good, 1977) and the processual (Christman, 1977; Friedson, 1960) have been used in medical anthropological researches by different scholars. This diversification in research approach has enabled them to gain more depth in the subject matter.

Medical Anthropology: Basic Premises

Three basic 'empirical generalisations' in medical anthropology which guide the research work are:

a. Illness as a ubiquitous entity is not necessarily a biomedical deviance (disease) but in reality a socio-psycho-bio-cultural entity (illness) and is present if and only if the affected person and the surrounding social group recognises it so.

b. Every society is capable of constructing cultural frameworks—set of ideas, beliefs, norms and values—in their past and persisting encounters with illness episodes. Thus, illness has a cultural domain, which means that illness experiences are not individual, impersonal and objective encounters but are subjective, shared and social experiences and therefore, are understood, labelled, communicated and expressed in cultural specific (relativistic) manner.

c. Every society also develops means to cope with these situations. This is the social domain of illness. In this domain, the pivotal attention is the affected person, surrounded by his/her family and other significant persons, (Therapy Management Group) at one end and the socially recognised health actors (Popular/professional/Lay healers) on the other. These culture-specific sets of roles and statuses are placed in a particular institutional setting.

Holism dominates the theoretical perspective in medical anthropology. There has been a shift in the emphasis in recent times and as such Colson and Selby's (1974) narration of finding a paucity of theory in medical anthropology no more appears to be so prominent. What we find today is the emergence of various schools of thought and overall development in the theoretical orientations of medical anthropology. Medical systems have been quite distinctively perceived as social systems (Paul, 1955), as cultural systems (Kleinman, 1979), as adaptive systems (Alland, 1970; Dunn, 1976) but always within the purview of *holism*. Finally, another apparent objective of medical anthropology is in the direction of cross-cultural generalisations, which have a direct bearing on the international health care planning.

Medical Anthropology Defined

A number of scholars have attempted to limit the subject matter of medical anthropology within a definition. The earliest definition of medical anthropology was given by two Indian scholars namely, Hasan and Prasad. They defined medical anthropology on the grounds of its broad objectives as "that branch of 'science of man' which studies biological and cultural (including historical) aspects of man from the point of view of understanding the medical, medico-historical, medico-legal, medico-social and public health problems of human beings" (Hasan and Prasad, 1959 : 21–22).

In a much later definition, Lieban (1974) primarily touched upon the inter-relationship between medical and social sciences, which was partially hinted, by Hasan and Prasad earlier. He defined medical anthropology as one which "... encompasses the study of medical phenomena as they are influenced by social and cultural features, and social and cultural phenomena as they are illuminated by their medical aspects" (Lieban, 1974 : 15). Both of these definitions merely inform us about the broad viewpoints in medical anthropology. The subject matter and the orientations are not clearly specified. The basic lacuna in a number of such definitions is of confining medical anthropology to the extent of their scholarly needs. For instance, Weaver defined it as"... that branch of applied anthropology which deals with various aspects of health and disease" (Weaver, 1968 : 1). But, medical anthropology is not only limited to the extent of providing fruitful strategies to the health care planners. But also contributed greatly in the theory-building process of general anthropology. To quote Lieban again"... medical anthropology is not only a way of viewing the state of health and disease in a society but also a way of viewing society itself' (Lieban, 1974 : 15).

Horacio Fabrega's (1972) definition of medical anthropology was slightly different, for he defined medical anthropology on the basis of content of the work done. According to him "medical anthropology... (a) elucidates the factors, mechanisms and processes that play a role in or influence the way in which individual or groups are affected by and respond to illness and disease and (b) examines these problems with an emphasis on the pattern of behaviour" (Fabrega, 1972 : 167). George M. Foster's (1978) two fold definition highlights the "bicultural inter-relationship between human behaviour" and "health and disease", as theoretical exercise and the utility of this knowledge in health-related planning "through changing of health behaviour in direction believed to promote better health" (Foster, 1978 : 10).

In the light of the above definitions, we might attempt at a fresh definition of medical anthropology as follows:

Medical anthropology is the holistic study of health, illness and related misfortunes, as these are culturally perceived, labelled, classified, experienced and communicated on one hand and socially constructed roles, statuses and institutional networks which are believed to help in the health-enhancing process, on the other, with a view to identify cross-cultural similarities and variations in patterning of such behaviour.

The Scope of Medical Anthropology in India

Medical anthropology is a newly emerging sub-discipline in India. Though the term medical anthropology was first used in India itself, it could not be pursued systematically in this country. At present, we have a modest database in the form of ethnographic notes with medical anthropological contents but a systematic appraisal of what should be done and how it should be done has yet to be established. The work done in India further suggests that our studies are heavily influenced by the ideas and approaches developed outside. As a result, its utility in Indian context is being increasingly doubted. We have yet to change our orientations to adapt to the present needs of our country.

Despite diversions in the National Health Care Policy, our planners are accused of being urban oriented and favouring allopathic model. In the name of indigenisation, they have merely erected parallel systems of medicines. Consequently, the expectations of cooperation and of being complementary are converted into a feeling of jealousy and competition. All this has occurred because the change was not initiated on systematic and scientific grounds but was merely an expression of medical revivalism (Leslie, 1976). I would like to mention at this juncture that no medical system could be perfect in catering to the total needs of a particular cultural setting. India is a country of diversities which is also reflected in the realm of medicines. This situation is referred to as *medical pluralism*. Besides Allopathy (in the scheme of Dunn 1976, as cosmopolitan medical system), we have well developed medicinal traditions like Ayurveda, Homeopathy, Siddha, Unani, Yoga and Nature Cure as our regional medical systems. At the bottom of all this, we find myriad local traditions—the realm of home-medicines, folk medicine, shaman, diviner, peer, herbalist, midwife, mantra and sundry others. A sum of all these categories would form the actual resources in a given cultural setting. A dynamic understanding of this pluralism is of utmost importance for any health care planning.

Our point of departure from the contemporary planning is that the non-allopathic resources should not just be discarded because they cannot be fitted into the so-called scientific framework dominating the minds of professionals today. We also argue that the local medical systems have enormous resource potentials, which should be incorporated systematically and acknowledged properly in the health care planning. It is possible only when we understand them as adaptive responses to the health related needs of a particular micro-level cultural matrix. It would be wrong to consider the traditional systems as mere assemblage of few plant remedies and traditional birth attendants. The psychological, social and cultural contributions are equally impressive in such parochial groups. In an exhaustive study of North Indian healers, Sudhir Kakar (1982), a trained psychoanalyst, found out that the non-allopathic healers can also administer psychoanalytically potent therapy despite great differences in their style of treatment.

Anthropology strongly advocates that the cultures should be studied as wholes. A holistic study of traditional medicines, at methodological front, would require that the researcher is not only eliciting informations by asking people (interviewing) but also learning about culture-specific ways by means of actually living with the people. Such an approach can reveal how the health-related beliefs and practices are intimately related to other spheres of socio-cultural life. In other words, how these ideas are patterned in a culture. Further, through this methodology, we can also know about *emic* view in the study of medical care.

A therapy in traditional setting quite often has greater implications than just healing the symptoms of an ill individual. In the study of Ndembu, Turner (1966) found out that the onset of illness generally points towards cleavage in the social solidarity. Consequently, the therapeutic activities in such situation are primarily oriented towards cementing the social ties. In all the traditional systems, we can find the aetiology of illness explained in the realm of breach of taboo and divine punishment. Here, the beliefs and practices actually act as culture-specific mechanisms for perpetuation of norms and maintenance of social control.

The therapeutic efficacy of traditional remedies can be evaluated fruitfully if such a task is accomplished in an interdisciplinary manner. For plant medicines, in particular, anthropologists can cooperate with botanists and pharmacologists. But, an identification of just plant species is not sufficient in evaluating its medical potency. Though, the chemical potency of a particular herb may be found in some plant medicines, its actual efficacy could only be revealed if we exactly know its quantity of intake, the situations when it is used and the manner of its application. Besides chemical properties, the mystification through which a herb is often administered is also of great relevance in judging its efficacy. A herbal medicine cannot simply be equated to the intake of tablets and capsules. The practice and paraphernalia, which generally accompany it, have great placebo implications.

Divination is also an important component of the traditional system. Diviners are the healers who mediate between the culturally postulated superhuman and the society. Besides carefully examining the circumstances and problems where such healers are used, an understanding of the process of becoming a diviner also has medical significance. In traditional societies, every individuals does not become a diviner. It is believed that such individuals are specially selected by the divine powers. It is also a ubiquitous phenomenon that such persons pass through a phase of experiencing non-ordinary behavioural symptoms. This entire sequence is systematically related to the stress and strain, which a culture induce over its members. Thus, the process of becoming a diviner is also a therapeutic action where a person with inner conflicts finds a culturally prescribed medium for channelising frustrations and aggression.

Integration of diverse systems of medicine into the official health care is a recent idea. For a developing poor nation like India, it is very important that the expenditures are economised. But what and how of the integration has to be planned out very carefully. We should be modern in our approach. The term 'modern' is used here to connote a very specific meaning. In a situation of multiplicity of options (medical pluralism), modern action should be of the kind which appropriately suits the local conditions. Integration would not mean that we legitimise and license the traditional systems but an inventory of potent elements in such systems has to be prepared beforehand. At the same time, we should also know what are the harmful elements in a traditional therapy. Integration has to be an interdisciplinary exercise where social scientists (anthropologists), doctors, psychiatrists, botanists and pharmacologists would work together. Such a task would further require that the potent elements of traditional medicines are promoted, healers are trained effectively of treatment and finally, people are made aware of the dangers of employing harmful therapeutics in the treatment.

In their latest edition of *Anthropology*, Ember and others (2002), after reviewing useful studies over the past two decades, have suggested some useful points related to the fast growing sub-field of medical anthropology (see pp. 514–15).

SUGGESTED READING

Urban Anthropology

- Barnes, J.A., "Class and Community in a Norwegian Island Parish", *Human Relation,* 7, 39–58, 1954.
  There is a suggestion that the traditional holistic approach is untenable in understanding social interaction in a fishing community of Norway. Barnes developed the use of network analysis.
- Bott, Elizabeth, *Family and Social Network in Urban Families*, Free Press, New York, 1955.
  Bott analyses operation of social network in selected families of urban London.
- Epstein, A.L., *Politics in an Urban African Community*, Manchestor, 1958.
  In this study of the growth of Unionism and intertribal relationships in an African mining town, the author shows how social structure is developed in response to the action of the mine-owning group.

- Cox, R.E., *Urban Anthropology*, Prentice Hall, New Jersey, 1977.
- Friend, John and Noel J. Chrisman (Eds.), *City Ways: A Reader in Urban Anthropology*, Harper and Row, 1975.
  This is the most comprehensive volume consisting of research papers that come under urban anthropology. Some articles on problem areas in the study of urban cultures are by Elizabeth Bott (*Urban families*), Richard Fox (*Rational in Urban Anthropology*), Oscar Lewis (*Culture of Poverty*) and John Fried and N.J. Chrisman (*Themes in Urban Anthropology*). The above edited volume lists comprehensive bibliographies with annotations.
- Harris, Marvin, *Cultural Anthropology*, 2nd ed., Harper and Row, New York, 1987. Chapter 16 (Anthropology of an Industrial Society) depicts emics and etics of the system of social stratification in modern U.S. Alienation, poverty, unemploy-ment, concentration of wealth, race relations, crime, welfare, sex roles and new forms of religion are covered well.
- Mitchell, J. Clyde (Ed.), "Analysis of Personal Relationships in Urban Families," *Social Network in Urban Situations*, Manchestor, 1960.
  This is a collection of original articles using network analysis in African urban studies done during 1955-1960. This is also one of the best resource materials on urban anthropology.
- Whyte, William Foote, "The social structure of an Italian slum," *The Street Corner Society*, Aldine, Chicago, 1955.
  This is a classical study of an Italian slum. The second edition includes an appendix on "the Evolution of Street Corner Society", with a note on urban field research technique.
- Vidyarthi, L.P., *Rise of Anthropology in India*, Concept Publisher, New Delhi, 1978. Volume II contains anthropologicol studies done in Indian town and cities (1955–75).

Ecological Anthropology

- Damas, David (Ed.), *Contribution to Anthropology: Ecological Essays*, National Museum of Canada, Bulletin No. 230, 1969.
- Eggan, Fred, "Social Anthropology and Method of Controlled Comparison", *American Anthropologist*, **56,** 444–456, 1954.
- Forde, C. Daryll, *Habital, Economy and Society,*: Dutton, (First published in 1934), New York, 1963.
- Greetz, Clifford, *Agricultural Involution: The Processes of Ecological Change in Indonesia.* University of California Press, Berkeley, 1963.
- Helm June, "The Ecological Approach in Anthropology", *American Journal of Sociology*, **64**, 630–639, 1962.
- Hardesty, Donald L., *Ecological Anthropology*, Wiley, New York, 1977.
  This book combines theoretical perspectives with broad problem areas.
- Kroeber, A.L., *Anthropology*, Harcourt, New York, 185–186, 1923 (1950).

Cultural and Natural Areas of North America, University of California Press, Berkeley, 1939.

- Lee, Richard B., "What Hunters Do for a Living, or How to Make Out on Scarce Resources", Richard B. Lee and Irven DeVore (Eds.), *Man the Hunter,* Aldine Chicago, 1968.
- Mencher, Joan P., "Kerala and Madras: A Comparative Study of Ecology and Social Structure", *Ethnology*, **5**, 135–171, 1966.
- Netting, Robert, "The Ecological Approach in Cultural Study", *McCale Module in Anthropology*, Addison-Wesley Publishing Company, Boston, 1971.
- Nicholas, Ralph W., "Villages of the Bengal Delta: A Study of Ecology and Peasant Society", Unpublished Ph.D. Thesis, University of Chicago, 1962.
- Pospisil, L., *Kapauku Papuan Economy*, Yale University Publications in Anthropology, **67**, 1963.
- Rappaport, Roy A., *Pigs for the Ancestors*: *Ritual in the Ecology of a New Guinea Village*, Yale University Press, Yale, 1967.
  Nature, Culture and Ecological Anthropology, See Shapiro, 237–257, 1971.
- Sahlins, Marshal D., "Cultural Environment: The Study of Cultural Ecological", *Horizons in Anthropology*, Sol Tax (Ed.), Aldine, Chicago, 132–147, 1964.
- Shapiro, H.L. (Ed.), *Man, Culture and Society*, Oxford University Press (Revised), New York, 1971.
- Srivastava, A.R.N., "Rise of Ecological Studies in Cultural Anthropology", *Man in India*, **70**, 269–287, 1990.
- Steward, Julian, *Theory of Culture Change*, University of Illinois Press, Urbana (Paper back 1968), 1955.
  The concept and method of culture ecology are dealt with at length.
- Stoddart, D.R., *Geography and the Ecological Approach*, Warner Modular Publication, Massachusetts, 1973.
- Vadya, Andrew P. (Ed.), *Environment and Cultural Behavior*, Natural History Press, Garden City, New York, 1969. A collection of essays on relationships between societies, cultures and environments.
- Wissler, Clark, *The Relation of Nature of Man in Aboriginal American*, Oxford University Press, New York, 1926.
- *Journal of Human Ecology*, Kamala Raj Publication, Delhi, 1990.
  This is a trendsetter in Anthropology of Ecology.

Visual Anthropology

- Agrawal, B.C., *Anthropological Methods for Communication Research*, Rawat Publishers, Jaipur, 1990.
- Arora, Sushil, "The Movie Films in India and its Socio-Cultural Context: An Anthropological Study" (unpublished), University of Ranchi, 1988.

- Collier, John, Jr., *Visual Anthropology: Photography as a Research Method.* Holt, Rinhart and Winston, New York, 1967.
- Heider, Karl, G., *Films for Anthropological Teaching,* (5th ed.,) American Anthropological Association, Washington, D.C.,
- Hockings, Paul (Ed.), *Principles of Visual Anthropology*, Mouton, The Hague.
- Mead, Margaret, 'Anthropology and the Camera', *Encyclopedia of Photography*, Edited by W.D. Morgan, National Educational Alliance, 1963, New York. Also Introdution in Hockings, 1975.
- Sahay, K.N., "Ethnographic Films in India: Prospect, Priorities and Proposal", *Methodology in Anthropological Film-making*, N.C.R. Borgat and H.W.E.R. Karclaar (Eds.), 1983. Gottings: Herodo, *Visual Anthropology*, New Delhi, Gyan Publishers, 1963.
- Srivastava, A.R.N. and Rai, Samir, *Readings in Visual Anthropology,* Papers in Social Anthropology, University of Allahabad (1996).
- *Visual Anthropology: A quarterly Journal,* Harwood Academic Press, Founder Editor: Jay Ruby, New York, 1985.

Medical Anthropology

- Ackerknecht, E.H., *Primitive Medicine's Social Function*, 1958.
- Alland, Alexander, "An Approach to Medical Anthropology," *Adaptation in Cultural Evolution*, Columbia University Press, New York, 1970.
- Avezard, Claude, *Whispers from the Hills:* (A photographic Journey into the Tribal Areas of Andhra Pradesh and Orissa). Arabian Heritage Sponsored by Naandi Publication, Dubai and Hyderabad, 2003.

  This is an excellent piece of work on visual anthropology by a non-anthropologist, in collaboration with the Nikon Digital, Japan.
- Christman, Neol, "An Approach to the Natural History of Illness, Culture, Medicine and Psychiatry", *The Health Seeking Process*, 25–58, 1977.
- Clements, F.E., "Primitive Concepts of Diseases," *University of California Publications in American Archaeology and Ethnology*, **32**, 185–252, 1932.
- Cochrane, A.L., "Random Reflections of Health Care," *Effectiveness and Efficiency*, Nuffield Hospital Trust, London, 1972.
- Coe, R.M., *Sociology of Medicine,* McGraw-Hill, New York, 1979.
- Colson, Anthony and K.E. Selby, "Medical Anthropology", *Annual Review of Anthropology,* **3,** 245–262, 1974.
- Dunn, F.L., "Traditional Asian Medicine and Cosmopolitan Medicines as Adaptive systems", *Asian Medical System: A Comparative Study,* C. Leslie (Ed.), University of California Press, Berkeley, 1976.
- Eisenberg, Leon, "Disease and Illness: Distinctions Between Professional and Popular Ideas of Sickness", *Culture, Medicine and Psychiatry,* **1**, 9–23, 1977.

- Fabrega, H., "Medical Anthropology", *Biennial Review of Anthropology,* 167–229, 1972.
- Fabrega, H. and D. Silver, "An Ethnomedical Analysis", *Illness and Sharmanistic Curing in Zinacantan:* Stanford University Press, Stanford, California, 1973.
- Foster, G.M. and B.G. Anderson, *Medical Anthropology*, John Wiley and Sons, New York, 1979.
- Freidson, Eliot, "Client Control and Medical Practice", *American Journal of Sociology,* **65**, 374–382, 1960.
- Haggerty, Robert J, "The Boundaries of Health Care", *Pharos,* **35,** 106–111, 1972.
- Hasan, K.A. and B.G. Prasad, "A Note on the Contributions of Anthropology to Medical Sciences", *Indian Journal of Medical Association,* **33,** 182–190, 1959.
- Illich, Ivan, *Medical Nemesis,* Pantheon, New York, 1976
- Kakar, Sudhir, "A Psychological Inquiry into India and its Healing Traditions", *Shamans, Mystics and Doctors,* Oxford University Press, Delhi, 1982.
- Kleinman, Arthur and L.H. Sung, "Why Do Indigenous Proctioners Successfully Heal," *Social Science and Medicine,* **13,** 7–26, 1979.
- Lieban, R.W., "Medical Anthropology", *Handbook of Social and Cultural Anthropology,* Rand, McNally & Co., Chicago, 1974.
- McCorkal, James, *Dewesternizing Medicine*, Paper read at the Xth ICAES at Poona, 1978.
- McKeown, Thomas, *The Role of Medicine: Dream, Mirage, or Nemesis,* Nuffield Provincial Hospital Trust, London, 1976.
- McKeown, Thomas, *The Modern Rise of Population,* Academic Press, New York, 1977.
- Mead, Margaret *Cultural Patterns and Technological Change,* UNESCO, Paris, 1953.
- Paul, B.D., *Health, Culture and Community: Case Studies of Public Reactions to Health Program,* Russel Sage Foundation, New York, 1955.
- Powles, John, "On the Limitations of Modern Medicines", *Science, Medicine and Man,* **1,** 1–30, 1973.
- Turner, V.W., "An Ndembu Doctor at Practice", *Magic, Faith and Healing,* Ari Kiev (Ed.), The Free Press, New York, 1964.
- Waltzkin, Howard, "A Marxist Analysis of the Health Care Systems of Advanced Capitalist Societies." *The Relevance of Social Science for Medicine,* L. Eisenberg and A. Kleinman (Ed.), 333–369, 1980.
- Weaver, Thomas, "Medicial Anthropology: Trends in Research and Medical Education", *Essays on Medical Anthropology,* T. Weaver (Ed.), University of Georgia Press, Athens, 1968.
- Wellin, Edward, "Theoretical Orientations in Medical Anthropology: Continuity and Change Over the Past Half-Century", *Culture, Disease and Healing,* David Landy (Ed.), McMillan Publishing, New York, 1977.

Chapter 13

Cultural Change

Anthropological perspective on cultural change includes the theme of stability and change in simpler societies. This theme falls into a different category from the topics we have discussed so far in this book. We have already touched upon the subject of change at many places in Chapter 3. Earlier in Chapter 2, we have examined the concept of culture and society and related concepts. Now, we need to understand that in every culture, there is both 'stability' and 'change', and without some degree of change, adaptation would be impossible (Barber, 1971).

MEANING OF SOCIAL AND CULTURAL CHANGE

Alterations in the culture, which includes not only systems of ideas, values and aesthetics but also the material things people have created, are referred to as *cultural change*. 'Social change', as used here, refers to alterations in social relations and social organisation. Although social change may result from changes in the natural environment, it is typically due to alterations in cultural values and meanings. The latter bring about new patterns of interaction among the members. For example, the invention and popularisation of the automobile has been associated with changes of great significance in family life. Cultural change is generally associated with social change, but it does not necessarily result in social change. Causal connections between cultural and social changes are exceedingly difficult to establish.

Social change alters the 'normative' or characteristic patterns of behaviour of individuals and groups. It redefines the relations of persons in the social structure. In the final analysis, it involves the creation of new values, new meanings and new definitions of human interactions. Social change, therefore, always involves the creation, borrowing, development or popularisation of ideas, beliefs, myths, ways of doing (technologies) or material things.

Social change can only come from the following three sources:

(1) discovery, a new addition to existing knowledge;

(2) invention, a new application or combination of previously existing knowledge; and

(3) borrowing, by which a social arrangement is taken from another society and applied intact or in some modified form.

DIFFERENCE BETWEEN APPROACHES OF SOCIOLOGISTS AND ANTHROPOLOGISTS

After noting the relationships between social change and cultural change, it would be worthwhile to examine the ways experts of the two areas differ from each other. It must be noted here that a very few professionals claim that they are studying only social change and not cultural change and vice-versa. It is left to the readers to ponder over who is doing what. For example, see the title of the book *Social Change in Tikopia* by Raymond Firth. What Firth is trying to study are the changes in all aspects of Tikopian life—social as well as cultural, but the title is social change as if Firth is talking about only social change and not cultural change (see also Eggan, 1966).

Most sociologists agree that the problem of social change involves the task of uncovering generalisations, and ultimately discovering general laws governing the operations of variables that contribute to change. Anthropologists, in the eyes of the present author, look for variables which contribute to stability. However, their ultimate goal is to understand the processes involved in the change.

The second major difference between the two approaches is with regard to the subject matter. Most of the sociologists base their arguments on changes in complex (industrial-western) societies; on the other hand, anthropologists are oriented mainly towards the simple/non-industrial societies. Obviously, the contents of these societies are different and the professionals look for these contents.

The third major difference between the two traditions is that sociologists, interested in study of social change prepare *a charter* for considerations they look for such as:

1. Identification of units of analysis,
2. Specification of determinate relationships,
3. Intensity and magnitude of change,
4. Direction of change and
5. Planned and unplanned changes.

To study these factors, sociology developed appropriate research designs suited to the nature of the problem.

Field anthropologists, on the other hand, base their analysis on ethnographies. American anthropologist David Mandelbaum (1970), in his two-volume book on India, has devoted three chapters on cultural change. He focussed on the content, degree and direction of changes in tribal and peasant societies (1970 : 636–659). This, however, does not mean that anthropologists do not make use of survey and experimental research designs. Anthropologists involved in studies of cultural change rely much on informants' description or their memories or at best, on local history, if traceable.

POPULAR THEORIES OF SOCIAL CHANGE

Since the time of ancient Greece, philosophers and thinkers have asked more specifically, "What is the pattern of social change?" For some, all social change has been *progress*; according to them, things are getting better and better or at least, are proceeding in some specific direction and are motivated by some determining power hidden deep among the secrets of nature, perhaps in the obscure nature of man. Such theories of change may be called *linear* and are clearly expressed in the works of a number of early sociologists, notably Herbert Spencer.

Spencer asserted that the history of societies is the story of their evolution from a 'lower' (homogeneous) to a 'higher' (heterogeneous) stage. He recognised, however, that social evolution is not merely 'progress' from the homogeneous (simple primitive society) to the heterogeneous (complex modern society); it also can happen that 'the cosmic process brings about retrogression as well as progression where the conditions favour it'. Spencer's total view of change remains linear. He argued that the evolution of societies is governed by an immutable natural law which man can tamper with but never permanently alter. The *status quo,* then, by one interpretation of this formulation, is merely a stage through which a society must pass in the inevitable course of its evolution. (see Chapter 3, Classical Evolutionists.)

One of the important criticisms of Spencer's theory of social evolution points out that it fails to account for different societies at the same 'stage' or place in the evolutionary process are not necessarily similarly structured; they do not exhibit similarities in economic, political, moral, religious, artistic and other forms.

Another set of theories holds that social and cultural changes are neither progressive nor linear. Their patterns of change are more like the swinging of a pendulum. Extremes in meanings, values and social organisations are accepted for a time and then, rejected by a reverse process. The opposite extremes are sought. A society, like the pendulum, moves from one extreme to another. Arnold J. Toynbee, who theorises that 'civilisations' go through a 'life cycle,' asserts that typically a few centuries after its origin, a civilisation passes through a period in which it 'breaks down', then 'disintegrates,' and eventually 'dissolves'. (see Chapter 2, civilisation.)

One of the criticisms of Toynbee's theory is that his conclusions are based on the analysis of only 21 societies, mostly Hellenic and Western. It is, at least, questionable that his generalisations are true for other societies. At best, Toynbee's theory has not had sufficient empirical test to justify its uncritical acceptance.

Pitirim A. Sorokin's theory of social change asserts that societies fluctuate between what he calls 'ideational' and 'sensate' cultures. Societies in which people emphasise on the importance of faith in their lives are ideational. Ancient Greece, Sorokin held, was such a society. If people believe that their senses are the ultimate source of what is valid, then their society is sensate. This polar extreme is exemplified by the Roman Empire from the fourth century B.C. to the fourth century A.D. A society in which the sensate and the ideational are merely thrown together and are not harmonised has a mixed culture. Such culture was found in western society during the fifth and sixth centuries B.C. If the sensate and ideational emphases are harmonised, then the culture is said to be 'idealistic'. Western society in the thirteenth century had such a culture.

One important criticism of Sorokin's general theory of social and cultural changes suggests that the basic differences in societies which are considered to represent the same phase of fluctuation between the ideational and sensate are overlooked or oversimplified.

Anthropologist A.L. Kroeber concluded that there is no such thing as a 'law' of cultural growth of decline. From a study of historical data on the growth and decline of philosophy, science, painting, drama and other cultural creations, he stated that cultural growth and decline are attributable not to any one factor but to a multiplicity of factors.

After this brief review of the theories of social and cultural changes, some conclusions can be drawn. First, there is no known law of cultural and social changes which holds for all the cultures and societies at all times. Second, if change is linear, then it must be admitted that the final goal towards which the man and his creations are progressing is not known. Third, if it is cyclical, then the nature of the cycles is not agreed upon, and there is no known way of predicting the distant future of societies. Finally, if cultural and social changes are totally unpredictable, then it is futile to search of order, yet the changes must be orderly because some reasonably accurate, though relatively short term, predictions of changes have been made and continue to be made.

Each of the theories of social and cultural changes mentioned above can provide only oversimplified answers to exceedingly difficult and complex questions about the course of human history.

Various deterministic explanations of social change have been offered. According to some geographers, social change springs from climatic changes or has its roots in the physical environment and the movement of people from place to place. Some theorists have held the view that biology is the determinant of social change. Of more concern to both the sociologists and the anthropologists are three sets of social factors, which are especially significant to the nature, and the direction of social change—cultural diffusion, technological change and social movements. We have already discussed classical and multilinear evolutionists in Chapter 3 in some details. (For detailed analysis of social change see Wilbert Moore's *Social Change*, 1963).

HOW TO STUDY CHANGE?

There are two ways of looking at social/culture change. One is to ask what produces change. This is a theory of change, and it implies that we are asking why it should occur. Another way is to identify common trends over a period of time in different parts of the world. Experts, in particular sociologists, have sought answer to these issues, but they took little interest in folk/pre-literate societies. Most of the anthropologists have taken the view that stability and change, norm and deviance can be examined together. "There need to be no treatment of social control apart from social conformity," remarked Mandelbaum, 1970 : 60.

Conceptual Elements Involved in Social-Cultural Change

In the remaining pages of this chapter, we will examine the phenomena of stability and changes in pre-literate/tribal/traditional societies to which anthropologists are more concerned with.

Most of the cultural anthropologists maintain that culture is an adaptive system with relation to the environment and as such, cultural change is the result of the cumulative effects of its interaction with the economic system. In this sense, the neo-evolutionists such as Julian Steward, Leslie White and Marvin Harris analysed changes in societies. Cultural anthropologists use a host of terms, viz. *acculturation, innovation, diffusion, syncretism,* etc. to examine trends in cultural change.

Here, we will limit our discussions to cultural stability and changes based on the ideas contained in a masterpiece work *Innovation: The basis of culture change* by a philosopher anthropologist H.G. Barnett published in 1953. In a way, the following account may be viewed as a summary verbatim of this book, especially from Chapters 2 to 6.

ORIGINATION, SOCIAL ACCEPTANCE AND ACCULTURATION

Origination

Historical accounts provide evidences of change. In every society, there are some cultural differences between the generations, with the older generation expressing its displeasure over the new one and the younger generation regarding the old people as too conservative. Moreover, in all over the world, large areas can be found, in which there is gradual variability from one culture to another within the area. Cultural change, thus, is a constant of culture, and anthropologists are much interested in understanding the processes involved. It should be remembered that a given person ultimately brings a trait into being. The process of bringing into being a trait that may become a part of a culture may be called origination. This is essentially a psychological process in which the individual perceives a new relationship between two or more pre-existing ideas or portions of them that he combines into a new idea. What happens in origination is that the individual substitutes a part of one mental configuration for a part of another mental configuration, thereby bringing into being something psychologically new to him into their elements and the identification of one of the elements in a familiar configuration with one in a different configuration. The identification is possible because the originator experiences the elements of the analysed configurations as similar to one another in some respect.

An origination is not a part of the culture, in the view of most of the anthropologists, until it is multi-individual. Other people than the originator must accept the new custom. There is no doubt that many originations, perhaps the vast majority, do not spread to other members of the society. They remain unique and personal.

ACCULTURATION

Some of the anthropologists have been interested to explore *how* and *why* customs spread or diffuse from one culture to another. This situation is called acculturation. This term is also applied frequently to the reciprocal diffusion of customs between cultures. An alternative term, not widely used, seems to be somewhat more descriptive, namely *interculturation*.

Some Conceptual Issues Involved in Acculturation

Students of culture change often confront with the problem of defining the term acculturation. It would be worthwhile to examine its historical background. In 1936, Melville J. Herskovits, Ralph Linton, and Robert Redfield, as members of a committee of the Social Science Research Council (USA), studied the question carefully and prepared '*A Memorandum on Acculturation*,' discussing the need for a definition and offered the following:

"Acculturation comprehends those phenomena which result when groups of individuals having different cultures come into continuous first hand contact, with subsequent changes in the original cultural patterns of either or both the groups. Under this definition, acculturation is to be distinguished from *culture-change*, of which it is but one aspect, and *assimilation*, which is at times a phase of acculturation. It is also differentiated from *diffusion*, which while occurring in all instances of acculturation, is not only a phenomenon which frequently takes place without the occurrence of the types of contact between the people specified in the definition given above, but also constitutes only one aspect of the process of acculturation" (Redfield, Linton and Herskovits, 1936 : 152).

Generally, this definition continues to be used in establishing the fact that what kind of a situation is under consideration when a study is labelled acculturation. But, scholars still debate what kinds of subsequent changes are likely to occur and in which group. In 1938, Herskovits published a small volume entitled *Acculturation* in which he reviewed a number of anthropological reports pertinent to the question of acculturation, pointing out problems for further study. He concluded that things are never just accepted from one group by another, but are *reinterpreted* to suit the accepting group; acculturation is a two-way street and changes worthy of study occur in both the groups that have continuing cross-effects.

In 1953, the American Social Science Research Council sponsored a summer seminar on acculturation to examine ideas and information (Barnett et al. 1954 : 973–1002). The participants admitted that the discipline was still far from a coordinated analysis of the subject, but concentrated their attention on types and situations of contact. Acculturation was redefined as:

"...Culture change that is initiated by the conjunction of two or more autonomous cultural systems. Acculturative change may be the consequence of direct cultural transmission; it may be derived from non-cultural causes such as ecological or demographic modifications induced by an impinging culture; it may be delayed, as with internal adjustment following upon acceptance of alien traits or patterns; or it may be a reactive adaptation of traditional modes of life. Its dynamics can be seen as the selective adaptation of value systems, the processes of integration and differentiation, the generation of developmental sequences, and the operation of role determinants and personality factors."

In regard to both the social acceptance and the diffusion, it is important to remember that two kinds of persons are involved. There are at least one objectifier and one respondent. The problem is to determine why a respondent accepts or rejects a custom objectified by someone else and to understand what he does by way of reinterpreting a custom he accepts. In a sense, these are psychological problems, but they also are cultural and, therefore, anthropological, because the respondent's reaction is determined in significant measure by the multi-individual esotraits he shares with other members of his society.

It is also significant that origination—unintentional and often unnoticed—takes place during acculturation. This is one of the major sources of cultural change and the cultural differences found between the generations in all societies.

Cultural Conditions for Origination and Change

It should be understood that cultures vary from one another in these conditions not only from society to society but also from one time level to another in the same society. Before an origination can occur, the prerequisite esotraits must be available, and most of the elements employed by inventors are drawn from their culture. Other things being equal, a complex culture should change more rapidly than a simple one.

The presence of the necessary ideas in a culture does not itself guarantee that the origination will occur. Individuals originate, not cultures as such; and if there is no one in the society who has the prerequisite elements concentrated in his mind, then the origination cannot take place.

There may be more than one member of the society with the same or similar ideas concentrated in their minds. This is true particularly if there are many opportunities for collaboration provided by the culture, that is opportunities for originators to exchange ideas or to draw on the same sources of information. The result of such a situation is the development of simultaneous inventions.

Cultures also vary a good deal in respect to the degree of contact with alien cultural esotraits. Until recently, the societies in marginal geographical areas such as the Australians, the Bushmen of the Kalahari desert, the Shoshones of the arid Great Basin of North America and a number of others have had little opportunity to contact with the people very different from them culturally. This seems to be one of the reason why their cultures have been changed more slowly than less isolated groups. By contrast, the areas where the world's most complex civilisations were originated are those areas in which many people of a variety of cultural backgrounds came into contact with one another, stimulating a ferment of change. It happened in the river valleys of the subcontinent of India and Pakistan and also, in Middle America and the congrous region of South America.

Syncretism

One of the most common results of intersocietal contact has been called *syncretism*. Syncretism is a term applied to those culture complexes that are known to be a blend of elements of different cultures. An excellent example is of the Zinacantecos of southern Mexico. These natives of highlands of Chiapas (Zinacontan) have traditional Mayan ceremonial life combined with Spanish-Catholic elements of Christianity. Thus the natives have associated Sun with God and Moon with the Virgio Mary. This and other rituals of the Zinacantan represent syncretism (Vogt, 1970).

Among the Dahomo, Christian Saint Patrick is identified with rainbow-serpent, portrayed in his role. Similarly, among the House of West Africa, the pagan 'iskoki' is identified with the 'Jinn' of the Koran (Islam).

Many of the component complexes of present-day Indian cultures of Latin Americans are international blends of pre-Columbian Indians and Spanish customs. The same is true for the cultures of the New World Negroes. Herskovits has identified the West African Dahomean ancestor religion elements and the Catholic features in the Vodun cult of Trinidad, the West Indies (Herskovits, 1947). According to Herskovits, syncretism is one of the forms of cultural *reinterpretation*. Reinterpretation is a process by which old meanings are ascribed to new elements by which new values change the cultural significance of old forms. It operates internally, from generation to generation, no less than in integrating a borrowed element into a receiving culture (1955 : 492). It is both interesting and significant that a syncretism often consists of many linkages between overt forms borrowed and existing in the culture.

Competition, either between groups quite different culturally or among subgroups of the same society, varies in extent and intensity from one society to another. Origination may occur in the development of means of defeating one's competitors; or one group may borrow something from the rival society in order to compete with them on equal terms.

Another condition stimulating change is *deprivation*, which is defined by Barnett as the elimination of something to which people feel they have a right. War and such threats to security are, generally, known to precipitate originative activity. One of the most widespread consequences of acculturation has been the felt deprivation of subordinate groups, which in turn, has prompted the cultural reactions sometimes known as *nativistic* movements. These reactions emphasise on the restoration or perpetuation of certain cultural elements highly symbolic of valued life ways. Linton has referred the movements emphasising on a return to former ways as *revivalist* movements, and those which attempt to preserve the status quo as perpetuities movements (1943 : 231). One of the best examples of revivalist nativism is the *Ghost dance* religion that swept through the western American Indian tribes during the last decades of the nineteenth century. The major prophet of the Ghost Dance predicted exclusion of the whites and called for a return to ceremonial aspects of the old way of life. The widespread acceptance of his doctrines testifies to the appeal of his programme.

In many parts of the world, so-called *Cargo cults* have sprung up, calling for the provision of goods and services for which the people have acquired tastes as the result of contact. The reason that this type of reaction is called a cargo cult is that a common element in the acculturative responses of New Guinea tribes is the prediction that a ship will arrive bearing the desired goods (see Chapter 9, section on revitalisation movement).

Among the most common conditions making for cultural change is the modification of some element of the culture or of its field, which is interdependent with various other traits. Barnett calls such an element the *dominant correlate*, dominance being understood in terms of the trait being the first modified in the situation in question. Changes in the culture of the North America Shoshone Indians due to the introduction of horse riding illustrates well the chain of reactions which may result from such a modification. Change in the natural habitat also may have cultural repercussions, whether it is due to indigenous activity, contact with a culturally alien group, or is independent of cultural activity.

Acceptance and Rejection

One of the major tasks facing cultural anthropologists is identification of factors and the development of effective means for assessing their relative effects. A few of the factors that have been explored are as follows:

1. ***Objectification*** is a respondent who has not observed an action, artifact, or utterance that expresses that the custom cannot accept a necessary prerequisite to acceptance, for a custom.
2. ***Advocacy*** may also be a determining factor. Sometimes, a custom is not borrowed or diffused because none is advocating that anyone should accept it, and no effort is made to convince a respondent of its desirability.
3. ***Personality*** is often of great importance. Many times, a custom has been rejected because the respondent found the objectifier's personality offensive, even in cases when the respondent was actually attracted to the custom.
4. ***Personal relations*** comprise another variable that is often of importance. It refers particularly to friendship and kinship. Many respondents will accept a custom advocated by a friend or relative and reject it if is proposed by a stranger.
5. ***Majority affiliation*** is for many respondents a recommendation for acceptance. Many people accept a new idea because 'everyone else' is doing so. Majorities tend to be intimidating.
6. ***Compatibility*** is a cultural factor of considerable importance in understanding a respondent's reaction. Often, an alien custom is simply out of harmony with the respondent's culture, and the proposed trait simply cann't co-exist with present items in his way of life. The women of the Yurok tribe of Northern California were unable to accept women's hats with feathers on them because, by aboriginal definition, only Yurok men could wear feathers on their heads. There are many examples of incompatibility in the anthropological literature. Compatibility, of course, may constitute a recommendation for acceptance.
7. ***Efficiency*** frequently is a factor-recommending acceptance. The issue is whether or not the proposed custom does the job it is alleged to do and how well it does it.
8. ***Cost*** is one of the commonest deterrents to acceptance. Sometimes, an item has been rejected because it requires too much money or the draining off of too many other valued resources in order to put the custom into effect.
9. ***Penalty,*** if it is a necessary concomitant of acceptance, may influence the respondent to reject a custom. Commoners on the island of Palaun in the western Pacific failed to accept American sun helmets because the Palauan chiefs threatened reprisal on anyone who wore them.

10. ***Advantage*** is another factor of widespread significant. Some of the customs are accepted simply because they provide the respondent some sort of gain which cannot be obtained otherwise. Some people have accepted Christianity openly in order to acquire the material benefits available from the missionaries.
11. ***Mastery of a custom*** is a significant determinant of a respondent's reaction. His talents and cultural background may be such that to provide little of no satisfactory basis for learning the custom.
12. ***Functional repercussions*** may result in rejection (culture). It has been emphasised in this volume. They are not composed of discrete elements but are systems composed of traits which are functionally linked to one another; and a change in one custom may result in a chain reaction in other parts of the culture. If the respondent is unwilling to undergo the secondary changes, then he may reject the custom that would precipitate them.

These are only a few of the factors that may be considered by students of culture change.

DIRECTED CHANGE

Directed change is also known as planned or social planning. It is a process involving a series of related activities or steps. The four steps in the planning process are:

(i) Definition of the problem,
(ii) Investigation of the total situation,
(iii) Agreement on policy, and
(iv) Collective action.

The objectives of this process is to solve existing social problems or to forestall predicted ones.

Anthropologists are now rather frequently called upon in directed change programme to predict the increasing number of cases in which efforts are being made to persuade people to accept new ideas. The anthropologists are able to answer questions concerning whether or not proposed changes can be accomplished, and the possible or probable effects upon a given culture. The notion that social scientists can predict human behaviour seems strange to some people but it should not in view of the fact that human beings predict one another's behaviours daily and govern their own actions and reactions accordingly. Edward Spicer and Benjamin Paul (1952) have cited several sources of difficulty that appear over and again as agents of change.

One of the most elementary principles of change, but one which seems to be difficult to get across to many agents of change is the fact that the customs which comprise a culture are linked to one another and to elements of the cultural field. The fact that cultures are systems, and any modification of parts of a culture may have repercussions which are destructive either to the goals of the agents of change or those of the people undergoing change often goes unappreciated until some serious mischief is done.

To Sum Up

1. Social scientists have found that one of the most effective ways of securing agreement to a desired change is to work through the proper social units. Frequently, this is not done. In South America, the people of a village refused to use the water from the wells drilled for them by the government, in spite of the fact that the water was wanted desperately. The source of the problem was that the directors of the project failed to secure the cooperation and approval of the large landowners and the priest, who were the people of power and prestige in that community. S.C. Dube in his evaluation of community development projects in Indian villages has cited several examples of this type of rejection (see *India's Changing Villages, 1962*).
2. The nature of the relationship between objectifiers and respondents has been found to be one of the most relevant issues of all.
3. Misinterpretation of the customs of culturally different groups is an exceedingly common source of trouble.
4. A common source of difficulty is the failure of agents of change to bring the members of the respondent's society in the planning and carry out a programme. Effective agents of change often encourage people to make their own decisions with minimum possible guidance, and many a change has been rejected because of failure to do so.
5. Finally, almost in all anthropological studies on culture change, the researches have confined to one or more of the following factors:
   a. Acculturation, (fully defined earlier and in Appendix I).
   b. Diffusion (refer to above and Chapter 3).
   c. Cultural convergence or convergent cultural evolution. It refers to the development of similar traits and institutional patterns by the separate groups as a result of adaptation to ecology.
   d. Urbanization and industrialisation: Processes of leading urban and industrial way of life.
   e. Globalisation: The process that links people of the nation states economically through the modern mass media and information technology.

SUGGESTED READING

- Barber, Bernard and Alex Inkles, *Stability and Social Change*, Little Brown Beacan, Boston, 1971.
  This is an edited volume; it has a few anthropology-oriented articles.
- Barnett, H.C., *Innovation: The Basis of Culture Change,* Macmillan, New York, 1953.
  This is the most intensive effort so far at systematic analysis of the process of culture growth. Because this book is not easily available, its several chapters are reproduced in abridged form in textbooks.

- Eggan, Fred., *The American Indians; Perspective for the Study in Social Change*, Aldine, Chicago, 1970.
- Foster, G.M., *Applied Anthropology,* Little Brown, Boston, 1969.
  The author answers the issues related to applied anthropology as an agent of culture change.
- Goodenough, Word H., *Cooperation in Change: An Anthropological Approach to Community Development*, Russel Sage Foundation, New York, 1963.
  This is an excellent volume by a leading theorist in Anthropology on conceptual analysis of culture and culture change.
- Lippitt Ronold, J. and Waston, Bruce Westley, *The Dynamic of Planned Change*, Macmillan, New York, 1958.
  Although the orientations of authors are more sociological, several issues related to agents of culture change are clarified well with suitable case studies.
- Mandelbaum, David, *Society in India: Continuity and Change*, University of California Press, Berkeley, 1970. Indian reprint is available with Manohar Publication. It examines trends in Indian societies, including the tribal communities.
- Moore, W.E., *Social Change,* Prentice Hall of India, New Delhi, 1963.
  It is a low-priced paper back easily available. It presents a modern sociological view of social change.
- Spicer, Edward H., *Human Problems in Technological Change*, Russell Sage Foundation, New York, 1952. Case studies on introducing change in traditional societies of Latin America and India by leading specialists.
- Vogt, Evon Z., *The Zinacantecos of Mexico, a modern Mayan way of life.* New York, Holt, Rinehart and Winston series in cultural anthropology. 1970.
- Wagner, R., *The Invention of Culture*, University of Chicago Press, Chicago, 1981. The revised edition includes culture creativity and self.

Note: Students are encouraged to go through the *Journal of Human Origination* published by the American Applied Anthropological Society, Washington for lively case studies on cultural change and applied anthropology. *Social change*, a periodical published from New Delhi is also useful for the students of Indian universities. Anthropological case studies are included in *Applied Anthropology in India,* Edited by L.P. Vidyarthi, Kitab Mahal, Allahabad (1968, 1990).

Appendix I

Selected Terms and Concepts in Anthropology

ACCULTURATION

The term refers to a change that occurs when groups of individuals with different cultures come into continuous first-hand contact. Many anthropologists have used this term while describing the changes that have arisen out of contact between different societies. Acculturation studies also focus on the 'process of change'. Traits borrowed by one culture in what order and in what degree are accounted for culture change.

A Short History of Acculturation Studies

Because of political and technological changes in the past six decades, isolation and independence of the indigenous population all over the world are losing their identities. This state of affairs was anticipated by the anthropologists of earlier generations. The term 'acculturation' covers this process of change, and it has become a major area of anthropological research.

Anthropological studies of acculturation date back to 1935 when a group of scholars in response to the American Social Science Research Council submitted their memorandum outlining the areas and problems of acculturation. According to this memorandum, "acculturation comprehends those phenomena which result when groups of individuals having different cultures come into continuous first-hand contact, with subsequent changes in the original culture patterns of either or both of the groups". (Memorandum on the study of Acculturation, *American Anthropologist*, **38**, 149, Redfield, Linton and Herskovits, 1936).

Herskovits, one of the earliest scholars of the acculturation study, suggested a model for comparative researches on the subject (see also Herskovits, Appendix II of this book). His study on Africa and the Caribbeans (the Black communities resettled in Haiti, Trinidad, Surinam and Brazil) suggests that acculturation operates by means of three analytically distinct but interrelated processes—*Retention, syncritisation* and *reinterpretation.* Retention refers to the persistence of both the form and meaning of a traditional trait in a situation of culture change. Syncritisation is the process denoting fusion of two distinct systems of beliefs and practice. It was Brazilian anthropologist Arthur Ramos (1936) who first used this term to designate the identification of migrants from West Africa and their tribal deities with Catholic saints. (see preceeding chapter page, 193)

Reinterpretation refers to an aspect of the process of cultural transmission in which old meanings are ascribed to new elements of culture or vice versa.

It is worth noting that in the Indian context, K.N.Sahay examined the above cultural processes in his pioneering work on impact of Christianity on the Oraons of Ranchi district, South Bihar. (See *Under the Shadow of Christ,* K.N. Sahay, 1965; republished in 1985. Concept, New Delhi).

APPLIED AND ACTION ANTHROPOLOGY

Anthropological connotation of 'applied anthropology' (sometime called Practical anthropology) has two meanings— in a narrower or conventional sense, it means utility or usages of anthropological insights in various facets of human life. In this context, the four core branches of anthropology have application of their data (conclusion) not only in the academics but in non-academic instances as well. Linguistic anthropologists, for example, are now interested more in developing methods and materials for forms and instructions for pre-literate members. Tribal communities all over the world have and are being benefited by the linguists for they have prepared text materials suited to a particular society or cultural life. One of the examples of such materials is a textbook written in Khasi language for Meghalaya.

Likewise, physical anthropological skills are used in fields of forensic medicine (identifying human remains) for legal purposes. Osteometric and somatometric measurements are useful in dress and furniture-industries. Through their studies, physical anthropologists are now counselling certain hereditary diseases of a defined human population. Archaeological anthropological data are limited, even though they are applied to preservation of monuments and artefacts. Now, the well-known countries of the Third World are motivating the tourists of the industrial world, who visit sites in large numbers to see and enjoy the places of historical importance. Therefore, the role of archaeologists cannot be underestimated.

However, cultural anthropology is deeply involved in *direct application* (definite or specific gool) of its findings. Evans-Pritchard has indicated that the growth of anthropology especially in England and America was due to potential demands of cultural data of the countries that were under the colonial administration. This trend still persists; independent nations including India together with developed countries now employ anthropologists in their development programmes. The idea is that the professional anthropologists have special skills of understanding societies at all level of technological development.

In broader context, the meaning of applied anthropology is the use of anthropological concepts, theories and findings for specific purposes. In this sense, a trained anthropologist after completing his/her educational career, i.e. M.A./Ph D. in Anthropology, need not be personally involved in the actual application of anthropological conclusions. Other professionals/agencies may use the findings in their own ways.

In brief, however, applied anthropology is defined, the potential usages of anthropology have appealed to a wide variety of public and private organisations.

Related to Applied anthropology is *action anthropology*. The originator of this terminology was Sol Tax, the celebrated American cultural anthropologist. He and his followers believe that the only legitimate professional function of the applied anthropologists is to provide administrators, politicians and project aids suppliers with an objective analysis of a situation (society, organisation), and that, *atmost actions should be limited to suggesting but not implementing a plan*. Sol Tax used the term 'action' paraphrasing Max Weber's actor-oriented meaningful behaviour. His famous case study on the Fox Indians of America has been in Vidyarthi's edited volume (1968).

SUGGESTED READING

A large number of books are available under the title Applied-action anthropology. Some popular text books on cultural-social anthropology also have separate treatment on the subject; a few notable are:

- Clifton, James (Ed.), "Readings in the Uses of Science of Man", *Applied Anthropology*, Little Brown, Boston, 1970.
- Foster, G.M., *Applied Anthropology*, Little Brown, Boston, 1969.
- Fried, Morton H., *The Study of Anthropology*, T.Y. Crowell, New York, 1968.
- Srivastava, A.R.N., *Applied Anthropology and Tribal Welfare in India*, Allahabad University, 1990. (in Hindi).
- Vidyarthi, L.P., *Applied Anthropology in India*, Kitab Mahal, Allahabad, 1990. (First Published in 1968) A number of essays on theoretical in nature including case studies are included in this edited book.
- Vidyarthi, L.P., *Tribal Development and their Administration*, Concept, New Delhi 1980. (A collection of articles by the specialists on aspects of more anthropology and its implication in administration in Indian situation). For more references see popular texts by Harris, Hoebel, Evans-Pritchard, Fried and Lucy Mair.

BRIDEWEALTH AND DOWRY

In many societies, the transfer of women in marriage is associated with the payment of various forms of wealth to the kin group of the bride. This is often said to compensate her group for the loss of her economic and reproductive services. Such payment is known as bridewealth. Bridewealth is especially prevalent in patrilineal societies and is much less common in societies having matrilineal, double or bilateral descent. Van den Berghe (1979) reports that 71 per cent of patrilineal societies make use of bridewealth, compared to only 37 per cent of matrilineal societies and only 32 per cent of societies with double or bilateral descent. It is not at all difficult to see why bridewealth should be much less frequently found among matrilineal societies. What somewhat surprising is why bridewealth exists at all in matrilineal societies.

Far less common is dowry, a system whereby a woman takes property with her into a marriage. While dowry seems to mean the opposite of bridewealth, this is not quite the case. Dowry actually means that a woman receives an early inheritance from her parents, and she is able to use this inhertiance to contract a marriage.

This practice is almost exclusively restricted to complex agrarian societies characterised by intensive social stratification. Its function appears to be to allow a woman to obtain a husband of equal or higher status (Van den Berghe, 1979); thus, it serves to preserve the social and economic standing of whole families.

Some important studies of bridewealth and dowry have been carried out by Jack Goody (1976) and by Alice Schlegel and Rohn Eloul (1988). Goody found that bridewealth was the principal mode of contracting marriage in Africa, while dowry was widespread throughout European and Asian agrarian societies. In attempting to explain these observations, Goody relied heavily on the fact that the African societies practiced horticulture, while in Europe and Asia, plough agriculture predominated. The African societies were less stratified and had less population densities and more available land. By contrast, the Eurasian agrarian societies had intensive social stratification, high population densities and scarcity of land. These divergent features of the two regions make bridewealth adaptive in one region, but dowry much more adaptive in the other.

CROSS-CULTURAL STUDY (CCS)

(This is a revised article of A.R.N. Srivastava, *Man in India* published in 1978).

The CSS simply means comparing two or more societies together. It could be either synchronic or diachronic study. Two major types of cross-cultural studies are 'descriptive analytical' and 'co-relational'. A descriptive-analytical cross-cultural study involves comparison of two or more cultures (societies). Examples of such studies are Margaret Mead's *Sex and Temperament*, or Ruth Benedict's *Patterns of Culture*. A descriptive-analytical cross-cultural study is different from an intensive ethnographic study of a society in the sense that it seeks to examine the range of diversity with respect to one or more aspects of societies concerned.

A co-relational cross-cultural study differs from a descriptive-analytical cross-cultural study in the sense that it employs statistical measures to determine the degree of relationship between the cultural traits or institutions of societies. Another major distinction between these two sorts of study is with respect to the method of collection of data. A trained anthropologist carries out a descriptive analytical cross-cultural study, while an investigator who may or may not be a trained anthropologist carries out a co-relational cross-cultural study.

During the mid 20th century, Kluckhohn and others had developed a methodological scheme to study variations in value-orientations in five major rural communities of southwest North America. Since then, some of the scholars continued to use the same method while studying European peasants with little modifications.

The essence of a cross-cultural study, however, is the scientific comparison of ethnographic data. Earlier, anthropologists like E.B. Tylor and Franz Boas, to name a few, were interested in cross-cultural comparison. Murdock gave co-relational cross-cultural comparison a distinctive flavor in his *Social Structure* (1949). His method of cross-cultural study is based on statistical correlations designed for testing hypotheses. It rests squarely on description and taxonomy of ethnographic data.

According to Murdock's technique, the cross-cultural survey is a classified repository of ethnographic data. In this technique, the data are indexed in such a way that even a non-anthropologist interested in knowing what has been reported on any aspect of culture can select the coded cards of subjects of his interest in no time. Each card contains a verbatim reproduction of ethnographic facts included in book or article. The cultures included in the Yale Survey represented all the geographical areas of the world and societies of all levels of development. Murdock's famous handbook *Outline of Cultural Materials* (first published in 1938, and revised thereafter in 1940) provided a standard scheme to be followed in indexing the cards. In 1940, Murdock wrote that his survey "should prove useful in nearly every type of research which anthropologists and other social scientists have hitherto pursued (1940 : 363; see also preface of *Social Structure*).

The value of the Yale cross-cultural Survey was realised by the professional anthropologists of that time. In 1949, it was made available to many U.S. universities and research institutions in the form of the *Human Relations Area Files (HRAF)* with the support of the Carnegie Corporation. With the increase of more ethnographic facts, the Files were and are being revised even today.

Both the Survey and the Files were designed to facilitate the testing of hypotheses formulated on some cross-culturally theoretical ground. At the time of preparing materials for his book *Social Structure*, Murdock used a sample of 250 societies, of which 85 were taken from the above-mentioned survey. Presently, more than 1000 societies are indexed in HRAF.

The logic behind the cross-cultural co-relational method is to discover some 'regularities of form' or a process which will show a functional relationship between the custom (cultural trait) under study and some other parts of the cultural system.

In *Social Structure,* Murdock used the co-relational approach in testing many different hypotheses systematically (in statistical terms) including 120 tests on the determinants of kinship terminologies. We may, just by way of illustration, note his conclusions on the relationship between kinship and rules of social structure (social norms). One such hypothesis suggests an association between the marriage custom (sister exchange) and a kinship terminology for the wife of the brother of Ego's wife is his own sister.

After testing the above hypothesis (Wi Br Wi = Si) for a sample of 65 societies, Murdock found that there are only 7 societies in the sample having the custom of sister exchange, the association is highly significant (the probability of this arising by chance is less than one in 100). Therefore, the functional relationship is confirmed. Following this several conclusions about the *relative effect* of structural factors upon kinship terminology can be studied.

The Strength and Weaknesses of Co-relational Cross-cultural Methods

One of the advantages of the co-relational method is that it encourages the formulation of hypotheses and the efforts to test them. The vital question is how successfully they are tested. To be sure, co-relations do not speak for themselves. If two variables are associated in a number of societies, then this may be due to a number of different causes, not necessarily because the same factor led to the associations in each case. Statistics tells us only how close to the truth a certain outcome is. It can never certify the truth.

Despite the above drawbacks, cross-cultural surveys seem to have been a useful methodology for comparative study. In anthropological writings, we often come across the frequent use of the expressions 'usually', 'commonly', and 'rarely'. By the use of Murdock's cross-cultural co-relational analysis, one can state social phenomena, with some confidence, in probability term. In reviewing the Murdock's statistical approach to social organisation, Marvin Harris (1968 : 612–13) has accepted, with some reservation, the utility of such study as a 'method for revealing *unsuspected connections* among the institutions, for identifying exceptions to regularities, as 'measure of probability and as an indicator for research needs'.

CORPORATE SOCIAL GROUP

A corporate social group, in the context of tribal and peasant world, displays one or all of the following characters:

(a) Its members can collectively hold title to land and other property.

(b) The members can exploit their resources by cooperative labour.

(c) The members have status of being legal individuals of the group; they can conduct litigation and make treaties, conduct feuds and wars and can also enter into contracts.

(d) Since corporation continues despite the death and replacement of individual members, the group is said to be enduring and stable.

It should be noted that in the tribal world, worship of individuals of a group is always defined with reference to an *ancestor*. In other words, only descendants of an ancestor claim to be the legal individuals (members) of that group. Obviously, there is more than one way to define the mode of relationship. This is called rule of descent. A rule of unilineal descent (matrilineal or patrilineal, defined earlier) is eligible for membership in a corporate descent group.

By contrast, cognatic descent (non-unilineal descent members) does not successfully encompass explicit criteria of corporateness. But, studies completed during 1950–1965 clearly demonstrate that the cognatic descent groups do produce discrete or quasi corporate group.

CULTURE RELATIVISM

This term refers to the idea that behaviour in a society should be evaluated in terms of the society's own cultural values. In other words, understanding of the behaviour of any culture (society) should be based on people's standard, not researcher's (or external) standard. The root of cultural relativism goes back to Boasian era. Since then, cultural anthropologists have been using this concept during collection of field data. Modern cultural anthropologists continue to practice cultural relativism. While studying other cultures, they combine it with holistic view. But, in cross-cultural studies, when anthropologists want to compare the activities in different cultures in order to arrive at some general conclusion, they may find it useful to look at the results the behaviour produces, instead of what is meant to the people themselves.

CULTURAL UNIVERSALS

This refers to the basic solutions to the problem of living that are found in different forms in different societies/cultures. G.P. Murdock (1945) has made up a list of cultural universals what he called 'cultural universals' (*The common denominator of cultures*). This list gives a general feeling of closeness among *Homo sapiens;* that is, how human beings, no matter where they come from, share different kinds of behaviour. Some examples of cultural universals are:

age grading	*community organisation*
bodily adornment	*education* *play*
hair style	*division of labour*

CULTURE OF POVERTY

A celebrated American anthropologist, Oscar Lewis (1966) developed this concept in his study of poor urbanities of Latin America. Lewis found a feeling of helplessness, a withdrawal from political activity, and an orientation towards immediate consumption of goods produced by the people. Though this sort of condition does exist in some parts of non-western industrialising populations of South America, it cannot be generalised for Asian and African societies that are under the grip of modernisation. In a country like India, poor slum dwellers actively participate in country's political and economic development programmes.

In brief, in situation of culture of poverty, each social class leads its own life-style carrying a popular idea that people in the lower strata are kept poor by their own behaviour. Current researches using Lewis ideas have yielded a little theoretical value in anthropology.

EMIC AND ETIC APPROACH

Unlike other social scientists, research anthropologists have been confronted with the problem of translating the cultural world of the natives into the idiom of professionalists. The problem of translation occurs at both ends of one's research— learning about the people which is investigation, and then communicating what one (thinks one) has learnt about these people to one's professional colleagues. Confronting these views, some of the anthropologists wish to keep 'perspectives' and 'world views' separately—the perspective of the people being investigated is called emics and the perspective of social science in general (and anthropology, in particular) is called etics. Keeping these 'folk' and 'analytical' perspectives separate, whether one is engaged in field research or the subsequent analysis of data, is very difficult.

In short, 'emic' is inside or native view; while 'etic' is anthropologists or social scientists. Derived from Linguistics after *'phoneme'* and *'phonetic'* some of the cultural anthropologists have viewed this approach as objective as this is based on the linguistic model. But, a close examination of use of this concept reveals totally different (M. Durbin 1975 : 384–386, see Chapter 3).

EGO AND ANCESTOR FOCUSED KIN GROUPS

In reckoning kinship affiliation a distinction is made between *ego-focus* and *ancestor-focus* kinship. The former is traced from a living person, rather than focusing an ancestor, i.e. downwards from a common ancestor (male or female). Examples of an ego-focused kingroup is 'kindred'; whereas ramage, clan, lineage are ancestor-focused kingroups.

ENCULTURATION

This term, which refers to the process of learning one's culture, is often (but by no means universally) distinguished from socialisation, which means the general process of learning culture. Enculturation is most often applied to childhood learning.

In the anthropological usage, enculturation is not limited to childhood, but like socialisation is a life-long process. Each time a novel situation is encountered in which the content and rules of new rules must be learned, it may be said that enculturation is taking place. One has to learn how to become an acceptable patient in a hospital, how to think and act like a professional and how to interact as a spouse, father/mother, grandfather/grandmother or in law. We all must learn how to grow older and prepare to die, each within the acceptable limits of behaviour and within the context of our own culture.

ETHNOGRAPHY

Ethnography literally means a portrait of people. Currently, it refers both to a particular strategy in anthropological research and also to its products. This brief definition raises important questions about ethnographic studies. Why is the research done? Who does it and how? What kinds of information were obtained? Whose viewpoints are reflected in the final portrait—those of the ethnographers or of the subjects? The traditional ethnography is a synchronic (same time) study.

In another way, ethnographic research may be comparative. Often, the ethnographer treats the commonly studied communities as a special sample of a larger universe. This larger universe may be other community in the same region or tribe of nation, or it may consist of communities with special (e.g. peasant) characteristics.

Some widely known ethnographies are:

Allan, W.	*The African Husbandman* (1965)
Barth, Frederick	*Nomads of South Persia* (1961)
Bateson, Gregory	*Raven* (1936)
Berreman, Gerald D.	*Hindu of the Himalayas* (1963)
Embree, John F.	*Suye mura* A Japanese Village (1939)
Evans-Pritchard, E.E.	*The Nuer* (1940)
Firth, Raymond	*We, the Tikopea* (1936)
Holmberg, A.R.	*Nomads of the Long Bow* (1950)
Lewis, Oscar	*Five Families* (1959)
Lowie, R.	*The Crow Indians* (1935)
Malinowski, B.	*Argonauts of the Western Pacific* (1922)
Pitts-Rivers, J.	*People of the Syria* (1954)

Redfield, Robert	*Chankom,* A Maya Village (1934)
Tumball, Collin	*The Forest People* (1961)
Wagley, Charles	*Amazon Town* (1953)
Wilson, Monica	*Good Company* (1951)

Over Sixty short ethnography on communities across the world has been prepared by the anthropologists during 1960–1990 under the series *Case Studies in Cultural Anthropology* published by Holt, Rinehart and Winston, Inc. of New York.

ETHNOGRAPHIC INFERENCE

Ethnographic descriptions are based on records of social interactions together with native judgements of appropriateness of such action (*emic view*). From these concrete cases and evaluative statements, the ethnographer (social-cultural anthropologist) *infers* the shared social rules (expectation) that govern the group under study. This is known as ethnographic references. In social analysis, says Philip Bock, the relevant units to be considered are kinds of people (roles), kinds of groups, institution, conception of space and the time and the principles of organisation which guide the way in which the structure is put into action.

In brief, ethnographic inferences help in discovering 'functional relationships within a given society'.

ETHNOGRAPHIC PRESENT

Anthropologists study and write about the simple societies in terms of what is known as the ethnographic present. In other words, they write in the present tense as if now the situation were as it was at the time they saw it or even as some old informants remembered it.

THE NEW ETHNOGRAPHY

In recent decades, there has been increasing emphasis on the formulation of hypotheses and theories to govern data collection processes. A hypothesis to account for the cultural behaviour of the group under study is set up, and a fact to test the hypothesis is gathered. Another aspect of the new emphasis is view things from the point of view of the people being studied rather than imposing the categories obtained externally. The so-called new ethnography is actually rather old, but the consistency and explicitness with which the new approach is set forth among the anthropologists is new. (See Chapter 3, Cognitive anthropology, and also Ethnoscience, Ethnosemantics, Componential analysis, Etic and Emic).

ETHNOLOGY

Anthropologists have defined this term in several different ways. It is sometimes used broadly as a synonym for cultural anthropology, and in the past it has also been employed to refer to the historical approach to the study of cultures. In recent decades, however, a more systematic meaning has emerged which identifies ethnology with a general strategy in the search for knowledge about cultures. In this sense, now accepted widely ethnology is the comparative study of cultures. The field of ethnology utilises various sources of data. Ethnological hypotheses may be synchronic or/and diachronic; but are always *comparative*. The American anthropologists use Ethnology for cultural theory; for example, Robert Lowie's *A History of Ethnological Theory* (1937).

ETHOS, EIDOS

Gregory Bateson (1904–80) US anthropologist developed an interest in understanding the relationship between communication and anthropology. He introduced several concepts viz. eidos, Schismogenesis, ethos. In his ethnographic work, *The Naven* (1958) used the terms *ethos* and *eidos* to designate the general principles which gave coherence to a belief system and those which gave coherence to a value system respectively. These were later on used by some American anthropologists.

ETHNOCENTRICISM

The belief that one's own patterns of behaviour are superior to those of other cultures is termed ethnocentricism. The idea that every culture is unique in its own way and anthropologists must be strictly neutral in describing and comparing other societies is referred to cultural relativism. Cultural relativism is based on the idea that all values are relative, and there are no absolute standards that are valid in all cultural settings. Anthropologists discard ethnocentricism and follow cultural relativism.

ETHNOSCIENCE

Study of folk conceptual system of classification (folk taxonomy) is called ethnoscience. With such study, it is hoped that one can penetrate into deeper understanding of culture. The basic assumption of ethnoscience is that the things and events in people's conceptual world will be reflected in their linguistic categories. It is relevant to note here that the eighteenth century theorest Wilhelm von Humboldt and his successors in Germany were ahead of in developing the notion of semantic fields, but the concest was made popular in the work of Sapir, Jakobson, Harris, among others. Stephen Tyler, Charles Frake, R. Berlin, Ward Goodenough are among a few who have used this kind of strategy in understanding culture and society. Ethnoscience sometimes called ethnosemantics, now comes under purview of cognitive anthropology.

Ethnosemantics is the study of the ranges of meaning attached to specific terms and classes or terms by members of a group. The prefix 'ethno' refers to the fact that a study of segment of reality from the perspective of the people being studied. The suffix 'semantics' refers to meaning. Thus, ethnosemantics concentrates on the meaning of categories of reality, folk taxonomies to the people who use them as their bases of action. The underlying assumption of ethnosemantics is that the categories designated by a language adequately reflect the entire range of things important to people within a socio-cultural system. This assumption is far from universally accepted fact. (See Tyler's *Cognitive Anthropology,* N.Y., Harper and Row, 1969, there are over dozon cultural anthropologists have contributed to this volume. Tyler's Introduction (1–21) is probably the best piece on cognitive anthropology.

FOLK-URBAN CONTINUUM

This evolutionary scheme was developed by Robert Redfield to explain differences between various communities of the Yucatan peninsula of Mexico. In 1941, Redfield published a summary of a city (Merida), a town (Dzitas), a peasant village (Chankom) and a tribal village (Tusik). Merida was placed near one end of the continuum and Tusik near the other Dzitas and Chankom were regarded as intermediate types. Redfield found that as one moves along the continuum from folk communities, to urban communities, there is increasing group size, disorganisation, role segregation, individualisation and secularisation. Redfield's theoretical construct provided a model for culture change as rural communities come into increasing contact with urban communities.

PEASANT SOCIETY

Over five decades back, the *The Encyclopedia of Social Sciences* (1960) wrote about historical, social and economic aspect of life of peasants. In Europe, in the middle ages, when agricultural serfs clustered around manors, or marginal farmers lived closer to towns and cities; they come to towns to sell their produce and buy the items which they could not buy themselves. Today, anthropologists and other scholars see peasants as a *Socioeconomic category* and understand it in a wider perspective.

Kroeber wrote: "Peasants constitute part-societies with part-cultures; they are definitely rural yet live in relation to market towns; they form a class segment of a larger population" (1948 : 284). Anthropologist Clifford Geertz has written: "The peasant is an immemorial figure on the world social landscapes, but anthropologists noticed him only recently," (1962 : 1).

Robert Redfield has pioneered peasant studies in America who first called peasant as 'folk' (see his *Tepoztlan* and its subtitle, 'a study of folklife'), but subsequently he recognised the concept differently. Many scholars describe a folk life in such a way as if they are writing about peasants.

Most of the researchers today analyse peasant societies in terms of structural relationships between village and city. In doing so, they emphasise on social, economic, political and religious characteristics. Eric Wolf, the foremost specialist on peasant and peasantry, does not look for a definition. Rather, he sees that the word "indicates a structural relationship, not a particular cultural content"...and a peasant society can be understood only as *it relates to some larger integral whole*" (Wolf, 1955 : 454). George Foster has refined his old version and is of the opinion that "it is really not important *what* peasants produce; it is *how* and *to whom* they dispose of *what* they produce." (1967 : 6). In this sense, a farmer, a potter, a basket-maker and even, some tribes in changing situation are peasants because they as Wolf said, "are subject to the demand and sanctions of power-holder outside (their) social strata. Redfield thinks of peasants 'intermediate' and places them between folk and urban; and thus, developed the notion of 'folk-urban continuum'.

Alfred Kroeber defined peasant society as *a type* and suggested that peasants are rural groups who live near market towns and form a segment of a larger population that also has urban centres or even metropolitan capitals. Peasants are not isolated, as are tribal groups, and they lack the tribe's political autonomy and self-sufficiency even though they do retain much of the same identity with and attachment to the land.

George Foster expanded Kroeber's suggestion when he described peasant society as a 'half-society'—one that is part of a larger unit (generally a nation) in both a horizontal and a vertical sense. The peasant part of this larger unit is related in a symbiotic way to the more complex part, which is composed of the upper classes of the pre-industrial centre. Peasant groups and urban groups are, therefore, not desparate concepts. Instead, both are integral constituents of a particular type of sociocultural unit to which the pre-industrial city is central. In fact, the existence of the peasant society depends on the presence of this type of urban unit.

In *Peasant Society and Culture* (1956), Robert Redfield further explored the relationship between the peasantry and the elite. He pointed out that in trying to understand the peasant way of life, an anthropologist must integrate his/her research with the traditional humanities, inasmuch as studies of history, literature, art, religion and philosophy are all necessary for comprehending the culture of the elite. In particular, he felt that the study of peasant cultures must follow two important guidelines that are not relevant to the study of an isolated primitive band or tribe.

First, a peasant culture cannot exist without communication with the local urban community. Because the intellectual and often, religious and moral life in the peasant village is not self-contained, the anthropologist must know the influence of the remote teachers, priests and philosophers whose thinking affects and may be affected by the peasantry. Second, the study of a peasant village (the little tradition of the 'unreflective many') invites study of the long history of its interaction with local centres of civilisation (the great tradition of the 'reflective few').

Eric Wolf places greater emphasis on the existence of the state as the crucial factor in defining and characterising peasant society. According to Wolf, the birth of the state was paralleled by the birth of a peasantry that occupied a social stratum separate from that of the holders of power. Customs and institutions of the peasants are, in part, a response to the forms of economic and political control exercised by the elite. Thus, administrative forms, modes of tax collection and types of land tenure all influence the little tradition by asserting the limits within which the peasants must work, marry, market and worship. In a feudal barony, for instance, or in a village controlled by conquerors, a group of peasants may be treated as a single entity in the legal system, so that each peasant is responsible for the deeds of all, and a failure by one individual to adhere to the strict order is punished by sanctions against all.

Above we have noted the anthropological, notion of peasants. Sociologists define and analyse "peasants" and "peasantry" in terms of "Agrarian class-models" (Daniel Thorner, 1956; Bèteille, 1974; Dhanagare, 1983). Readers should read sociological paper carefully.

SUGGESTED READING

- Arensberg, Conard, *The Irish Countryman: An Anthropological Study*, Macmillan, New York, 1937.
- Bèteille, A., *Studies in Agrarian Social Structure,* Oxford University Press, Delhi, 1974.
- Dhanagare, D.N., *Peasant Moments in India*, Oxford University Press, Delhi, 1983
- Firth, R., *Malay Fisherman: Their Peasant Economy*, Oxford University Press, London, 1946.
- Foster, George, "What is a Peasant", *Peasant Society*, Jack M. Potter, Mary N. Diaz and George Foster (Eds.), Little Brown, Boston, 1967.

  (Most comprehensive current ideas about peasant society and culture in anthropological perspective.) The editors have compiled almost all the important references on peasants area-wise, see above book, pp. 438–52.
- Geertz, Clifford, "Studies in Peasant life", *Biennial Review of Anthropology*, 1961.
- Kroeber, A.L., *Anthropology,* Macmillan, New York, 1948.
- Redfield, Robert, *Peasant Society and Culture,* An Anthropological Approach to Civilizations, University of Chicago Press, Chicago, 1956.
- Thorner, Daniel, *The Agrarian Prospect in India,* School of Economics, University Press, Delhi, 1956.
- Wolf, Eric R., *Peasants,* Prentice Hall, New Jersey, 1966.

PRIMITIVE SOCIETY

The anthropologists usually use the word 'primitive' to refer to primitive society, primitive culture, primitive art and primitive religion. But, anthropologists are not happy with the word primitive used in this way, and 'the primitives' probably won't be happy with it as well when they find out about it. The term came into use at a time when it was commonly assumed that the way the so-called primitives live today represented the way the 'early man' was supposed to have lived.

Various other terms have been suggested such as simple, pre-literate, non-literate and small-scale, but none of these designations is wholly satisfactory. In this book, the word primitive has been avoided except in a few instances when nothing else seems to fit.

Primitive Culture of North America, Asia, Africa and Oceania

North America	*Primary subsistence activities*
Eskimo	Hunting and fishing.
Athapaskans and Algonkians	Hunting and fishing.
Northwest Coast Indians	Dependence on sea food; somewhat hunting.
Plains Indians	Dependence on bison.
Shoshonean Indians	Hunting and gathering (mainly the later).
Pueblo Indians	Sedentary agriculture.

Iroquois League	Hoe cultivation and hunting.
Creek Natchez	Intensive cultivation of maize, corn, pumpkin etc.
Asia	
Mongols	Horse milk, sheep, goats, and camels.
Chukchee	Hunting, fishing on coast and reindeer domestication. (in interior).
China	Millet and wheat farming in North and wet rice in south.
India	Farming of rice, barley and legumes.
Arabs, Afghani	Wheat and barley agriculture. Goat and sheep domestication.
Africa	
Moroccan peasants	Wheat and barley agriculture. Goat and sheep domestication.
Berbers	Camel and horse pastoralism. Oasis cereal cultivation.
Hausa, Tallensi	Intensive cultivation of yams, bananas, sorghum, millet, maize and manioc.
Swazi, Nyoro	Cattle herding and cultivation.
Bushmen	Hunting and gathering.
Oceania	
Truk, Paiuau, the Carolines, etc.	Coconut, pandanus, breadfruit and taro, fishing, domestication pigs.
Tahiti, Samoa	Fishing; cultivation of taro, breadfruit, coconuts, bananas, yams and sugarcane.
Malaya, Java, Bali	Cultivation of dry rice domestication of water buffalo, cattle, sheep, goats, chickens and pigs.
New Guinea, Admiralty islands	Cultivation of taro, yams and sago, domestication of pigs, fishing and hunting.
Australians	Hunting and gathering.

For a discussion on 'primitive society', see E.E. Evans-Pritchard's *Social Anthropology* (1955: 7–10) and Herskovits (1955 : 358–363)

VALUES, CULTURAL

One of the functions of culture is to provide answers for many questions which do not have any objective answer, but which must be answered if the human society is to function. *Cultural values* include all kinds of socially transmitted ideas, what we often call 'belief system'. Cultural anthropologists have used the term 'value' in more than one ways and have also used other terms to describe and analyse values or belief system of cultures. Such terms are *ethos, themes, world-view, style* and so on.

Writing on the concept of values in cultural anthropology David Bindley (1953 : 698) notes: "The most important and difficult task which confronts the cultural anthropologists is that of making an ethical and comparative study of values." This is because it is directly related to the belief system of a culture or society. Belief systems include all kinds of historically developed and culturally transmitted ideas. Most of the small societies studied by the cultural anthropologists have shown a relatively homogeneous core of shared beliefs and a variable amount of specialised beliefs.

Integrating Patterns of Value

Anthropologists have used some general conceptions to describe the integration of a value system though it is difficult on a comparative scale because of complex nature of value.

Ruth Benedict's *Patterns of Culture* (1937) is an attempt to describe whole cultures (*configuration*) in terms of their general emotional approach to the world and to human relationships. Borrowing from the field of Psychology and Social philosophy, she used the 'Apollonian' terms (peaceful, cooperative, etc.) to describe patterns of culture of some Southwest American Indians.

Anthropologists including Benedict and Kroeber have used 'ethos' for the above terms. To quote Kroeber (1948 : 294):

"Ethos deals with qualities that pervade the whole culture... the ethos includes the direction in which a culture is oriented, the things it aims at..."

Morris Opler has suggested that cultural patterns should be studied and described in terms of several *themes* (cultural ideals)–which control behaviour or stimulate particular kind of activity. To Opler, cultural integration is the outcome of the interplay among the different themes. Some of the themes reinforce one another while others limit each other. Thus, for the Chiricahua Apache American Indian society, he characterised themes such as "men are physically, mentally and morally superior to women. Long life and old age are important goals" (Opler 1945, 1968).

Philip L. Newman in his study of the Gururumba culture has used the concept 'cultural theme'.

The study of value system of five communities of America by Florence Kluckhohn (wife of C. Kluckhohn), Fred Strodbeck and their research team at the Harvard is a classic example of comparative studies on the belief-system. Their approach is known as '*dominant*' and '*variant*' value-orientations (1961).

In India, a study of value-orientations of two tribal communities (the Munda and the Oraon of Chotanagpur) has been completed by A.R.N. Srivastava (1992). Attempts to characterise the ethos of the Munda and Oraon in terms of dominant and variant value-orientations, the outcome of Srivastava's study is summarised in the following table:

M = Munda O = Oraon

Universal problems	Overall Orientations
Man-Nature	M Subjugation > With > Over O Subjugation > With > Over
Time	M Future > Present > Past O Present > Future > Past
Activity	M Doing > Being O Being > Doing
Relational	M Lineality > Individualism > Collaterality O Collaterality > Individualism > Lineality

Although the fundamental cultural differences cannot be explained in one or all of the above-mentioned terminologies but anthropologists hope to explain the differences among the value-system of societies across. The approach developed by the F. Kluckhohn and her group seems to account for judgements, evaluations and choices made by the members in various aspects of social life. Anthropologists must pursue intercultural understanding.

WORLD-VIEW (WELTANSCHAUUNG)

This is an anthropological perspective on culture/society that entails that most of the members of a society have a common outlook to nature, values, attitudes, morals, beliefs and so forth. In other words, the members of a society resemble in their own way. Though Malinowski did not use the term world-view, his approach to ethnography clearly demonstrated the idea of world-view of the native. He said, "...an ethnographer should grasp the native's point of view, his relation to life, to realise his vision of his world..." (Malinowski, 1922 : 25). Robert Redfield insisted in studying the 'world-view' of a folk or peasant society. We may also state that a world-view is an 'emic' interpretation of the society concerned. (See also entry under Emic and Etic).

The term world-view came into common usage since the appearance of Redfield's famous work *The Primitive World and its Transformation* (1953). Earlier, in one of his articles, Redfield had defined the concept as follows:

"World-view... is the picture the members of a society have of the properties and characters upon their stage of actions... It refers to the way the world looks to that people looking out... It is that organisation of ideas which answers to a man the question: where am I? Among what do I move? What are my relations to these things?"

In other words, 'world-view' is a heuristic device to conceptualise the relationship between socio-cultural and ideological (religions) systems. It conveys a message that folk religions are to be understood as an intellectual system of the natives.

Two Categories of World-view: Primitive and Modern

Modern cultural anthropologists classify the world-view into two categories—primitive and modern. The 'primitive world-view' is associated with non-western/small-scale societies in which face-to-face relationship predominate (see above Redfield's folk-peasant societies). The 'modern world-view' is associated with Western/industrial/large-scale societies, where social relationships are of less personal nature, i.e. impersonal nature of social relationships. It is to be noted that the anthropologists do not make any value-judgement that one type of world-view is better than the other (for detail, see Howard 1990).

Appendix II

Pioneers of Cultural Anthropology

The purpose of this appendix is to introduce the readers to the works of some of those anthropologists who have prominently contributed to the field of Anthropology. Reference to them has been made in various chapters of the present textbook.

Franz Boas (1858–1942)

Born in Germany, Franz Boas was the father of American anthropology. He nourished and trained the first generation of anthropologists in America. In 1883, he began his studies in Baffinland, North America. In 1886, he joined the staffs of the American Museum of Natural History and Columbia University where he remained until his death.

Boas insisted upon the rigorous field-based ethnographic study that was lacking in behavioural science at that time. He was against the sweeping generalisations about human behaviour made by cultural evolutionists. He insisted upon sophisticated observation of cultural variability. He stressed on the value of native language being studied by anthropologists. Boas, in true sense, stood for understanding alien cultures in terms of native categories and not those imposed by outsiders (including anthropologists). The school of historical particularism is associated with Boasian period.

This approach has been characterised by its rejection of the comparative method of unilinear evolution. Some of the well-known concepts, viz. cultural relativism, cultural determinism, relationship between race and culture, linguistics, etc. are associated with Boas. Among his students, Kroeber, Wisseler, Lowie, Radin, Herskovits, Sapir, Spier, R. Bunzel, Linton, Benedict and Mead were prominent. For many years, Boas' edited volume *General Anthropology* (1940) remained the only classroom text in anthropology. For Mead, Boas was 'the man who made anthropology into a science'. In the words of Goldenweiser, Boas was anthropology's 'cultural hero'.

Boas' lengthy bibliography ranges across the entire field of anthropology. Some of his famous works are:

(i) *The Central Eskimo* (1888)
(ii) *The Kwakiutl of Vancouver Island* (1909)
(iii) *The Mind of Primitive Man* (1911)
(iv) *Primitive Art* (1927)
(v) *Race, Language and Culture* (1940)

Paul Bohannan (1920–2000)

The major contributions of Paul Bohannan, a leading American social anthropologist, include theoretical considerations of the study of legal processes cross-culturally, the development for legal ethnography and economic anthropology. His work involves issues related to culture and culture theory. Some of his popular works are:

(i) *African Suicide* (1960)
(ii) *Social Anthropology* (1963)
(iii) *The Tiv Economy* (1970)
(iv) *Markets in Africa* (1992)

Emile Durkheim (1858–1917)

The master French sociologist Durkheim is regarded as one of the founders of modern social science. He had profound influence not only on sociology and psychology, but also on anthropology. The most important impact on anthropology resulted from his works is 'functional approach'. He argued forcefully that the social phenomena could usefully be analysed in terms of the functions they serve in maintaining the system as a whole.

Durkheim's most significant application of the functionalist approach was his study of religion (*The Elementary Forms of Religious Life*, 1917). Religious beliefs and rituals, he contended, serve an important social function in enhancing the solidarity of members of a group. He believed that a shared belief system–a religion or some functional equivalent–was essential for a social integration. Without such a system, social order would tend to disintegrate, leading to a situation of societal and individual anomie or normlessness.

In *Division of Labour in Society,* he contrasted two types of societies by patterns of social facts. Primitive of pre-modern societies are held together by *mechanical solidarity*, which is based on the similarity of persons in the society. The collective conscience is characterised by strong consensus, since everyone thinks and acts in the same way. With the increase in the division of labour found in advanced societies, people are bound together by *organic solidarity*.

Fred R. Eggan (1926–1991)

Eggan, a celebrated American social anthropologist greatly influenced by A.R. Radcliffe-Brown, has combined structure-function theory with historical analysis. In 1954, his methodological contribution to 'controlled comparison' in the studies of social organisation of North American Indian tribes was published. His other major contributions include *Social Anthropology of North American Tribes* (1955) and *the American Indians: Perspective for the study in Social Change* (1966).

Sir E.E. Evans-Pritchard (1902–1974)

Professor of Social anthropology at Oxford University (1946–1970) Evans-Pritchard was one of the founders of the British school of social anthropology. He conducted fieldwork in East Africa in 1920s and 1930s among the Nuer and Azande tribes. His researches owe more to Emilie Durkheim and his school than to Bornislaw Malinowski's functionalism to which he remained hostile. Evans-Pritchard insisted on the link between History and Anthropology and identified a humanistic and descriptive approach whose task was to interpret one culture. His notion on 'Time' and Lineage is appreciated well. His widely-known works are:

(i) *Witchcraft, Oracles and Magic among the Azande* (1936)
(ii) *The Nuer* (1940, 1969)
(iii) *Social Anthropology and Other Essays* (1951 Paperback 1955)
(iv) *African Political Systems* with M. Fortes (1940, 1969)
(v) *The Institution of Primitive Societies and the Positions of Women in Primitive Societies* (1980)

Raymond Firth (1902–1994)

Professor Firth was a British social anthropologist with extensive contributions to fields of economic anthropology, social change and anthropological theory (specially social organisation, see Chapter 3 of the book.) His area of specialisation, is tribal-peasant economic system. He has made major ethnographic contributions to the southeast Asian and Polynesian studies. His major works include:

(i) *We, the Tikopia* (1936, 1957), Republished in 1957, Beacon Press, Boston
(ii) *Primitive Polynesian Economy* (1939),
(iii) *Malay Fisherman: their peasant economy* (1946),
(iv) *Elements of Social Organisation* (1959),
(v) *Social Change in Tikopia* (1959, 1966),
(vi) *Social Organisation,* **Man** (1964)

Sir James Frazer (1854–1941)

The Scottish-born anthropologist Frazer was one of the influential persons of his time due to his monumental work, *the Golden Bough* (published in several volumes between 1890–1915) on the development of world religion. Frazer traced the evolution of human culture through the successive stage of magic, religion and science. One of his many important contributions to anthropology concerned the distinction between the different types of magic—imitative magic such as the use of a doll to imitate a desired result upon a person and contagious magic, where a severed portion of a person (a piece of hair, nail) could be used to practice 'black' magic upon the person.

Frazer viewed religion as the propitiation of supernatural natural laws.

Meyer Fortes (1906–1980)

Fortes, a student of both A. R. Radcliffe-Brown and Malinowski, developed new insights, especially in the field of kinship studies. His work on the Tallensi and the Ashanti of Ghana has served as a model for all subsequent studies of African social organisation. His work on ancestor worship is also of great significance which combines psychoanalytical insights with the study of its social function. Fortes headed the Anthropology Department of Cambridge University, England from 1950 to 1973. Among his works, the major ones are:

(i) *The Web of Kinship among the Tallensi (*1949)
(ii) *Kinship and Social Order* (1975)
(iii) *Social Structure* (1970)

Marvin Harris (1927–1999)

Marvin Harris, a cultural theorist, is remembered for his writings on 'etic' ethnography cultural materialism, economic anthropology the history of anthropology and race relations.

Some well-known works of Marvin Harris are:

(i) *The Cultural Ecology of India's Sacred Cattle* (first published in Current Anthropology, 1966, now reprinted in *Inquiry and Debates in Human Sciences*, 1991, edited by Sydel Silverman, pp. 261–276. Wener Grain Foundation, New York. In modified form, it has appeared in *Anthropology: Contemporary Perspectives*, 6th edition, 1990, Editors: Whitten and Hunter.
(ii) *The Rise of Anthropological Theory* (1968)
(iii) *Cultural Materialism* (1980)
(iv) *The Nature of Cultural Things* (1964)
(v) *The Cannibals and Kings: The Evolution of Culture* (1978)
(vi) Man, Nature and Culture*: 'An Introduction the General Anthropology'* (1971, 1979). Revised in 1985 retitled *Cultural Anthropology.*

Melville J. Herskovits (1895–1963)

Herskovits, internationally celebrated American anthropologist, was one of the earliest anthropologists concerned with the process of acculturation. He had defined 'acculturation' as 'the study of cultural transmission in process' (1950). His work both in West Africa, and among the descendants to West Africans forcibly resettled in the America (the Caribbean), provide 'classic' illustration of the design of acculturation (1958, 1966). Herskovits also classified the culture areas of Africa (1930) and wrote major text books in cultural anthropology (1950, 1952).

His major books are as follows:

(i) 'Culture Areas of Africa', *Africa,* Vol. 3, 59–77 (1930).
(ii) *Man and His Work,* Knopf, New York
(iii) *Cultural Anthropology,* Knopf, New York, (1955).
(iv) *Dahomey*, New York (1938).
(v) *Acculturation: The Study of Culture Contact,* Gloucester, Mass (1958).

Alfred L. Kroeber (1876–1960)

Kroeber, Cultural anthropologist, ethnohistorian and linguist, has often been considered the maker of the American anthropology. He was, probably, the last anthropologist whose interests and contributions extended over the entire range of anthropological subjects (including physical and cultural ecology, folklore, kinship and prehistory). He helped to stimulate the development of academic anthropology and its emergence as a professional field of scholarly investigation. Kroeber is often criticised for being a cultural determinist for his 'superorganic view of culture'. He introduced certain terms like *culture age area, configurations, styles, culture climax* and *culture intensity*, etc. His most influential book, *Anthropology* (1948) was the major source from which scholars in other fields as well as the general public learned about anthropology.The essays included in *Anthropology Today* (1955) are recognised as a compendium of world anthropology. In 1973, one of his students, Julian Steward prepared a profile on him.

Clyde Key Maben Kluckhohn (1905–1960)

Kluckhohn was a major figure in American anthropology at the Harvard University, who made important contributions to the field of culture and personality, Navajo studies on witchcraft and religion and concept of culture and values. His *Mirror for Man* (1949) and numerous publications (concept of culture, Acculturation, cultural value) brought him with Kroeber on international map. He edited a volume on *Culture, a critical review* in 1952.

Edmund R. Leach (1910–1995)

A contemporary British social anthropologist, Leach is well known for his *Rethinking Anthropology* that appeared in 1961. This essay is thought-provoking since it deals with the idea of 'comparative generalisation'. Leach rejects the views of his teachers Malinowski and Radcliffe-Brown and their followers, i.e. analysis of cultural behaviour in 'significant social categories'. Some of the well-known works of Leach are:

(i) *Political System of Highland Burma,* 'A study of Kachin Social Structure' (1954)
(ii) *Social Anthropology* (1971) (Collection of six articles)
(iii) *Pul Eliya, 'A Village in Ceylon'* (1961)
(iv) *My Kind of Anthropology,* (1985)
(v) *Claude Levi-Strauss* (1975)
(vi) *Rethirking Anthropology.* (Collection of Articles), 1961.

Claude Levi-Strauss (1908–2009)

One of the great anthropologists of the modern time, Levi-Strauss propounded the view popularly known as 'structuralism' (or 'the French school of structuralism') different from British structure-functionalism. He introduced 'linguistic model' in analysis of mythologies. His popular texts are translated from French into English after sixties. Some of them are:

(i) *The Elementary Structures of Kinship* (1969)
(ii) *Structural Anthropology* (1958, 1963)
(iii) *Totemism* (1963)
(iv) *The Savage Mind* (1962)
(v) *Mythologiquei* (1964–72)
(Note: See Chapters 3 and 5 of the present book)

Oscar Lewis (1914–1970)

Oscar Lewis, an American cultural anthropologist, is best known for his historical functional researches on Mexicans, Americans and rural people of India. He had developed the concept of 'culture of poverty'. Lewis has also contributed a landmark paper on cross-cultural anthropological researches (comparative method) in Kroeber's *Anthropology Today* (1955). His major publications include:

(i) *Village Life in North India* (1958)
(ii) *Five Families, Mexican* case studies in culture of poverty, (1958)
(iii) *The Children of Sanchez,* Autobiography of a Mexican Family (1960)
(iv) *La Vida* A Puerto Rican family in the culture of poverty (1966)
(v) *Pedro Martines:* A Mexican peasant and his family (1969)
(All texts are published from the Random House, New York)

Ralph Linton (1898–1958)

Linton, an internationally known American psychological anthropologist, was a member of the team of the famous archaeological expedition during 1920–22 on Marques islands. He became interested in natives and switched on cultural anthropology. Linton is best known for his abilities of synthesising diverse anthropological data and for formally introducing the concepts of 'status and role'. The main published works of Linton are:

(i) *The Study of Man* (1936)
(ii) *The Cultural Background of Personality* (1945)
(iii) *The Tree of Culture* (1955)

Bronislaw Malinowski (1884–1942)

The Polish born and English-trained anthropologist Bronislaw Malinowski developed of his own functional approach. Malinowski's functionalism was less true to Durkheimian principles than to Radcliffe-Brown's. The function Malinowski sought to discover related to the biological needs of society's members—the need to eat, the need to reproduce, the need for shelter and so forth. Rather than viewing the function of institutions as responsive to the requirements of society, he viewed institutions as answering the primary or derived needs of people.

Among his works, the outstanding are:

(i) *Argonauts of The Western Pacific* (1922)

(ii) *A Scientific Theory of Culture* (1944)

(iii) *The Dynamics of Culture Change* (1945)

(iv) *Magic, Science, Religion, and Other Essays* (1955)

(v) *A Diary in the Strict Sense of the Term* (1967)

George Peter Murdock (1897–1969)

In true sense, Murdock is the representative of the contemporary American socialcultural anthropology. His *Social Structure* (1949) is one of the most influential works in anthropology of comparative study of family, marriage and kinship. Murdock and his associates had started indexing descriptions of all cultures at the Yale University that has since become the *Human Relations Area Files* (HRAF), a foremost institution of its own kind (see entries under Comparison, Appendix I). Murdock was the founder-editor of *the Journal of Ethnology* published from the University of Pittsburgh. He has also done significant work on African ethnology.

Margaret Mead (1901–1978)

The embodiment of anthropology Mead is, perhaps, the best-known world anthropologist. Her efforts to bring the results of anthropological research to the general public have made her books best sellers (*Anthropology, Male and Female, Cultural Patterns and Technological Change, The American Indians,* just to name a few).

While her interests are manifold, she has constantly focused on culture as learned behaviour and has especially studied institutions of cultural transmission across generations. Among the contributions she has made on this score is her demonstration that cultural transmission, especially in complex societies, flows in two directions—from parent generation to children, and vice-versa. In her early career, she studied native groups of New Guinea and Manus. Over the last thirty years, she has turned her attention to complex societies, especially the study of culture change in terms of generation gap in United States. She has insisted on 'actual process of change' as they occur in one generation to adjacent or next generations (1964–1970).

Mead's basic position is that of a cultural relativist, which insists that each culture must be understood on its own terms, and each culture forms a unique whole. This has especially characterised her work on male and female gender identity.

Some of her most important books are:

(i) *Coming of Age in Samoa* (1928).
(ii) *Growing up in New Guinea* (1930).
(iii) *New Lives for Old* (1956).
(iv) *Continuties in Cultural Evolution* (1964)
(v) *Culture and Commitment* (1970)
(vi) *Blackberry Winter: My Early Years* (1972)
(vii) *Letters of Margaret Mead: 1925*–1975, collected by Ruth Anshen (1971)

A.R. Radcliffe-Brown (1881–1955)

A.R. Radcliffe-Brown developed social anthropology in England following the principles of Durkheim. He began his career with training in the evolutionary tradition of anthropology. However, in his first ethnography, *The Andaman Islanders* (1923), he repudiated the evolutionary approach on two grounds—first, the historical reconstruction in absence of historical data is conjectural and unscientific, and second, the comparative method abstracted institutions from their social context and thus, divested them of their meaning. Instead, he embraced the organic model of society of Durkheim and explained the specific functions in maintaining the structure of that society. Because of their concern with the functional integration of social structures, Radcliffe-Brown and his followers are often called structural functionalists.

Radcliffe-Brown wrote a little but all of his books are outstanding. Some of them are: (i) The *Andaman Islanders* (1923), (ii) *Structure and Function in Primitive Society (1952),* (iii) *Methods in Social Anthropology* (Edited by M.N. Srinivas, 1958).

Robert Redfield (1897–1958)

During the period 1935-1955, Robert Redfield played a crucial role in shaping the course of cultural anthropology in America. He joined the University of Chicago in 1928 and remained there as the Head of Department till his death. Although his theoretical orientations reflected the influence of Boasian historical particularism, he was much influenced by the then sociological traditions of America. His major theoretical constructs were the folk and peasant society, folk-urban continuum, great and little traditions, social organisation of traditions and the world-view.

Redfield's major publications consist of books and several research papers, some of them are:

(i) *The Primitive World and its Transformations,* Ithaca, New York (1953)
(ii) *The Folk Culture of Yucatan,* Chicago, (1941)
(iii) *The Little Community and Peasant Society and Culture,* Chicago (1960)
(iv) The papers of Robert Redfield in two volumes, *The Social Usages of Social Sciences,* Chicago (1963)
(v) "The Cultural Role of Cities" (with Milton Singer), *Economic Development and Culture Change,* **3**, 53–73, (1954)

Redfield's view of 'folk society' developed during 50's is still considered to be a typical characterisation of 'primitive' community, viz. the community is usually quite small; kinship relations and close bonds extend throughout the community; the economic and social interests are homogeneous, and there are a few specialists; attitude and behaviour are dominated by religion and outer world. (For Rural-urban continuum, see Appendix-I)

The concepts of 'great and little traditions' have been adequately dealt in *Peasant Society and Peasant Culture* (1956). The term 'great tradition' refers to the formal, literate tradition of civilisation, which is maintained by the elites and formal traditions of urbanites. The term 'little tradition' refers to the culture of the rural villagers living within a civilisation. Elements of Little traditions are continually incorporated into the great traditions through the process of universalisation. Likewise, the elements of the great tradition filter down at village level, but by a specific process known as parochialisation; its elements are modified to fit the peasant tradition. It would be difficult to apply the concept to the tribal communities because their culture is thought to be autonomous. However, a link can be established with those who are living near the tradition.

With M. Singer, Redfield attemped to construct typologies of cities and finally, presented the role of cities in the creation and spread of a cultural tradition into the surrounding region. A distinction is made between cities in which great tradition is maintained (*orthogenetic*) and those in which new traditions are introduced (*heterogenetic*).

Redfield's powerful impact was on Chicago-trained anthropologists (including Marriott and L.P. Vidyarthi, Surajit Sinha, Cohen, to name a few) who have contributed to the study of Indian civilisation and have examined the interplay of folk-urban continuum.

Sol Tax (1907–1995)

Sol Tax, the internationally known American anthropologist, encouraged the worldwide exchange of ideas among anthropologists and non-anthropologists through the forum of the Wener Grain Foundation of America over a period of 14 years (1960–74). Tax has edited a volume for young students (*Horizon of Anthropology*), and more than 20 volumes on various aspects of anthropology for advanced researchers. All the valumes are published during 1975–1980 by the Mouton. Sol Tax's contributions to Anthropology, like M. Mead, are numerous and popular. He was propounder of 'action anthropology'. *Current Anthropology* (Vol. **36**, 1995) contains a life sketch of Sol Tax and his lifetime achievements.

His major works include:

(i) *Penny Capitalism: A Guatemalan Indian Economy*. Smith Sonian Institute, Paper 16, Washington, D.G., 1953.

(ii) *From Lafitau to Radcliffe-Brown. Social Anthropology of North American Tribes,* Chicago. (1955).

(iii) *Horizon of Anthropology.* Aldine (1964).

(iv) *Fox Indians Action Anthropology Project,* Chicago (1965).

(v) The Integration of Anthropology, *Yearbook of Anthropology,* Wenner-Green Foundation, New York, pp. 313–28 (1955).

Steward, H. Julian (1902–1972)

Julian Steward was an American evolutionary theorist and cultural ecologist who introduced the concept of levels of *sociocultural integration.* Given that not all people live in homogeneous (tribal) societies, the anthropologists must analyze different levels; each constitutes a distinct level of social and cultural integration. This operational concept enabled him to discuss evolution in terms of adaptation on comparative level. He was concerned with the adaptation of specific *ecological niches. Technology* offers a key to understanding adaptation to environment. In this way Steward introduced the *multilinear evolution.* (Italicized terms are defined and discussed in the main text, consult index).

Steward was interested in discovering processes of culture change across societies and argued that culture change consists of complex continuing processes rather than unitary in character. A good number of cultural and archaeological anthropologists have been influenced by his stimulating insight.

Steward's main works include:

(i) *Essays in Historical Anthropology of North America,* (Ed) Smithsonian Collection, v. 100, Washington DC.

(ii) Ed., The Handbook of South American Indians, *American Ethnology Bulletin,* 141, Washington DC, 6 vols., 1946–1950.

(iii) The Level of Sociocultural Integration, an operational concept, *Southwestern Journal of Anthropology,* 7:374–90, 1951.

(iv) *Theory of Culture Change: the methodology of multilinear evolution,* Urbana, The University of Illinois Press, 1955 (originally published in 1951), paperback edition, 1965.
This book includes essays like the Patrilineal Band, The Great Basin Shoshonean Indians, Development of complex societies, irrigation civilization, among others.

Tylor, Sir Edward Burnett (1832–1917)

The foremost British cultural evolutionist Tylor has been regarded as the founder of modern anthropology. His contemporaries referred to anthropology as "Mr. Tylor's science." He introduced a number of concepts, viz. culture, animism, cultural survivals, etc. He pioneered the field of cross cultural analysis investigating how cultural traits take parallel and independent evolution and diffusion.

Tylor's main works include:

(i) *Researches into the Early History of Mankind,* London, 1865.

(ii) On a method of investigating the development of institutions; applied to laws of marriage and descent, *Journal of the Royal Anthropological Institute,* 18: 1–45, 1888.

(iii) *Primitive Cultures: Researches into the development of mythology, philosophy, religion, art, and custom,* London, J. Murray, 1871 (Paperback edition, Harper Torchbooks, 1958).

Appendix III

Tribal Movement in India

TRIBES

In anthropological parlance, the term tribe connotes an ethnic group, large or small, geographically isolated or partially isolated, identified with a distinct territory following a distinctive way of life which includes language, custom, religious practice, economy, polity and folk tradition. The most important attribute of a tribal community is that it has a joint ownership of resources which invariably include forest and land for generations. These specified groups are popularly called *Adivasis* or *Janjati Adivasi* in Hindi. The British administrators addressed them as Aboriginal tribes, and put them under the category of backward community. In post-independence period, the term *scheduled tribe* has been used in the Constitution of India and has got a recognition.

Ignoring the controversy among the administrators and anthropologists for the proper use of the term tribe, it is seen that today we use the term to mean socially disadvantaged section of the population called the scheduled tribes which are specified by the President of India by Public notification under the Article 342(1) of the Constitution. To be sure, the Constitution does not define the term as such, but Article 366(25) refers to scheduled tribes as those communities which are deemed under Article 342 to be scheduled tribes. It is therefore relevant to note that although no fixed criteria are specified for the tribe, the administration for the purpose of declaring a group as a tribe, follow the following criteria:

1. Tribal origin
2. Primitive or pre agricultural way of life
3. Habitation in less accessible areas
4. Low level of educational and technological development

Distribution of Tribes in India

According to the 2001 census (2011 census on the tribal not yet released) scheduled tribes constitute 8.14% of country's total population. Keeping in view of their historical, ethnic and cultural relations the tribal communities can be classified into following geographical zones:

1. The sub-Himalayan zone comprising states of Jammu and Kashmir, Himachal Pradesh, Uttrakhand and Sikkim;
2. The North-eastern zone comprising states of Assam, Arunachal Pradesh, Nagaland, Meghalaya, Tripura, Manipur and Mizoram;
3. Western zone including Rajasthan, Gujarat and Maharashtra;
4. Central zone has several states, viz. Jharkhand, Odissa, West Bengal, Chhattisgarh, Madhya Pradesh;
5. Southern zone with Andhra Pradesh, Karnataka, Kerala and Tamil Nadu; and
6. Islands of the Andaman and Nicobar and Lakshadweep.

The census does not list any scheduled tribe in the States of Haryana, Punjab, Chandigarh, Delhi and Puducherry. Further, in regions like Goa, Daman and Diu and Uttar Pradesh tribal population is in lesser number. Therefore, it can be concluded that of the total scheduled tribal population (8.45 crore), nearly 74% exists in the central and southern zones while 14% is in sub-Himalayan and North-eastern zones.

Out of nearly 750 tribal groups (which include major tribe, sub groups, section within a group), the Gonds stand first in order with their population of 74 lakh. Next in the lot are the Bhils (55 lakh), Santhals (43 lakh), Mina (21 lakh), Oraon (19 lakh) and Munda (14 lakh). On the other hand, tribes like the Andamanese, the Sentelese, Shompen, Onges, Toda and Malakkuravan are in lesser number whose population varies from 42–945.

Classifying tribes on the basis of territory does not mean that they live in cultural isolation. Today, almost all tribes in the country are under the pressure of modern forces like rapid growth of urbanization, industrialization and democratization; they are passing through the phases of transition. The Constitution of India has provided special safeguards under its several Articles in social, economic and political spheres. More recently, the tribals have shown their position as a distinct ethnic, linguistic and cultural entity, and they like to be called *Adivasis* (the oldest inhabitants) irrespective of their constitutional identity as scheduled tribe.

It must be noted that tribals in India, do not represent homogeneous ethnic stock. They differ from one another in physical appearance, language and forms of socio-cultural patterns. Finally, a tribal community is structurally different from the Hindu caste or any other non-Hindu community. A Hindu caste is a part of a larger society called Hindu; the tribals are not a part of Hindu. Each is complete in itself. Each has its full autonomy.

RISE OF TRIBAL MOVEMENT

Against the above background we may now briefly note the tribal movements in India.

Meaning of Social Movement

The Oxford dictionary defines movement as a series of combined actions and endeavours of a body of persons for special object. In Chapter 9 of this book various types of movements under revitalization have been discussed. Each of these arises under special circumstances peculiar to the time of its own.

Ethnic movements

K.S. Singh in his *Tribal Situation in India* (Shimla, 1972, p.19) has stated,

"Broadly, there are two types of ethnic (tribal) movements, one marks a phase of expansion of tribal entities by creating united symbols and organs of command among erstwhile isolated tribal communities. In other type, the tribals are in close interaction with the larger nation society and are aware of national goals and symbols".

Here we will describe a few prominent freedom and reform movements among the tribals which emerged during the later phase of British administration in India. These movements may be roughly grouped into three phases.

1. *Phase I:* This phase saw movements up to 1857, during the regime of the East India Company. These were basically in the form of crude agitations of primitive character, often non-organized, securing some concessions from the rulers.
2. *Phase II:* This phase talks about movements from 1857 up to beginning of the 20th century against the British economic policy with regard to land tenure pattern. Both tribal and non tribals stood against the colonial power.
3. *Phase III:* This phase is marked by tribal struggles during the first three decades of the 20th century. These were economic struggle involving money lenders, *zamindars*, traders and administrators who tried to exploit the tribals. During this phase some of the them were much inspired by Mahatma Gandhi and his associates.

It is evident that all tribal movements were not politically motivated. They were close to what some scholars have called agrarian reform or religious revitalization type of movements. We may briefly present here some important case studies recorded in ethnographic studies and official papers.

The Kol and Santhal movements in Jharkhand

The earliest known tribal movements in the country originated in the region of Chotanagpur and Santhal Parganas which lie in the southern part of Bihar, now Jharkhand State. This region is dominated by the tribals as out of 67 lakh tribes of Jharkhand more than 90% are concentrated in various parts of Chotanagpur and Santhal Parganas alone. The famous groups are the Santhal, Ho, Oraon and Munda. Till India became a British colony in 1765 A.D tribals lived peacefully along with non-tribals. Soon an army headquarter was established at Ramgarh, a place close to Ranchi in 1772. This accelerated movements of outsiders in tribal territory. Tribals hailed them as *Dikus* (a local term for intruders). Over the years they exploited the tribals and demanded revenues. This goaded them to desperation so much that the entire tribal population of Chotanagpur stood up with traditional weapons (bow, arrow, axes, sickles) against the *Dikus* in 1831–32. This is known as the Kol insurrection. (Kol is a general term of address for the tribals in this region.) In parts of Santhal Parganas, Santal stood against the outsiders including the administrators. During the year 1855, the slogan of Santhals 'kill the police and *Dikus* and we will not pay the rent' was spread throughout the tribal land. Two Santhal brothers Sido and Kanhu were the leaders for uprisings. The British Army

Captain Sherwill led over hundred Indian sepoys in the region. Soon marital law was declared. Kanhu Santal was captured and executed in January 1856.

The Santhal with traditional weapons could not face the warfare weapons of the British troops and lost the battle. The administrators realised the pressing needs of the tribals. As an outcome, some measures were introduced to relieve the anxiety of the inhabitants. The bonded labour system was abolished and verbal complaints of the tribals were treated as valid in the English court.

Between the period 1872 and 1878 land ownership rights were settled throughout the district of Santhal Parganas. Thinking that socio-economic position cannot be regained by mere agitation tribals turned toward supernaturalism.

The Baghirathi Movement

A Santal headman by the name of Bhagirath called himself a representative of God, and directed the followers to slaughter the domestic animals and fowls. It is told that the villagers began paying him rent via the Hindu landlord ignoring the administration. Soon it met its natural death. This movement is also known as the *Kherwari* movement (Kherwar is an older term for the Santal).

The Birsa Movement

The so called *Dikus* had already penetrated into deep of Chotanagpur region. The Munda were losing their land day-by-day resulting a feeling of discontent and unrest among the people. At this juncture, a Munda youth–Birsa (b.1875) appeared and raised his voice against the exploitation and oppression of local landlords. Since the British rulers stood the side of landlords, the tribals were against them too. 'As long as foreign dominance was not uprooted the tribals could not be saved,' Birsa thought. Since Birsa was educated by the Christian teachers, and was in contact with non-tribals around the area, he organized a tribal wing to go against *Diku*-cum-rulers. The administration wanted to capture him but it was not very easy to arrest him, because he was well-verse with local forest ecology. After several months of chasing, Birsa was finally caught and sentenced to 30 months of imprisonment. On appeal, the period was reduced to 2 years. He was released in 1897 on eve of diamond jubilee celebration of Queen Victoria's rule.

The period of 1857–1899 was very unfortunate for Chotanagpur. Famine, diseases and scarcity of forest produce showed their ugly face. This gave Birsa and his team excellent opportunity to perform social services. He gained more popularity in the later days. The local landlords continued to oppress the tribals. On the eve of Christmas, 1899 the Birsa team decided to launch its mission. Soon Christian mission offices, police stations were under the attack of Birsa fighters. A couple of officers of Khunti police station were killed. Within no time the news reached Ranchi. The government announced a cash reward of ₹ 500 for the arrest of Birsa. Finally, Birsa was captured and brought to Ranchi. Here thousand of people were waiting to get a glance of their beloved leader Birsa. On 20th May 1900 he was convicted and was sent to Ranchi jail where he died on 9th June 1900 due to cholera. According to the official documents, more than 400 people (male and female) were arrested for trails and were convicted and acquitted. Capital punishments were awarded to the close associates of Birsa. Proudly, the tribals of Chotanagpur tell their children the story of Birsa. They worship him as Bhagwan (the God). A noted anthropologist and ethnographer of India, Professor Sachidananda writes:

"Birsa movement was an embodiment of the socio-economic and religious unrest among the Munda. Buffeted by the waves of repression and oppression and torn by despair, the tribes saw in Munda a prophet and a saviour. Birsa movement is (to be viewed) as a combination of Munda belief, Hinduism and Christianity. The movement had such a tremendous impact that the foundation of British rule in Chotanagpur was shaken for some time. (quoted in Srivastava, 2010, p.18).

The Bhagat movement

Bhagatism was essentially a religious movement which sprang up around 1914 in Oraon region of Chotanagpur. An Oraon, named Jatra, proclaimed that in a vision he had received a revelation of *Dharmes* (Oraon's supreme deity). Soon this spread to parts of Ranchi. In short, Jatra message was that the people should stop animal sacrifice and lead a vegetarian life avoiding wine, tobacco and even tribal dance and songs. They should not work for the zamindars, and so on. The annoyed British administrators arrested Jatra and sentenced to imprisonment. After completing the term, Jatra lived for a short period of time.

The followers of Jatra are called Tana Bhagat (Tana means pulling together and Bhagat means devotee). Jatra was trying to unite people into his fold. Around 1921, some Tana Bhagat participated in non-cooperation movement led by Mahatma Gandhi.

The Zeliangrong movement

Around 1832 the British reached North-eastern area. They administered this region as backward tracts till 1937. Soon the region was bifurcated as NEFA (North-Eastern Frontier Agencies) along with the Mizo hills, Naga hills and North Cachar hills, and were declared as *excluded areas* where as the Garo hills, the Mikir hills and Khasi Jaintiya hills as *partially excluded areas*. The entire hilly tracts were occupied by the tribes like the Naga, the Khasi, the Mikir, and the Garo, among others. The Zeliangrong movement started among three tribes, viz. Zemei, the Liangmei and the Rongmei. The prefixes of each of these (Ze, Liang, Rong) merged into one forms Zeliangrong. The inhabitants were forced to pay the tax to the British government and not to the Maharaja of Manipur. This created serious problems to leading their life smoothly. At the same time, the Christian missionaries began to bring the tribals into Christianity. At this stage Jadonang appeared on the scene. It is held that he had some supernatural blessings. His political actions were accepted by the people. His cousin sister–Gaidinliu too joined him. It is said that he was involved in human sacrifice. Jadonang was finally caught and sentenced to death in August 1931.

After Jadonang, the movement was converted into a peaceful movement under the leadership of Gaidinliu. She established a tribal organization in 1934. By this time she had heard a lot about Mahatma Gandhi, and told her people that that the British will soon be driven out of India. She had several secret agents; at one time her recruits exceeded 4000. The British force captured her. Mr Higgins, the British political agent of Manipur, imposed life imprisonment on her, in 1932. At that time she was merely 18 years old. She remained in prison for 14 years moving from one place to another, viz. Kohima, Guwahati, Shillong, Tura and Aizwal. During her long confinement Gaidinliu became more popular. At one time Pandit Nehru visited her in Shillong and addressed her as "Rani" (Queen). Since then she was known as Rani Gaidinliu. He also tried to help her in releasing with the help of some British ministers, but as Manipur was not a full fledged province his attempts failed. However, soon after the independence, Prime Minister Nehru directed the authorities of Assam to release her. In appreciation of her role in the tribal freedom movement Rani Gaidinliu was awarded a *Tamrapatra* by the Government in 1972. It is worthwhile to quote a few lines of her speech delivered in the seminar of Anthropological Survey of India, Kolkata:

"...Most of the problems concerning the tribals stem from the fact that very few people know the problems they face....In the past there had been bloodshed and rebellions, especially among the Naga and Mizo....I supported Indira Gandhi's 20-point economic programme because she knew our problems... My brother, Jadonang fought against the British for our rights. Now the British have gone, but our demand has still not been conceded..."

The above words reflect Gaidinliu's philosophy of tribal welfare. She has been a landmark in the history of North-east India. Today Zeliangrong term has been a very popular among the Naga. Students union, women organization, sport club and many cultural organizations are named after this term.

Narayan Singh—the Hero of Chhattisgarh

When Madhya Pradesh was occupied by the British in 1854 some of the *zamindars* prominently Narayan Singh, a local landlord did not like the policy of interference in local administration. He hailed from Binjhwar tribe and moved in Sonakhan of Raipur district. Around August 1856, the entire rural belt of Sonakhan and fringe areas faced acute shortage of grains due to failure of rains. Narayan Singh then decided to do something for the villagers as his granary was too empty. He approached a local merchant for grain, but the latter refused to do so. Narayan Singh got furious. He entered the warehouse and took bags of grain and distributed them among the people. Because of his link with the British officer, the merchant complained to the Deputy Commissioner of Raipur. The latter issued a warrant of arrest against Narayan Singh. He was brought to Raipur and was put into jail. Soon he managed to escape from the cell by digging an underground tunnel. He returned to Sonakhan and organized a local team consisting of tribals and peasants. The British government had already experienced tribal revolt in Bihar, and the great Sepoy mutiny. Therefore it directed the police and military authorities to suppress the patriotism in this region. Lieutenant C.B.L. Smith with the help of a local zamindar surrounded Sonakhan from three sides. There was heavy exchange of fires from both sides, finally Narayan Singh surrendered himself before the police for the benefit of the people. He was executed on 10th December 1857 at Raipur.

The people of Sonakhan and neighbouring states never thought such a cruel punishment would be awarded to Narayan Singh. He is still veneered as the first hero of the First War of Independence in Central India.

The Rajmohini Devi movement in Sarguja, Chhattisgarh

Several short-lived movements arose among the Gonds of Bastar and its adjoining states. They are not directly related to our theme. However one social movement is worth noting. This was led by a tribal lady Ramohini Devi. She hailed from a Manjhi tribe, a branch of Gond. She had no formal schooling. In 1951, a famine broke in Sarguja creating scarcity of food grains. This had a direct bearing on the rise of reform movement. For want of food, Rajmohini was moving here and there in forest. At this point, she saw a sage coming towards her. She asked her to return to the village showing them the path of truth as shown by Gandhiji. Having said this, the sage disappeared. She then returned to the village and got involved in social service. There are some other local versions of the story. But the message is clear— she was blessed with supernatural powers; soon she had many followers. In 1959, a full fledged Ashram (*Dharma Sabha Adivasi Seva Mandal*) was established by her, and this has been running with success till date.

Undoubtedly, there was imprint of Gandhian ideology on Rajmohini Devi.

Koya Revolt of Andhra Pradesh

Andhra Pradesh, one of the fourth largest tribal population region, has as many as 35 individual tribes. Their combined population is over 50 lakh or about 7% of state total population. Among all the Koya is a prominent one. It is to be noted that a considerable part of tribal region is concentrated in Agency district of Andhra Pradesh. In British system, agency was a country inhabited mainly by the tribal people with special legal position.

The revolt named Rampa *Fithui* (rebellion) took place sometime in 1862, by the Koya against the *Muttadars* or petty *zamindars*, who formed a chain of intermediary rent collectors appointed by the British administration. It has now been fully abolished.

Like elsewhere in north and central India tribals did not like the oppressive methods of the outsiders. The main cause was that the toddy trees, the most valuable property of the tribals were leased out to the non-tribals. The outsiders also tortured the tribals for not working for them, and not repaying the loans they had taken for their daily needs. Ultimately, the tribals under the leadership of Thamman—Deva of Koya tribe revolted against the prevailing system of exploitation. It was suppressed by the administration. Muttadars remained as ever powerful under the Britisers.

During 1922–24, a mass agitation was led by Alluri Sreerama Raju. This was synchronized by the Non-cooperation and Civil disobedience movements launched by Gandhiji. According to the available sources, the main causes were the strict restrictions imposed by the forest departments for not allowing slash and burn (podu) cultivation, and extraction of free labour force in the agency for construction of a proposed highway from Narsipatnam to Chintapalli. Mr. Bastian, a Tahsildar, began using all sort of methods to achieving government objectives.

In August 1922, Alluri Raju with his followers, attacked police station. In another encounter Raju's forces killed commanding officer and the police men. In December, the British administration announced cash reward on the head of Raju and against the rebels. The agency area was almost sealed and cut-off from all connections. Looking at the miserable condition of his fellowmen, Raju surrendered before the police headquarter. Instead of protecting Raju, a policeman was asked by the superior officer Major Godall to shoot him. It was a clear cut case of cold-blooded murder. But the administrator put it differently. In the official record it was declared as death in the encounter. Thus, the life of a great leader of freedom struggle ended. By September 1924, the rebellion was all over. Alluri Raju was not a tribal by birth, but the tribals made him immortal Raju of west Godavari district.

TRIBALS: THE PIONEERS OF NATIONALIST MOVEMENT

During the last 100 years of Britsh rule, there had been increasing encroachment on the tribal hills and plain areas by the outsiders. This category included *jagirdars*, *zamindars*, *landlords*, merchants and Christian missionaries. Many of them were geared by the British system. When the tribals found that their way of life is being jeopardized by the outsiders they arose against them. One or two of them motivated their people and fought with the system. Initially, the tribal uprising was reformatory in character, but later on, due to continued suppression by the administration they turned into rebels.

Tribal freedom fighters are the precursors of the revolutionary nationalistic leaders who ultimately forced the Britishers to quit India. The point to be emphasised here is that these fighters shook the British Empire of its foundation, before the national political parties raised their slogan of Swaraj.

Appendix IV

Selected Social-Cultural Anthropology Textbooks 1970–2003

- Barnouw, Victor, 1978: *An Introduction to Anthropology*, (Vol. 1 *Ethnology* and Vol. 2 *Physical Anthropology and Archaeology*). The Dorsey Press, Illinois. (First published 1971). The two-volume work is designed as a general introduction to the field of anthropology.
- Clifton, James A. (Ed.), *Introduction to Cultural Anthropology* (Essays in the scope and methods of the science of man), first published in 1968.
  This is a valuable collection of up-to-date statements on the experts of cultural anthropology. Strongly emphasises on approaches and major fields in cultural anthropology in 18 separate chapters. Each chapter is written by a specialist of the field. Some of them are Dundes (Oral literature), Bradfield (Economic anthropology), Pospisil (Law), Price-William (Ethnopsychology), Cohen (Ethnology), Sturtevant (Ethnoscience), Vayda (Ecology) and Berreman (Ethnography).
- Ember, C.R., M. Ember and Peter M. Perigine, *Anthropology,* 10th ed., Indian reprint, Pearson Education Inc., Patparganj, Delhi, 2002. Also translated in Hindi by the same publisher (2004).
- FriedI, John, *The Human Portrait: Introduction to Cultural Anthropology,* Prentice-Hall Inc., New Jersey, 1976.
  It is a comprehensive textbook in cultural anthropology, written for the undergraduate courses. American universities. Some of the crucial terms are defined at the end of each of 16 chapters. It also contains references.
- Gluckman, Max, *Politics, Law and Ritual in Tribal Society,* 1970 (Orig. 1965), Professor Gluckman of Victoria University of Manchester, England illustrates the general problem of rule and disorder in social life. All chapters are neatly written.
- Kottak, Conard Philip, *Anthropology: The Exploration of Human Diversity*, 7th ed., The McGraw Hill Inc., New York, 1996.

This is a good textbook. It contains the chapters found in many texts. It also has four new chapters, viz. Ethnology, Human Biologically Diversity and the Race Concept, Gender and Cultural Exchange and Survival which are not found consistently in many books.

- Lewis, I.M. "The relevance of social anthropology," *Social Anthropology in Perspective*, Cambridge, 1985.
  Skillfully wearing together the theory and ethnographic data, Lewis advocates an eclectic approach to anthropology. He combines the strengths of British structural function with ideas of Marx, Freud and Levi-Strauss.
- Hoebel, E. Adamson, *Anthropology, The Study of Man,* 4th ed., McGraw Hill, Bombay, 1988.
  The most popular textbook in anthropology. All core branches are dealt with in greater details including titles for the further reading.
- Harris, Marvin, *The Cultural Anthropology*, Harper and Row, New York 1988. A text in its own style up to date and well written. Harris earlier wrote a comprehensive text on general anthropology entitled *Man, Nature* and *Culture,* 1973.
- Howard, Michael C., *Contemporary Cultural Anthropology*, 3rd ed., Scott, Foresman and Company, Illinois, 1989.
  This is comprehensive, coherent and readable introduction to cultural anthropology. Throughout the text, cultures are examined through an ecological perspective. Twelve anthropologists have contributed original essays under 'Focus on People' that describes a wide variety of fieldwork experiences.
- Hunter, David E. and Whitten, Philip, *The Study of Anthropology*, New York, 1976.
- Mair, Lucy, *An Introduction to Social Anthropology*, Oxford University Press, 1975. Hindi translation of this book is available from the Bihar Hindi Granth Academy, Patna, 1975.
- Miller, Elmer S., *Introduction to Cultural Anthropology*, Prentice-Hall Inc., New Jersey, 1979.
  It is a comprehensive and up-to-date textbook.
- Scupin, Raymond and Christopher R. De Corse, *Anthropology: A Global Perspective*,. Prentice Hall, Inc., New Jersey, 1992. Available under EEE series of the PHI Learning (P) Limited, New Delhi, 2010.
  The authors have presented text-materials in ecological and comparative perspectives. Important terms are defined in a coherent manner.
- Whitten, Philip and David Hunter, *Anthropology: Contemporary Perspectives,* 6th ed., Harper Collins Publisher, 1990.
  This is an excellent edited book containing 49 articles which highlight the major topics of anthropology much discussed during the past three decades of 20th century. Over 60 per cent articles date from the 1980. Among the prominent anthropologists, authors of these articles, are B. Bogin, Laura Bohannan, N. Chagnon, Y. Coben, E. Friedl, M. Harris, W.W. Howells, R. Lee, D. May Bury-Lewis, Eric Wolf, Peter Worsley. Over 90 per cent articles were published in major textbooks, journals and popular periodicals such as *Science, Scientific American, Natural History and Nature.* The editors have introduced topics in a very lucid way making anthropology as an exciting discipline of the twentieth century.

Appendix V

Universities with Anthropology Department and Research Institutions (India)

1. Allahabad University	Allahabad (U.P.)
2. Andhra University	Waltair (A.P.)
3. Bastar Vishwvidyalaya	Jagdelpur, Chhattisgarh
4. Calcutta University	Kolkata (W.B.)
5. Delhi University	Delhi (Delhi)
6. Dibrugarh University	Dibrugarh (Assam)
7. Doctor Hari Sing Gour University	Sagar (M.P.)
8. Gujarat Vidyapeeth	Ahmedabad (Gujarat)
9. Guru Ghasidas University	Bilaspur (Chattisgarh)
10. Guwahati University	Guwahati (Assam)
11. H.N.B. Garhwal University	Srinagar (Uttara khand)
12. Hyderabad University	Hyderabad, (A.P.)
13. International Hindi Vishwavidyalay	Wardha, (Maharashtra)
14. Karnataka University	Dharwar (Karnataka)
15. Lucknow University	Lucknow (U.P.)
16. Madras University	Chennai (Tamil Nadu)
17. Manipur University	Imphal (Manipur)
18. Mysore University	Mysore (Karnataka)
19. North Bengal University	Siliguri (W.B.)
20. North Eastern Hill University	Shillong (Meghalaya)
21. Orissa Central University	Kalahandi (Odisha)
22. Pandit Ravishankar University	Raipur (Chattisgarh)
23. Pondicherry University	Puducherry
24. Poona University	Pune (Maharashtra)
25. Punjab University	Chandigarh (Chandigarh)

26. Punjabi University	Patiala (Punjab)
27. Ranchi University	Ranchi (Jharkhand)
28. Sido Kanhu Murrmu University	Dumka (Jharkhand)
29. S.V. University	Tirupati (A.P.)
30. Utkal University	Bhubaneshwar (Odisha)
31. Vidya Sagar University	Midnapore (W.B.)
32. Vinoba Bhave University	Hazaribagh (Jharkhand)
33. Viswa Bharti University	Santiniketan (W.B.)

Note: Some universities offer special programmes in Social anthropology, Tribal Studies and Applied anthropology under Sociology (Arunachal University, Kashi Vidyapeeth, Varanasi and Rani Durgawati Jabalpur University, Barukhtulla University, Bhopal).

State Government Research Institutions for Tribal Development

1. **Anthropological Survey of India**, Indian Museum, Calcutta-70016. Regional stations at Mysore, Shillong, Ranchi, Mysore, Udaipur, Dehradun, Nagpur, Jagdalpur and Port Blair.
2. **Tribal and Harijan Research-cum-Training Institute**, Government of Odisha, Bhubaneswar-751014.
3. **Tribal Welfare Research Institute**, Government of Jharkhand, Morabadi Road, Ranchi-834008.
4. **M.P. Tribal Research and Development Institute**, Government of Madhya Pradesh, 35 Simla Hills, Bhopal-462001.
5. **Cultural Research Institute**, Scheduled Castes & Scheduled Tribes Welfare Department, Government of West Bengal CIT, Scheme No. VII M., VIP Road, Dandurgachi, Kolkata-700054
6. **Tribal Research Institute**, Government of Maharashtra, 28 Queens Road, Pune-411001.
7. **Tribal Research and Training Centre**, Gujarat Vidyapeeth, Ahmedabad-380014.
8. **Tribal Research Institute**, Government of Assam, New Sarania, Guwahati-781003.
9. **Tribal Cultural Research and Training Institute**, Government of Andhra Pradesh, Telegu Samkshema Bhavan, Masab Tank, Hyderabad-500028.
10. **Manikya Lal Verma Tribal Research and Training Institute**, Government of Rajasthan, Udaipur-313001.
11. **Kerala Institute for Research Training and Development Studies of Scheduled Castes and Scheduled Tribes**, Government of Kerala, Kozhikode.
12. **Scheduled Tribes and Scheduled Caste Research and Training Institute**, Government of Uttar Pradesh, Vishal Khand, Lucknow-266001.
13. **Tribal Research Centre**, Tamil University under Fell Bungalow, Missionary Hill, Udhagamandalam, Tamil Nadu-600001.
14. **Tribal Research and Training Institute**, Govt. of Chhattisgarh, Raipur-400009.

Appendix VI

Major Anthropological Journals

NATIONAL LEVEL

1. *Man in India* (Ranchi)
2. *Eastern Anthropologist* (Lucknow)
3. *Indian Anthropologist* (New Delhi)
4. *Manav* (Hindi) (Lucknow)
5. *Vanyajati* (New Delhi)
6. *Journal of the Indian Anthropological Society* (Kolkata)
7. *Journal of the Anthropological Society of India* (Kolkata)
8. *Journal of Social Research* (Ranchi). Also, from Ranchi, *South Asian Anthropologist.*
9. *Journal of Human Ecology* (New Delhi)
10. *Journal of Physical Anthropology and Human Genetics* (Lucknow)

INTERNATIONAL LEVEL

1. *Current Anthropology* (USA)
2. *Man* (United Kingdom)
3. *American Anthropologist* (USA)
4. *Human Organisation* (USA)
5. *American Physical Anthropology* (USA)
6. *Journal of Anthropological Research* (USA)
7. *Ethnology* (USA)
8. *Contributions to Indian Sociology* (India)
9. *Annual Review of Anthropology* (USA)
10. *Anthropos* (Austria)

Index